Queering Theology Series

Editors
Marcella Althaus-Reid
Lisa Isherwood

Associate Editors
Robert Goss
Carter Heyward
Beverley Harrison
Ken Stone
Mary Hunt
Tom Hanks
Gerard Loughlin
Graham Ward
Elizabeth Stuart

D1615596

Practicing Safer Texts

Food, Sex and Bible in Queer Perspective

Ken Stone

T&T CLARK INTERNATIONAL
A Continuum imprint
LONDON • NEW YORK

Published by T&T Clark International
A Continuum imprint
The Tower Building, 11 York Road, London SE1 7NX
15 East 26th Street, Suite 1703, New York, NY 10010

www.tandtclark.com

All rights reserved. No part of this publication may be reproduced or transmitted in any form or by any means, electronic or mechanical, including photocopying, recording or any information storage or retrieval system, without permission in writing from the publishers.

Copyright © Ken Stone, 2005

British Library Cataloguing-in-Publication Data
A catalogue record for this book is available from the British Library

Typeset by Fakenham Photosetting Limited, Fakenham, Norfolk
Printed on acid-free paper in Great Britain by Cromwell Press, Wiltshire

ISBN 0-567-08182-6 (hardback)
      0-567-08172-9 (paperback)

CONTENTS

ACKNOWLEDGMENTS

During the period that I worked on this project, several people took the time to read portions of the manuscript or respond to oral presentations of material found here. For the helpful feedback and encouragement that resulted, I want to thank Wil Brant, Scott Haldeman, Tat-siong Benny Liew, Dale Martin, Michael Mendiola, Laurel Schneider, Yvonne Sherwood, Daniel Spencer, and students in my course on 'Lesbian and Gay Studies for Theology and Biblical Interpretation'. Students in my course on 'Homosexuality and Hermeneutics' endured rough drafts of several chapters and forced me to clarify my arguments. Julianne Buenting and Theodore Jennings went even further, reading penultimate drafts of multiple chapters and making numerous suggestions for improvement and clarification. Gabriel Calderón proved to be invaluable as a research assistant, turning earlier drafts into a form acceptable for the publisher and subjecting the entire manuscript to a reading that made me account, literally, for every comma chosen or rejected.

Several people contributed to the completion of this project in other ways. Suzanne Vega, whose gifts as a lyricist capture the relationship between food and sex more powerfully than any academic discourse, gave permission to reprint the lyrics to 'Caramel'. Marcella Althaus-Reid and Lisa Isherwood solicited the manuscript for their series, and Robert Goss encouraged its publication. The completion of the project was assisted greatly by a sabbatical granted to me by the Chicago Theological Seminary. For that sabbatical and other kinds of support I wish to thank the President of the Seminary, Susan Brooks Thistlethwaite; the Board of Trustees; and all of those faculty colleagues who encouraged my research on food, sex and biblical interpretation for a number of years. Joan Blocher, Rinnie Orr and Emma Rasoarivonjy filled my incessant requests for interlibrary loans. Several people engaged me in conversations that seem, in retrospect (and perhaps without their knowledge), to have stimulated my thinking about particular parts of this project at particular moments in particularly helpful ways: Matthew Cockrum, Neil Gerdes, David Gregg, David Kern, Julie Kilmer, Judith Phillips, Daniel Sack, Timothy Sandoval, Daniel Schlorff, BoMyung Seo and Lisa Wolfe. To the students in my classes at Chicago Theological Seminary, who have listened to me bring up food and sex in all sorts of probable and improbable contexts, I can only express my apologetic gratitude.

Finally, I need to thank Horace Griffin in particular, for all that he gave to my work.

Introduction: On Practicing Safer Text

It won't do to dream of caramel,
to think of cinnamon and long for you.
It won't do to stir a deep desire,
to fan a hidden fire that can never burn true.
I know your name, I know your skin,
I know the way these things begin;
But I don't know how I would live with myself,
what I'd forgive of myself if you don't go.
So goodbye, sweet appetite, no single bite could satisfy ...
I know your name, I know your skin,
I know the way these things begin;
But I don't know what I would give of myself,
how I would live with myself if you don't go.
It won't do to dream of caramel,
to think of cinnamon and long for you.

Suzanne Vega, 'Caramel' from *Nine Objects of Desire*[1]

'And indeed,' said Colonel Galliffet, 'this woman is now turning a dinner at the Café Anglais into a kind of love affair – into a love affair of the noble and romantic category in which one no longer distinguishes between bodily and spiritual appetite or satiety!'

Isak Dinesen, 'Babette's Feast'

I

Several years ago, while attending a conference on sexuality and theological education, I listened to a Christian ethicist encourage other ethicists to take into account contemporary research on sexuality and gender. The ethicist, who stood in the Roman Catholic tradition, was concerned about the tendency of thinkers within that tradition to make hasty appeals to 'nature' while arguing over sexual ethics. As the ethicist saw it, research on the social construction of gender and sexuality reveals the inadequacy of attempts to ground sexual ethics in simplistic appeals to 'nature'. The ethicist therefore went on to recommend a number of ethical principles that might be applied by Christians to sexual disputes, including the principle of 'sexual monogamy'; but attempted to ground those principles in 'tradition' and 'reason' rather than 'nature'.

In the wake of that presentation, I approached the ethicist to ask whether sexual monogamy was really as securely grounded in tradition and reason as the

---

1.   Reprinted by permission of the author.

presentation had implied. After all, I pointed out, the Hebrew Bible (or Christian Old Testament)[2] seems to presuppose views on marriage and sexual practice that cannot be characterized, strictly speaking, as 'monogamous'. Could this fact not be taken as an indication that 'tradition' is less monolithic on the issue of monogamy than Christian thinkers imagine?

In the course of responding to my question the speaker made an observation, almost as an aside, that I have reflected upon ever since. As a result of our growing awareness of the socio-cultural shaping of sexual meanings, Christianity, the ethicist suggested, stands 'at a crossroads'. On the one hand, the historicizing approach taken toward gender and sexuality in much contemporary research could lead Christians to accept a certain amount of 'relativism' with respect to sexual ethics. In that case, the ethicist opined, Christians would be tempted to follow the advice of those who recommend that sexual practices should be treated 'like food', deciding as a result that variable sexual arrangements are simply products of custom and pluralism. On the other hand, contemporary Christians could accept that sexual matters necessarily constitute a special case for ethical and theological reflection. Sexual practices, according to this latter view, are, for Christians, inherently more significant than food matters and always have to be evaluated with this difference in mind, though now with an awareness that such evaluation cannot be grounded in simplistic appeals to 'nature'. In the opinion of the ethicist this latter course was clearly the course to be adopted. As if to buttress the view that sexual matters must be treated with more caution than food, the ethicist pointed out to me that research into such phenomena as sexual abuse has uncovered numerous dangers often associated with sex.

Although aspects of the present project were already on my mind at the time of this conversation, it is fair to say that the comments of the ethicist helped to produce this book. They became a sort of challenge; for it was not apparent to me then, and is even less apparent to me now, that the sharp contrast drawn by the ethicist between food and sex is a helpful presupposition with which to approach either our contemporary ethical decisions or those religious texts from the past that play such a large role in Judaism, Christianity and much of Western culture. Thus, as someone whose professional identity involves the practice of biblical interpretation, I set myself the task of re-examining a number of biblical texts using this comparison between food and sex as a lens for reading. The essays that follow are products of that re-examination.

My hunch that it might actually be productive to think about food and sex in relation to one another, rather than treating them differently and separately as the ethicist recommended, is no doubt derived in part from widespread cultural associations between sex and food that are clearly on display in many of the texts of popular culture. Such associations are also frequently found in a wide variety of academic sources, including sources emerging from particular fields of study

---

2.   Though I make frequent use of the term 'Hebrew Bible' to refer to those texts that serve as 'Tanakh' for Jews and 'Old Testament' for Christians, Levenson (1993) has shown that the term is not without difficulties. In several places where a specifically Christian context of reading is in mind, I retain the term 'Old Testament'.

outside of biblical and theological scholarship that have proven to be useful dialogue partners in my own practice of biblical interpretation. Within those fields of study – and especially within the discourses of cultural anthropology and of lesbian and gay studies and queer theory – one encounters both passing references to, and extended discussions of, structural, metaphorical and other relations between, on the one hand, eating, hunger, diet and food production and, on the other hand, sexual activity, desire, identity and reproduction. Texts from both popular culture and academic writing seem to support an assertion made several years ago by the anthropologist Donald Pollock. Pollock, attempting to understand the relationship between food and sex among peoples of the Amazon, recalls the statement of Claude Lévi-Strauss that the significance of totemic animals lies not in the fact that they are 'good to eat' but, rather, in the fact that they are 'good to think' (Lévi-Strauss 1963: 89). Playing rhetorically upon Lévi-Strauss's formulation, Pollock suggests that, in South America, food and sex are in fact 'each "good to think" the other' (Pollock 1985: 25). That is to say, we can best understand the role of food, and the role of sex, when we take seriously the tendency to use food matters and sexual matters as metaphors for one another. Following up on this suggestion, I want to consider what might happen if we took this recurring tendency to 'think' food and sex together and deployed it in the context of biblical interpretation. Thus the chapters that follow will all approach food, sex and biblical interpretation, but will do so from a number of different perspectives and in relation to several different biblical as well as non-biblical texts.

In order to avoid misunderstanding, it is important to stress from the beginning that to argue that is *valuable* to think of food and sex in relation to one another is *not* to conclude that sex is, therefore, a trivial matter. Exactly this assumption seemed to trouble the ethicist with whom I spoke, but one doesn't have to inflate the seriousness of sex in comparison with food in order to see flaws inherent in this assumption. The supposed triviality of food is itself far from self-evident. Indeed, one of the most striking impressions to emerge from a study of food practices is the gravity of such practices in certain times and places – including certain times in the histories of Judaism and Christianity and certain places in the Bible. One can make plausible arguments that many of us should take food practices far more seriously than we normally do. As one historian puts it, food 'has a good claim to be considered the world's most important subject. It is what matters most to most people for most of the time' (Fernández-Armesto 2002: xi). For many people around the world, food – especially its scarcity – continues to be as significant as, if not more significant than, the sexual matters with which it will here be compared. If it is true that more explicit anxiety is now expressed over sex than over food in some parts of the contemporary West (which is my own context for writing), this difference may well be an effect of global and local inequalities in the distribution of resources that allow some people to worry less about food than others.

Of course, hasty conclusions about the relative significance of food or sex in particular contexts can be misleading. It is, for example, necessary to guard against underestimating the importance of sexual matters even in contexts where the struggle for daily sustenance is severe. Marcella Althaus-Reid, writing in part out of her experiences in Argentina and in dialogue with liberation theologies, has reminded us that 'the poor' are also gendered and sexual beings, and not only their economic, but also their sexual stories challenge many dominant assumptions and so need to be told (Althaus-Reid 2000). Such calls for attention to interrelations between economic and sexual realities might suggest that we should not be too quick to accept the notion that the poor, preoccupied with struggles for food, are less likely to be engaged in struggles for or about sex.

At the same time, it is important to remember that food matters also cause significant concern and anxiety in contexts where food scarcity is less prevalent. 'Food moralism', for example, has been a recurring feature of so-called 'mainline Protestantism' in the United States (Sack 2000). Outside of explicitly religious contexts, food has taken on new but significant meanings in postindustrial capitalism. Sociological studies point out that class distinctions are often negotiated and reproduced by upwardly mobile Westerners in relation to such matters as culinary skill and experimentation, the ability to entertain at dinner, the consumption and implementation of knowledge found in cookbooks, the deployment of codes of style in the preparation, presentation and consumption of food, the development of particular relationships to discourses on 'nutrition' and so forth (see DeVault 1991: 203–26; cf. Bourdieu 1984). Eating disorders are widespread in the West, and have received much attention in relation to matters of gender and body. In the United States it is nearly impossible to turn on the television or peruse the shelves of bookstores without being made immediately aware that the food-related phenomena of weight gain and weight loss have become social, and not simply individual, obsessions. Some writers suggest that food anxieties and 'food guilt' are very much on the rise in the West (e.g., Iggers 1996) and the preoccupation with 'proper eating' is so intense in some circles that one writer has coined the term 'orthorexia nervosa' to discuss it (Bratman 2001). To say, then, that it might be useful to think about sex in relation to food is certainly not to argue that sex should become a trivial matter; for food matters are themselves anything but trivial.

Having made these qualifications, however, I would also go on to suggest that, at least within contexts influenced by Christianity, and at least so long as basic needs for nutrition and health are met, it often appears that food practices as such are not automatically viewed with the same degree of ethical suspicion as sexual practices. Food pluralism seems not to be a major source of strife or conflict in most Western religious contexts. Many persons in the West who identify with Christianity, for example, or who live in contexts influenced by Christianity, appear to assume that food preferences and practices carry no *universal* moral weight but rather take many different legitimate forms in various contexts. Most of us would probably agree that everyone should have access to food, and to plenty of it. Apart from that conclusion, however, most of us would be content either to allow other differences of custom and interpretation that surround food to flourish, or at least to negotiate among these differences and their effects in a calm and pragmatic manner that relies upon persuasion and reasoned argument rather than condemnation and hyperbolic rhetoric.

With sex our attitudes are generally quite different, and nowhere more so than in contexts shaped by Christianity. Indeed, all one has to do to recognize the distinction between common attitudes toward food and common attitudes toward sex is imagine likely responses from most religious communities if we were to assert, by way of comparison with the statement I just made about food, that from now on the only ethical point which we will insist on universalizing with respect to sex is that everyone should have access to it, and to plenty of it. Such a statement would seem ridiculous, even offensive, to many Christians. Sexual practice is a matter about which Christian denominations still argue, and over which some of them threaten to split. In contrast, practices associated with food and eating, while still treated with great seriousness by certain streams of Judaism or within particular religious groups such as the Adventists, are more often considered matters that can safely be left either to individual choice or respectful dialogue.

Some observers might attempt to explain the differences between attitudes toward food and attitudes toward sex by suggesting that, if food is necessary for individual survival, sex is not. According to this argument, put to me by more than one person during the writing of this book, the importance of food for human survival not only calls into question the value of making comparisons between food and sex; it may also account for the fact that many cultures are willing to tolerate a greater degree of pluralism and variety with respect to food than with respect to sex. As our existence depends upon the adequate intake of a certain number of calories and nutrients, we have, according to this view, rightly recognized both the need to eat a range of different kinds of food and the fact that different people in different circumstances have access to different sorts of food (and so receive their calories in different ways).

Now it is not really the case, as this argument implies, that human beings take advantage of the wide range of ways in which calories can be obtained in any given situation. One of the phenomena emphasized by studies of food and eating is the tendency for both cultures and individuals to avoid certain potential food sources, readily available in their context, which other cultures and individuals would utilize (e.g., Simoons 1994; Capaldi 1996). It is, however, obviously true that at the level of the individual human organism food is necessary for survival in a way that sex is not. Indeed, this is a convenient point at which to dispel another possible misunderstanding of my project. While I do intend to explore, in relation to biblical interpretation, the implications of Pollock's suggestion that food and sex are 'good to think' one another, it is certainly not my view that the significance and effects of food and sex are ever completely identical. There are clearly many dimensions of sexual practices and meanings that cannot be accounted for adequately by thinking about them only in relation to food, and there are clearly many dimensions of the practices and meanings associated with food that cannot be accounted for adequately by thinking about them only in relation to sex.

Nonetheless, we should not forget that, while food is necessary for human survival at the level of the individual organism, sex is also necessary for human survival at the level of the species. Although developments in reproductive technology may be changing this fact, a minimum level of sexual interaction has been as necessary as a minimum level of food consumption for the survival of the human race as a whole. I am therefore not convinced that differences between attitudes toward food and attitudes toward sex can be accounted for solely in terms of their distinct contributions to human survival. In any case, such a focus on minimum required levels of either food or sex for human survival seems to me to lead to a rather impoverished way of approaching human life. Surely we are better served by asking about the ways in which both food and sex can contribute not simply to human survival, but to human flourishing and pleasure.

Even if we should be persuaded by the argument that our decisions about the relative significance of food and of sex ought to be linked to their respective contributions to the survival of the human organism, this would seem to me to be an argument in favor of worrying much *more* than many of us currently do about food arrangements and much *less* than many of us currently do about sexual arrangements. In other words, a plausible case could be made that the argument would lead in a direction quite opposite to that taken by my ethicist interlocutor, and that it is food rather than sex which ought to be receiving more attention than it currently does within religious, and especially Christian, communities in the West.

Thus, the anxiety expressed by the ethicist about the possibility that sex and sexual pluralism would be treated 'like food' seems to me to be largely an effect of what Gayle Rubin calls a 'fallacy of misplaced scale'. By using this phrase, Rubin points out that sexual activities are frequently given symbolic value and provoke emotional responses far out of proportion to any inherent meaning or necessary effects. In order to drive her point home, Rubin, too, contrasts attitudes toward sex with attitudes toward food: 'Although people can be intolerant, silly, or pushy about what constitutes proper diet', she notes, 'differences in menu rarely provoke the kinds of rage, anxiety, and sheer terror that routinely accompany differences in erotic tastes.' Rubin therefore concludes that sexual acts are too often 'burdened with an excess of significance' (Rubin 1984: 279).

Now I am aware that important questions having to do with power relations and exploitation need to be raised today when sexual matters are considered. Such questions, which rightly concerned my ethicist interlocutor, necessarily impact the 'significance' with which we 'burden' issues related to sex (to borrow Rubin's language); and they need to be taken into account by anyone who argues that food and sex can be handled in comparable ways. I will address some of these questions further, especially in chapter 4. For the moment, however, I will simply note that questions about power relations and exploitation can and should be raised in connection with food as well; and that inequalities in access to food, for example, are at least as serious an area of ethical concern and arguably more serious than the sexual questions which so obsess religious denominations today. If exploitation is wrong (as I believe it is), then we should try to eliminate it whether it manifests itself in relation to food or sex or anything else.

Most of us already recognize, at least in our practice if not always in explicit statements, that we do not need to wait until problems such as world hunger have been solved in order to enjoy eating, to imagine that others should derive pleasure from eating, and to tolerate a fair amount of pluralism with respect to food. Quite the contrary: the pleasure and comfort that we derive from a good meal can actually become an incentive to remove the barriers that prevent other human beings from experiencing such pleasure and comfort. Our encounters with different types of eating experiences (that is, with various sorts of food, prepared or presented in various ways and eaten in various contexts, with others or alone, in a hurry or at a leisurely pace, making use of various kinds of implements, etc.) can lead us to understand that diversity with respect to the preparation, consumption and meaning of food is a positive rather than a negative fact of human existence. Why should it not be the case, then, that the pleasure and comfort that we derive from sex might also become an incentive to remove the barriers that prevent other human beings from experiencing such pleasure and comfort? Why shouldn't our encounters with alternative sexual experiences (in various positions, in various contexts, with various types and numbers of partners, together with others or alone, in a hurry or at a leisurely pace, making use of various kinds of implements, etc.) lead us to understand that diversity with respect to sexual matters can also be a positive rather than a negative fact of human existence? Discussions of the very important problem of sexual exploitation seem far too often to be overdetermined instead by the long Christian tradition of viewing sexual pluralism and pleasure with a suspicion that is much less often deployed in relation to food.

Throughout this project I will work to keep both food and sex firmly in my sights, resisting in particular the assumption that biblical texts unambiguously support the contention that sex is inherently more grave and significant than food. Through a series of readings – readings of biblical texts, of interpretations of biblical texts, and of certain texts of cultural analysis – I wish to suggest that, contrary to the assumptions of the ethicist, it would not be a mistake for contemporary religious communities that make use of the Bible – and, for that matter, non-religious communities as well – to begin to 'think' food and sex in comparable ways. At a time when sexual disputes threaten to tear apart religious denominations and local congregations, I believe that a great deal of insight can be obtained from careful consideration of the many possible relations that exist, have been thought to exist, or could be made to exist between food and sex.

II

It will quickly become clear that the essays which follow do not exactly constitute 'a theology of food and sex'. They are concerned first of all with, and take their point of departure from, biblical interpretation; and the close reading of biblical texts plays a major role in this study. At the same time, I am not interested here *simply* in uncovering 'what the Bible has to say' about food and/or about sex. A consideration of biblical attitudes toward sex and of biblical attitudes toward food will, of course, play an important role in the chapters that follow (though I make no pretense at covering all of the biblical passages that are potentially relevant for a thorough study of such attitudes). In my view, much work remains to be done by biblical scholars on each of these topics, in spite of the projects already produced that examine biblical views of either sexual practice (e.g., Carr 2003; Brenner 1997; Streete 1997; Stone 1996; Frymer-Kensky 1989) or food (e.g., Sharon 2002; Brenner and van Henten 1999; Soler 1997; Feeley-Harnik 1994). Nevertheless, I am concerned here not simply with what the Bible 'says' or assumes about food and sex but also, and more importantly, with the ways in which we interact with biblical passages that refer to food and sex. For in many Christian contexts, and in many non-Christian contexts influenced by Christianity, a preoccupation with sexual matters and a relative lack of concern about food matters already shapes the ways in which, and the frequency with which, certain questions – for example, questions about the Bible and homosexuality – are put to the biblical texts while other questions – for example, questions about food practices and food symbolism – are more often ignored.

As I have continued to reflect on ways in which we read biblical passages that refer to food or sex, moreover, I have increasingly come to believe that food and sex are not only 'good to think' one another, as Pollock suggests, but also that food and sex are 'good to think' the nature and goals of biblical interpretation in the contemporary world. Indeed, my title, 'Practicing Safer Text', is itself an example of the use of issues associated today with sex and/or food to 're-think' biblical interpretation. It is also an indication of my intention to argue in this book for a particular, and somewhat pragmatic, approach to biblical interpretation. As the pun indicates, this view of biblical interpretation as the development of practices of 'safer text' is modeled in part on the attempts by AIDS activists to respond pragmatically to the dangers of HIV transmission by developing and encouraging practices of 'safer sex'. Because my rhetorical appeal to 'safer sex' as a model for biblical interpretation will no doubt surprise some readers, I want to explain its rationale briefly here.

As is well known, the fact that the Human Immunodeficiency Virus, or HIV, can be transmitted from person to person through particular sexual practices contributed to an overrepresentation of gay men among those persons infected with the virus in the United States and Western Europe, especially in the first decade of the AIDS crisis, but to a significant degree still today. This overrepresentation helped to produce, in turn, a strong association between AIDS and homosexuality in the early years of the epidemic, an association made clear by such facts as early references to the medical syndrome as Gay Related Immunodeficiency (GRID) Syndrome, and identification by the US Centers for Disease Control of 'homosexuals' as, collectively, a 'high-risk' group. One by-product of this association was a strengthening of the stigmatization of gay male sexual practices, which social and cultural responses to AIDS both built upon and took in new directions (cf. Treichler 1999; Watney 1989, 1994). This process was no doubt exacerbated by interpretations of homosexuality as itself a form of sickness (cf. Terry 1999), and perhaps also by longstanding if implicit associations between death and desire (cf. Dollimore 1998; Clack 2002).

In this situation many forces conspire to send, above all to gay men but also to others, the message that the only appropriate sexual responses to AIDS are abstinence and monogamy, the twin pillars of an attitude toward sex that Cindy Patton calls 'sexual austerity' (Patton 1996: 104). Dennis Altman puts the matter well when he points out that 'for moral conservatives AIDS seemed almost tailor-made as a rebuke to those who argued that it was possible to regard sex as recreation, and in many parts of the world … it was argued that the only meaningful response to AIDS was abstinence, celibacy, or at best mutual monogamy' (D. Altman 2001: 69). Indeed, even certain gay writers have accepted or promoted some version of this message of 'sexual austerity', especially in recent years (e.g., Kramer 1997; Rotello 1997).

However, other lesbian and gay writers and AIDS activists refuse to adopt the position that 'homosexual sex' as such, or even so-called 'promiscuity', are themselves inherently dangerous. As advocates for this alternative position point out, since epidemiological research has shown that the overwhelming majority of cases of sexual transmission of HIV can be linked to quite specific sexual practices, it is important to stress that it is not the gender of one's sexual partners, the number of one's sexual partners, or the location of one's sexual encounters, but rather the avoidance and/or modification of particular practices in particular situations that are crucial for the prevention of HIV transmission. Attempting to come to terms with the fact that HIV can indeed be transmitted sexually, while also trying to avoid sex-negative and heteronormative messages, AIDS activists and public health workers advocate practices of 'safer sex'. Such an approach emphasizes that, even if some uncertainty remains about the circumstances under which HIV transmission could ever conceivably take place, our knowledge about HIV transmission is sufficient to allow us to determine that the risk of such transmission can be drastically reduced in the overwhelming majority of sexual contacts if only a limited number of practices are consistently adopted, avoided, or modified (cf. King 1993; Watney 1994; Odets 1995; Turner 1997). To be sure, as the language of 'safer' (as opposed to 'safe') sex acknowledges, debates continue to take place about the varying degrees of risk associated with particular practices and circumstances, and about the acceptable levels of risk that individuals are or should be prepared to live with (in sexual as in other matters of human life). Moreover, discussions about 'safer sex' continue to be caught up in political controversies, including controversies over public funding for explicit representations of sexuality. Nevertheless, the emphasis upon 'safer sex' did seem to contribute to a certain leveling-off in the number of new HIV infections in urban gay male communities in the 1980s, and allowed many members of these communities to avoid successfully the binary alternatives of either denying that HIV could be transmitted sexually or succumbing to rigid versions of 'sexual austerity'.

Recently in the United States there seem to have been disturbing trends toward a resurgence in the most risky forms of sexual contact among men who have sexual relations with men. There has also been a resurgence in new HIV infections among that same population (see, e.g., Okie 2001). Careful reflection on these trends is instructive. Some of the 'resurgence' appears to have taken place among men that have sexual contacts with men but who are positioned to some degree, on the basis of such factors as age, race, class or culture, outside the populations of urban gay men among whom norms of safer sex had an earlier level of success (cf. Steinhauer 2001; L. Altman 2001; Russell 2001). These developments may speak not to the failure of 'safer sex' approaches, but rather to the need for such approaches to be worked out continually in relation to particular populations who live and imagine their lives in diverse and ever-changing circumstances. Strategies for the communication and implementation of 'safer sex' approaches that have proven useful for white, middle-class men in Europe and North America who self-identify as 'gay' cannot always be applied in a straightforward way to other populations of men who have sexual contact with men in different contexts, and still less to women, IV-drug users, and so forth. One must seek instead to understand thoroughly, and then create new strategies appropriate to, such specific populations of men who have sex with men as African Americans (cf. Peterson 1997), Latinos (cf. Diaz 1997), or men from other cultural backgrounds who do not conceptualize their sexual experiences in terms of middle-class Euro-American 'gay identity' (cf. Parker 1994).

One must also take into account the fact that even Euro-American gay men in urban gay enclaves now face a new context in which to think about 'safer sex' practices, a context in which new medicines, fewer visible deaths among one's acquaintances, and sheer exhaustion can produce a less vigilant attitude with respect to the dangers of HIV infection (cf. Goode 2001). One must seek to understand and discuss openly the psychic and physical appeal of unprotected anal intercourse, as well as the complex role generally of sex in the lives of gay men inhabiting a homophobic world, which will always complicate efforts at HIV prevention (cf. Crimp 2002: 282–301; Goss 2002: 72–87). For the sake of increased flexibility one must be willing to acknowledge that even messages with widespread applicability – for example, the advice to use a condom in every instance of anal intercourse – might be safely renegotiated in particular contexts – for example, between gay male sexual partners who refrain from participating in unprotected anal intercourse with other partners. Equally recommendations for 'safer sex' aimed at lesbians or persons participating in heterosexual intercourse will need to be formulated with still other considerations in mind. In other words 'safer sex' messages and approaches cannot be simplistically universalized but must take into account the contingencies of context, culture and situation. This is a fact that we shall have to keep in mind when we use safer sex practices as a sort of model for re-'thinking' biblical interpretation.

In a study of food and sex it is also important to point out that if sexual activity has to be approached with some awareness of the potential risks involved in particular instances of sexual contact, so too the distribution, preparation and consumption of food constitute a field within which an assessment of risks is important. After all, a great deal of psychological pain, physiological dysfunction and social and economic oppression can be linked to food practices. The spread of eating disorders; the difficulty of determining and acting upon the relation between diet and health; the growth of ecological destruction and the inhumane treatment of animals under modern agribusiness; the reproduction of inequality between nations through the so-called 'free trade' of food; the reproduction of gender, racial and class inequalities through assumptions about who prepares food for, and serves food to, whom; the support for regressive labor policies in some sectors of the food processing and restaurant industries; and, worst of all, the continuing obscenity of malnutrition and starvation in a world that also contains economic prosperity – all of these examples illustrate the potential dangers of food practices. If we ignore these dangers and simply take for granted the beneficial nature of food practices, a potential source of nourishment can turn into an occasion for pain, oppression and even death. As with sex, so also with food, the importance of safer practice is clear.

Eric Schlosser, in his popular exposé of the global 'fast food' industry, explicitly compares some of the potential risks associated today with food and eating to the risks of HIV infection (Schlosser 2001: 196). The comparison may seem absurd until we recognize that, according to relatively conservative estimates (e.g. Mead, *et al.*, 1999), as many as 5000 people each year – between thirteen and fourteen people every day – die from food poisoning in the United States alone. Other estimates put the total number of food poisoning deaths in the United States as high as 9000 people each year, and the numbers would be higher in other parts of the world. While food poisoning has always been a potential risk for humankind, Schlosser points out that certain features of our contemporary industrialized world actually facilitate the spread of food-borne pathogens – just as certain features of our contemporary world facilitate both the spread and the impact of HIV (cf. D. Altman 2001: 70–3). We do not have to push Schlosser's analogy too far in order to draw from it the conclusion that, with respect to food as with respect to sex, the promotion of context-sensitive 'safer' practices is today a desideratum. It is obvious also that 'safer food', like 'safer sex', is a topic that cannot be understood adequately without taking into account political interests and controversies that both produce and restrict possibilities for the fostering of new and safer practices (cf. Nestle 2002; 2003).

Now it may be somewhat easier for us to draw a connection to biblical interpretation from this presence of risk within the domain of food than it is, at least initially, to draw such a connection from the presence of risk within the domain of sex. Eating and drinking, after all, have long provided a language with which to speak about religious experiences and the appropriation of biblical ideas. The roots of this phenomenon seem to lie within the Bible itself. It is not only the case that such central biblical rituals as the Passover meal and the Eucharist are founded upon food symbolism; certain biblical texts also speak about the message that God gives as something that one can eat. Thus, the prophet Jeremiah 'eats' the words of God (Jer. 15.16). Ezekiel is commanded to 'eat' the scroll which contains the message that God wants Ezekiel to proclaim; and, when Ezekiel does so, he discovers that the scroll is 'sweet as honey' (Ezek. 3.3) even though the message itself is unpleasant. Isaiah 55 compares its message of restoration to 'wine and milk', and food that is 'good' and 'rich' (Isa. 55.1–2). The gospel of John refers to Jesus as the 'bread of life' that, unlike the manna given to the Israelites, allows one who partakes to live forever (Jn 6.22–59). As this same gospel refers to Jesus not only as 'bread' but also as 'word'; and as Christians, especially Protestants, frequently speak about the Bible as 'the word of God', it is not surprising that popular devotional literature links these images by talking about Bible study as 'bread for the journey'.[3] Within Christianity, 'the Word' is spoken about as a sort of 'bread'. This popular metaphorical conceptualization of biblical interpretation as a practice that is or can be 'nourishing' is simply a logical extension of clusters of symbols and images found within the Bible itself.

To talk about biblical interpretation metaphorically as 'bread' is, of course, a way of underscoring its potential positive effects. One must also acknowledge,

---

3.   See for example
http://www.cpo-online.org/catalogue/Bible_Study/breadforthejourney1.htm

however, that even if biblical interpretation can be (like food) nourishing and generative of life, so also it can be (again like food) dangerous and productive of death. Indeed, the literary theorist, Mieke Bal, has gone so far as to state that 'the Bible, of all books, is the most dangerous one, the one that has been endowed with the power to kill' (Bal 1991a: 14). While some readers will be tempted to dismiss this assertion as exaggeration, it acquires a troubling credibility when considered in the light of such phenomena as the use of the Bible to legitimize violence against women (Thistlethwaite 1985; Fontaine 1997) or against gays and lesbians (Comstock 1991), or to justify slavery (Haynes 2002) or political and ethnic violence (cf. Schwartz 1997; Collins 2003). It is therefore easy to be sympathetic to Michael J. Clark when he asserts that 'I studiously avoid the Bible whenever I can.' Clark, an openly gay and HIV-positive theologian, goes on to justify what he cleverly refers to as his 'scripture-phobia' by emphasizing 'the extent to which the Bible has been used, over and over again, as a tool of oppression and even terrorism, as the ideological justification not only for excluding gay men and lesbians, but also for blaming the victim in the AIDS health crisis and for engaging in acts of antigay/antilesbian violence' (Clark 1997: 9–10). What we have here is a clear recognition of the risks of biblical interpretation.

But are avoidance and fear ('phobia') of the Bible the only ways of responding to such recognition? Bal, cited above, uses the dangers associated with biblical interpretation to justify her direct engagement with it. Indeed, if we think about the dangers of biblical interpretation in relation to the ways in which we handle risks associated with food and sex, we might conclude that the best course of action is neither to eschew biblical interpretation altogether nor to approach the Bible uncritically or with a blindness to its dangers but, rather, to concentrate on *the creation of safer practices of textual intercourse.*

A point of comparison for the argument I am trying to make is provided by the work of the feminist biblical scholar Elisabeth Schüssler Fiorenza, who, a number of years ago, gave a collection of her essays the title *Bread Not Stone*. The title is derived from a passage in the gospel of Matthew (7.9) in which Jesus asks his listeners whether they would give a stone to a child who asks for bread. The implied answer is, of course, 'no'; in a similar fashion, Schüssler Fiorenza argues that biblical interpretation should provide bread rather than stone for readers of the Bible (Schüssler Fiorenza 1984: xiii). Yet as she points out, the Bible, while ostensibly playing a positive role in the lives of readers (and thus serving as 'bread'), too often functions instead to legitimize oppression and discrimination, especially for women. Thus, Schüssler Fiorenza insists that readers must confront the risks associated with biblical interpretation while at the same time generating strategies for reading the Bible in ways that promote equality, justice and liberation. Her consistent call over many years for readers of the Bible to evaluate critically both biblical texts and their various interpretations can be understood precisely as one attempt to make the 'bread' of biblical interpretation 'safer' for women and others who turn to it for nourishment rather than poison.[4] Just

---

4.   While Schüssler Fiorenza continues to develop her approach to biblical interpretation (see, e.g., Schüssler Fiorenza 1992; 1998; 1999), her attention to the potential dangers of biblical texts and biblical interpretation is a consistent feature of her work.

as 'safer sex' practices seek to avoid the false alternatives of, on the one hand, excessive 'sexual austerity' and, on the other hand, refusing to acknowledge the real risks of sexual transmission of HIV, so also Schüssler Fiorenza argues that feminist practices of biblical interpretation must avoid the false alternatives of a total rejection of biblical interpretation due to its negative effects and refusing to acknowledge the real dangers posed to many people by biblical interpretation.

My rhetorical framing of interactions with the Bible as 'practices of safer text' therefore indicates a fundamental agreement with Schüssler Fiorenza and other feminist scholars[5] about the need for contemporary readers to make pragmatic assessments of biblical texts and their interpretations in terms of the potential of those texts and interpretations for both good and ill effects. Such an approach to biblical interpretation would insist upon evaluating particular acts of reading the Bible by asking how those acts of reading contribute to the creation and sustenance of positive effects (e.g., justice, pleasure, freedom and companionship) in concrete situations, and whether the acts of reading in question sufficiently recognize, avoid, combat, mitigate, or seek to transform the various dangers that confront readers of the Bible who approach it in multiple circumstances.

However, this evaluative process will not, and should not claim to, produce a completely 'safe' or sanitized biblical interpretation. Here again, an explicit comparison with 'safer sex' strategies is illuminating. As Samuel Delany points out, the fantasy of *total* safety informing some versions of 'safe sex' bears far too close a similarity to a certain nostalgic and destructive notion of 'safe neighborhoods, safe cities, and committed (i.e., safe) relationships, a notion that currently functions much the way the notion of "security" and "conformity" did in the fifties' (Delany 1999: 122).[6] In distinction from this restrictive fantasy of a completely 'safe sex', *safer* sex approaches acknowledge that pleasure always exists in relation to some degree of risk, and that attempts to reduce any risk whatsoever are not only naïve, but too frequently result in the elimination of pleasure as well. I wish to emphasize again that my goal is the development of a 'safer', as opposed to an absolutely 'safe', biblical interpretation. One can work vigorously for harm reduction in biblical interpretation without succumbing to the myth that potential negative consequences can ever be eliminated entirely, or without falling into the trap of domesticating our reading of the Bible. Carrying forward my analogy with 'safer sex' and its recognition of the importance of context-specific strategies, I want to be clear about the fact that I am not advocating a single approach to biblical interpretation that is applicable to all readers in all situations. The essays found here are offered as examples of ways in which safer practices of biblical interpretation might be fostered by readers such as myself, who are involved in contemporary religious disputes over sexual matters especially in Europe and North America. As it is neither possible nor desirable to articulate a model or method for biblical

5. Thus Tolbert has long noted that the necessity of reading 'the same Bible as enslaver and liberator ... is the paradoxical challenge of feminist biblical hermeneutics' (Tolbert 1983: 126). Cf. Tolbert 1990; 1995a; 1995b; 1998.

6. Delany published this sentence in 1999. More recent events that have brought 'national security' once again to the fore, especially in the United States, only underscore the wisdom of Delany's caution.

interpretation that is equally useful for all readers in all contexts, I assume from the beginning that different groups of readers will need to work out concretely the best ways of 'practicing safer text' in their own situations.

III

I will return to these issues at various points in the chapters that follow. Here, I want to point out that the growth of feminist analyses of the Bible (such as those put forward by Schüssler Fiorenza) is only one of a number of changes that have taken place within biblical studies over the last twenty years that have made possible the readings of the Bible found in this book. Biblical scholarship today is character-ized by an increased willingness to carry out readings of the Bible that transgress the boundaries of biblical, religious or theological studies as traditionally defined. Throughout the discussions that follow my readings of the Bible will be generated through a kind of dialogical interaction with a wide range of discourses, sometimes more and sometimes less conventionally associated with biblical scholarship, which seem to me to shed light on food, sex and biblical interpretation.

Among the discourses that play a role here, the ones that have been least directly engaged by biblical scholars until now are the discourses of lesbian and gay studies and queer theory. There are no doubt numerous reasons for this lack of engagement, including the relatively recent emergence of the discourses in question and the fact that, as Stephen Moore notes (2001: 8–9), academic trends seem to find a place within biblical studies only after they have long been established in other fields, or even on occasion after they have ceased to have much purchase there. However, it is important to consider in this context the complex relationship between biblical studies as an academic field (with its norms, publishing organs, scholarly networks, academic institutions and so forth) and religious institutions and denominations in which questions about sexuality in general, and homosexuality in particular, con-tinue to generate controversy. Mary Ann Tolbert has suggested that the tendency of even 'interdisciplinary' biblical scholars to align themselves with the more con-servative rather than the more radical forms of contemporary textual analysis often has less to do with 'thoughtful intellectual rejection of those trends' and more to do with 'the ideological avoidance of what may be perceived as potential threats to vested interests', including the interests of 'academic or ecclesial institutions or church-related presses whose vested interests run counter to the implicit cultural critique mounted by contemporary "theory"' (Tolbert 1991: 210). This suggestion seems especially apt as a partial explanation for the fact that, until quite recently, even the more adventurous and least conventional biblical scholars largely wrote as if lesbian and gay studies and queer theory did not exist. Until recently, the primary context in which such academic discourses have been brought into dia-logue with biblical scholarship has been the conversation about biblical attitudes toward same-sex relations. That conversation has produced interesting results,[7] but

---

7.   For exploration of biblical attitudes toward same-sex sexual contact, see Thurston 1990; Fewell and Gunn 1993: 105–8, 148–51; Olyan 1994; Boyarin 1995; Martin 1995a, 1996; Stone 1995; Brooten 1996; Brenner 1997: 139–44; Nissinen 1998; Carden 1999; Bird 2000; Schroer

the heavy emphasis upon such questions is clearly overdetermined by political and ecclesial conflicts over the morality of homosexuality and by particular assumptions about the Bible's religious authority. With such conflicts looming in the background, concentration upon the question of 'Bible and Homosexuality' tends to push readers into a false alternative where one's only options appear to be a denial that the Bible condemns homoeroticism or a rejection of the value of biblical interpretation altogether.

Luckily, there are signs that this situation may be starting to change and that greater efforts are being made to relate the larger fields of lesbian and gay studies and of queer theory to biblical interpretation in a wider range of ways.[8] At several points in this book the discourses of lesbian and gay studies and queer theory will move to the center of my analysis, while at other points they will lurk in the background. As I have discussed, in several other places, some of my views about readings of the Bible carried out in dialogue with lesbian and gay studies and queer theory,[9] and as some of these views will become apparent in the chapters that follow, I will not pursue the matter further here except to make two points.

First, the present study, though not primarily focused upon the Bible's attitudes toward homosexuality, can be characterized as a 'queer' project partly because I understand homosexuality to function in my own life and work as (to borrow from an important discussion of David Halperin) 'a position from which one *can* know, ... a legitimate *condition* of knowledge ... not something to be got right but an eccentric positionality to be exploited and explored: a potentially privileged site for the criticism and analysis of cultural discourses' (Halperin 1995: 60–1, original emphasis).[10] In part, I am concerned here to analyze critically those biblical discourses and discourses of biblical interpretation that involve food and sex as a way of challenging normative and heteronormative assumptions that are too frequently made about sex and the Bible by the Bible's contemporary readers. I do not claim that my own readings of the Bible and of its reception are necessarily representative of other gay male readers, or other gay male biblical scholars, for I am not confident about our ability to give such phrases as 'gay male readers of the Bible', or for that matter 'queer readers of the Bible', anything like a single, stable content. I do, however, believe that my own position as an openly gay man working in an academic discipline (biblical scholarship) and an institutional setting (theological education) that are frequently characterized by hostility toward sexual pluralism, offers me a specific 'eccentric positionality' from which heteronormative cultural and religious practices – including practices of biblical interpretation – can be contested strategically. It is a certain type of strategic reading rather than a potentially homogenizing – and exclusionary – gay identity politics that I most want to

---

and Staubli 2000; Jennings 2003. More conservative studies, containing both useful insights and flawed hermeneutical assumptions, include Wold 1998; Gagnon 2001.

8.   Cf., e.g., Moore 1998, 2001; Boer 1999: 13–32; Goss and West 2000; Schneider 2000; Stone, ed., 2001.

9.   Readers who wish to trace my ongoing reflections can consult Stone 1997a; 1999; 2000; 2001a; 2001b; 2002.

10.   Halperin's notion of 'eccentric positionality' builds upon a discussion of 'eccentric subjects' by Teresa de Lauretis (1990).

emphasize by characterizing this work as a project of 'queer' biblical interpretation. It is not accidental, for example, that I have chosen to frame this study of
biblical interpretation with an allusion to practices of 'safer sex' that have been
developed especially in relation to sexual activities taking place between men.
Such a choice reflects a conscious strategic decision to reconceptualize biblical
interpretation from a queer 'positionality' rather than, as is more often the case,
using the premises and procedures of conventional biblical interpretation to interrogate practices and persons that are sometimes called 'queer'.

Second, I wish to point out that lesbian and gay studies and queer theory[11] are
among those discourses in which appeals can already be found to the comparison
between food and sex that shapes my project. Rubin's use of such a comparison
has already been noted and will be considered again in chapter 4. So, too, Halperin
has used the comparison between food and sex to raise questions about the ways in
which preferences for sexual partners of a particular gender have come to be considered constitutive of a certain kind of 'identity' category ('sexual orientation') in
Western societies, while food preferences are less frequently given such a function
(Halperin 1990: 27–8).[12] Compelling arguments for the comparison of food and
sex can be found not only in the writings of Rubin, Halperin and other scholars
working in lesbian and gay studies and queer theory (e.g. Lee 1990: 579; Jakobson
and Pellegrini 2003: 136–9) but also in the work of Michel Foucault, whose impact
upon queer theory has been substantial. In *The Use of Pleasure*, Foucault notes
that, in many ancient Greek texts, food is nearly as important an issue for ethical
reflection as sex and is often discussed in strikingly comparable ways. While
similar observations have been made by classical scholars (e.g., Nussbaum 1990),
the conclusion that Foucault draws from classical problematizations of food and
sex deserves to be quoted here at length:

> It would be interesting, surely, to trace the long history of the connections
> between alimentary ethics and sexual ethics, as manifested in doctrines, but
> also in religious rituals and dietary rules; one would need to discover how, over
> a long period of time, the play of alimentary prescriptions became uncoupled
> from that of sexual morals, by following the evolution of their respective

11.   I realize that by using the phrase 'lesbian and gay studies and queer theory' I am glossing
over important issues having to do with the relations between these, arguably distinct, terms. But
although distinctions between 'lesbian and gay studies' and 'queer theory' might be necessary
in other contexts, the importance of allowing a range of heterogeneous resources that might fall
under one or another of these labels to have an impact upon biblical interpretation outweighs the
need for making fine distinctions here. In any case, I understand attempts to give 'queer' a firm
and dogmatic definition to stand in significant tension with the most productive energies set loose
by the emergence of what is now called 'queer theory'. Cf. Jagose 1996: 72–132; Halperin 1995;
Berlant and Warner 1995.

12.   In an important note, Halperin clarifies that he is not denying that particular food practices can be, have been, and indeed sometimes still are markers for specific classes of human
beings. His point, rather, is that historical and cultural variation in such dietary marking tends
to be taken for granted; and that the modern Western tendency 'to categorize people according
to sexual object-choice' is 'just as contingent, arbitrary, and conventional as are classifications
of people according to dietary object-choice. Both schemes are possible; neither is inevitable'
(Halperin 1990: 28).

importance (with the rather belated moment, no doubt, when the problem of sexual conduct became more worrisome than that of alimentary behaviors) and the gradual differentiation of their specific structure (the moment when sexual desire began to be questioned in terms other than alimentary appetite). In any case, in the reflection of the Greeks in the classical period, it does seem that the moral problematization of food, drink, and sexual activity was carried out in a rather similar manner. Foods, wines, and relations with women and boys constituted analogous ethical material; they brought forces into play that were natural, but that always tended to be excessive; and they all raised the same question: how could one, how must one 'make use' ... of this dynamics of pleasure, desires, and acts? (Foucault 1985: 51–2)

It is worth underscoring Foucault's acknowledgment, in this quote, of religion as one place where 'connections' have been made 'between alimentary ethics and sexual ethics'; one of my goals here will be to examine such 'connections' in so influential a religious text as the Bible. Of course, both the modes and the objects of the 'moral problematization of food, drink, and sexual activity' can take forms in the biblical texts that are different from the forms taken in the Greek texts with which Foucault was concerned. Nevertheless, Foucault's recognition that the tendency to make 'sexual conduct ... more worrisome than ... alimentary behaviors' is a contingent historical development, rather than the inevitable form which 'moral problematization' must take, has influenced the questions that motivate this project, and can stand as one example of the ways in which issues and approaches associated with lesbian and gay studies and queer theory underlie my own work.

If it is still rather rare to find biblical interpretation carried out in relation to lesbian and gay studies and queer theory, another one of my interdisciplinary dialogue partners – cultural anthropology – seems at first glance more traditional. There is, after all, a long history of interaction between biblical interpretation and the social sciences; and, during the last twenty years or so, the utilization of socioscientific insights in the context of biblical scholarship has increased significantly.[13] Much of the resulting material has focused on the reconstruction of the history and society of ancient Israel. But as I argue elsewhere (Stone 1996), insights from cultural anthropology can be used not simply to strengthen the questions and hypotheses that scholars generate as part of the task of reconstructing ancient history, though such a gain is indeed important (see, e.g., McNutt 1999). Anthropological insights can also provide a valuable reading lens, useful for the construction of a sort of 'thick interpretation' or 'anthropological reading' of the biblical text itself, even in cases where it seems clear that we are dealing with myth, legend and symbol rather than with sources for the structure of ancient society or for 'what really happened'.[14] Anthropology is valuable for such an endeavor in part because of what Kirsten Hastrup calls its 'sensitivity to unfamiliar modes of life and reasoning' (Hastrup 1995: 5). Reading the Bible in dialogue with

13. Cf. Rogerson 1984; Wilson 1984; Meyers 1988; Eilberg-Schwartz 1990: 1–102; Martin 1993; Tolbert 1993; Overholt 1996; Stone 1996; McNutt 1999: 14–31; Yee 1998, 2003.

14. My use of the phrase 'thick interpretation' to gloss the goal of an 'anthropological reading' of biblical literature is obviously indebted to Geertz's elaboration of 'thick description' in Geertz 1973: 3–30.

anthropology, or by use of what Bal calls an 'anthropological code', may help us
to foster a 'critical attitude' that does not, of course, remove the inevitable anachronism and ethnocentrism involved whenever we read ancient texts, but that does
help us at least to resist some of the more pernicious effects of such anachronism
and ethnocentrism (Bal 1988a: 73). While anthropology cannot provide us with
anything like an actual 'ethnography' of ancient Israel, its insights can allow us to
interpret biblical texts with greater sensitivity to the gap between cultural assumptions presupposed by those texts and cultural assumptions of our own – including,
I will be suggesting here, assumptions about food and sex. Thus, anthropological
investigations of both food and sex have a significant influence on the chapters that
follow.

Of course, anthropology's traditional goal of representing cultural difference,
which I have just presented as a strength, is not without difficulties. Questions
have long been raised about anthropology's history of entanglement with European
colonialism, for example, and recognition of the problem of the objectification of
cultural otherness has played a major role in stimulating contemporary critical
reflection on the rhetorical and literary conventions of ethnographic writing.[15] One
might think that the resulting 'crisis of representation' in anthropology is serious
enough to make it too problematic to be helpful as an aid in the interdisciplinary
reading of ancient texts.[16] Yet as George Marcus and Michael Fischer point out,
anthropology serves not simply to represent other cultures, but also as a kind of
'cultural critique' of the societies from which anthropologists themselves originate.
The juxtaposition of radically different ways of organizing human life contributes
to a 'disruption of common sense' among the ethnographer's readers, a 'defamiliarization' process in which 'substantive facts about another culture' are used 'as
a probe into the specific facts about a subject of criticism at home' (Marcus and
Fischer 1986: 137–8). One of my motivations for engaging anthropology as an
interdisciplinary reading partner for the current project is rooted in this impulse
toward critique by way of 'defamiliarization'. A review of anthropological research
reveals a recurring 'analogy found in many societies between sexual relations and
eating' (Tambiah 1969: 423).[17] By juxtaposing this cross-cultural 'analogy …
between sexual relations and eating' with the tendency of many Christians to treat
sexual relations as a special case for reflection and restriction, I hope among other
things to 'defamiliarize', and hence critique, our tendencies both to treat food and
sex in radically different ways and to assume that the biblical texts treat them in
radically different ways as well.

15. On anthropology and colonialism see Asad, ed., 1973. On the rhetorical and literary
conventions of ethnographic writing see Clifford and Marcus 1986; Marcus and Fischer 1986;
Clifford 1988; Geertz 1988; Rosaldo 1989; Hastrup 1995; Behar and Gordon, eds., 1996.

16. My acknowledgement of this possibility is largely rhetorical, for biblical scholars interested in the use of anthropology for biblical interpretation generally ignore the contemporary
discussions of so-called 'reflexive' or 'postmodern' anthropology to which I refer. See, however,
Segovia 2000, where the anthropological conversations in question are presupposed.

17. Other anthropological explorations of the relationship between food and sex include
McKnight 1973; Hooper 1976; Meigs 1984; Pollock 1985; Gregor 1985; Dubisch 1986; Fiddes
1991: 144–62; Kahn 1994; Counihan 1999; Farquhar 2001.

IV

Feminist and gender studies, queer theory and anthropology are all mingled promiscuously with biblical scholarship in the chapters that follow. However, the first chapter takes its point of departure from theories of reading. One significant change in contemporary biblical scholarship is the extent to which readers and practices of reading are taken seriously in discussions about meanings of the Bible, decentering, to some degree, earlier emphases upon authors, reconstructed historical contexts and 'the text itself'. This attention to readers and practices of reading will be especially important for my first chapter, which considers the story of Adam and Eve in Genesis. Instead of focusing exclusively on what the text 'really means', I also consider some of the ways in which the Genesis story has formerly been read, above all by readers whose interpretive lenses were shaped by preoccupations with food and/or sex. One of my arguments, in agreement with contemporary theories of interpretation, is that the 'meaning' of a text is far from self-evident, and shifts over time. As I hope to show, this fact about textual interpretation has implications for one's thinking about food, sex and the Bible, and it impacts one's interpretation of the story of Adam and Eve, a story frequently appealed to even today as a foundation text for attitudes toward sex and gender. After using a review of certain ancient interpretations to unsettle the assumption that the story is more clearly about sex than about food, I offer an interpretation that takes into account the sociocultural significance in the story of both food and sex.

Chapter 2 is concerned with the use of food and sex to mark the boundaries of identity. The chapter takes as its initial textual object that part of the Bible where questions about food have most often been raised: the 'laws' of the Hebrew Bible. Revisiting the analysis of biblical food laws carried out by Mary Douglas in *Purity and Danger*, I stress the fact that biblical discourse associates food and sex with one another by using them to construct ethnic and religious boundaries, and in particular the boundary between 'Israelites' and such neighbors and predecessors as 'Canaanites'. As I point out, this association is found not only in the biblical laws but also in certain biblical narratives in which food and sex both make an appearance. The chapter ends with a brief consideration of the story of Tamar the Canaanite in Genesis 38, a story that, in my view, offers queer readers a valuable resource for challenging boundaries used to construct 'identities' in our contemporary world.

Whereas, in chapter 2, my consideration of biblical texts begins in dialogue with anthropology and ends up addressing queer questions, in chapter 3 the movement runs in the opposite direction. Starting from contemporary queer questions about 'public sex', I consider certain biblical texts in which sex clearly serves public functions. Anthropological studies of honor, shame and hospitality allow me to draw a parallel between these representations of sex and certain biblical representations of food, for neither eating nor sex are, in most of their biblical occurrences, adequately characterized as intimate or 'private' activities. Thus, an analysis of biblical representations of food and sex can make a contribution to queer and feminist reconsiderations of the modern 'public/private' divide, a divide that is frequently used to relegate not only food and sex, but also religion and biblical interpretation, to the so-called 'private' sphere. This analysis of the public role of food and sex in biblical literature leads me to challenge readers of biblical texts to engage, in a creative fashion, contemporary debates around 'radical' sexual practices, including so-called 'public sex'. Once we recognize that biblical traditions already accept certain forms of 'public sex', we may be better prepared to consider the possibility that a wide range of sexual activities and modes of sexual relationality can be incorporated into the lives of those who identify with those traditions – just as a wide range of food practices is already so incorporated. Moreover, we may find that 'marriage', which is often assumed to have clear meanings that are found already in biblical literature, takes various forms that call into question assumptions about continuity between biblical and modern structures of sex, gender and kinship.

Biblical representations of 'public sex' and 'marriage' raise pressing questions about biblical gender assumptions. Thus, chapters 4 and 5 both approach food, sex and biblical interpretation by engaging more directly questions about gender that are explored today by queer theory, gender studies and feminist analysis. In chapter 4, I return to the questions about power relations and exploitation referred to earlier in this Introduction. Although the role that sex sometimes plays in oppression, and especially the oppression of women, might seem to some readers to undermine the view that it is useful to compare sex with food, I believe that just the opposite is true. The comparison between food and sex is useful in part because both food and sex serve as tools of oppression in a world of domination. On the other hand, one paradoxical characteristic of both food and sex is that they also serve, under the right circumstances, as sources of pleasure, agency and creativity, a fact which quasi-essentialist views of the relation between sex and oppression too often ignore. As I will show through a reading of two rather different biblical texts – the story of David's daughter Tamar in 2 Samuel, and the Song of Songs – this paradoxical parallel between food and sex as sources of both 'pleasure and danger' is evident in the Bible. My reading of the Song of Songs will partly be aimed, however, at showing that resources already exist within the Bible itself for fostering a positive approach to female sexual pleasure, an approach that does not ignore the reality of danger but rather contests the assumptions under which such dangers are allowed to continue to exist.

Both food and sex are utilized in the rhetoric and symbolism of various Hebrew prophets. Only occasionally, however, does such rhetoric and symbolism involve food and sex at the same time. Chapter 5 explores one prophetic text – the book of Hosea – in which such a conjunction takes place. I argue that an interpretation of Hosea which pays careful attention to the imagery of food and sex is able to shed an interesting, if troubling, light on the notion of God which Hosea presupposes, a notion that makes heavy use of gendered assumptions having to do with both sex and food. In this chapter, however, assumptions about gender are analyzed especially in terms of biblical notions of 'manhood'. In the wake of Judith Butler's influential theory of gender, I suggest that biblical constructions of manhood, such as that used in Hosea's characterization of God, need to be seen in terms of their tensions and instabilities if the contemporary attempt to ground compulsory heterosexuality in the biblical texts is going to be challenged effectively.

Chapter 6 brings me to a sort of conclusion, written in dialogue with the biblical wisdom traditions. Food and sex play a variety of roles in the wisdom books, including Proverbs and Qohelet (Ecclesiastes). Some of the views on food and sex found in these books will seem, from a modern point of view, more compelling than others. We can (indeed, must) be prepared to critique some of the assumptions underlying these views. Nevertheless, I argue that the biblical wisdom books, and especially the book of Qohelet, may point us toward an approach to food and sex which is far preferable to the excessive moralism so common in religious communities today. By reading portions of Proverbs and Qohelet to some degree against one another, I also make the argument, perhaps unexpected, that Qohelet can be read as something like a 'queer' biblical text.

Although particular New Testament texts will occasionally be referred to in the chapters that follow (along with a range of non-biblical ancient texts), the texts that are my primary interpretive objects are all taken from the Hebrew Bible. This restriction is due only in part to my own disciplinary training. I do not question the fact that, for Christians, the theological and ethical implications of the 'Old Testament' will usually be explicated in relation to the 'New Testament', just as, for Jews, implications of the Tanakh will usually be explicated in relation to the Talmud and other Jewish textual resources (cf. Levenson 1993). It certainly is the case that the New Testament contains much material relevant to an exploration of food, sex and biblical interpretation. Nevertheless, given the history of supercessionist readings of the 'Old Testament', and given the role of such readings in the history of Christian anti-Semitism, I am leery of setting up a reflection on food, sex and biblical interpretation that can be read as implying that problems perceived in texts from the 'Old Testament' are resolved by the 'New'. To put the matter another way, I am opposed to the notion that the way for Christians to make of the Hebrew Bible 'safer text' is to read it always in light of the New Testament. Thus, I concentrate here on working out suggestions for queer practices of 'safer text' by reflecting on a range of diverse texts within the Hebrew Bible itself. My own assumption is that reading procedures carried out here could also be carried out in relation to the New Testament, which would thus be read not as a solution to, but rather in many of the same ways as, the Hebrew Bible. I shall leave exploration of that assumption to others.

The chapters that follow, however, do not focus upon a single text or pursue a single line of argumentation. Rather than thinking of the chapters as steps in a linear argument, perhaps it would be more useful to understand them metaphorically as courses in a meal. As Margaret Visser points out, while the notion of a 'well-planned meal' varies greatly from culture to culture, still it generally 'evolves and progresses in an orderly fashion'. Individual courses can, in theory, be consumed independently of one another, and yet their sequence provides the diner with a kind of 'plot'. At the same time, such a meal, taken as a whole, 'must contrive to provide variety, contrast, and completeness, to range from liquid to solid, cold to hot, and through all the flavours from savoury to sweet' (1991: 196). So, too, while the chapters that follow can be read independently of one another, still some thought has gone into the order in which they are placed, and later chapters often presuppose digestion of earlier ones (though some of my readers will surely find particular chapters easier to digest than others). Moreover, while food, sex, biblical interpretation and 'queer' questions all play some role in every chapter, the structure of the relations among these elements varies a great deal from chapter to chapter, depending upon the specific texts and interpretive goals that motivate the chapter in question. That is to say, there are common ingredients here which form a kind of theme across the book, and yet the particular amount and treatment of any one ingredient can change dramatically from section to section, providing my reader, I hope, with that 'variety, contrast, and completeness' mentioned by Visser. Taken as a whole, all of the chapters attempt to contribute to my conclusion that food and sex are indeed not only 'each "good to think" the other', as Pollock suggests; but also that food and sex are 'good to think' the nature and goals of a safer biblical interpretation in the contemporary world. Whether they succeed will finally have to be determined, however, by the gratification, satiety and nourishment they produce.

CHAPTER 1

FOOD, SEX AND THE GARDEN OF EDEN;

OR, WHAT IS THE BIBLE 'ABOUT'?

Christopher Seitz has recently attempted to address what he refers to as 'the special case regarding human sexuality now confronting the church: homosexuality and homosexual behavior in specifically churchly contexts' (Seitz 1998: 263). The title of the essay in which Seitz examines this 'special case' – 'Human Sexuality Viewed from the Bible's Understanding of the Human Condition' – hints at the fact, which Seitz makes explicit elsewhere (e.g., 1998: 319), that Seitz believes the Bible should play a normative role in Christian deliberations over sexual matters. Starting out from this premise, Seitz chastises Christians who accept homosexuality within 'churchly contexts'; for, in Seitz's view, such Christians fail to acknowledge that 'scripture' is the 'avenue by which God makes the divine will known to Israel and to the church' (270).

In a postscript, Seitz singles out one portion of scripture that he seems to think is especially important for reflection on sexuality: the story of Adam and Eve and the so-called 'fall' in Genesis. This text, Seitz argues, tells us that 'the one ineluctable fact of human nature, of being human ... is that we are created male and female. More than this', Seitz continues, 'the opening chapters of Genesis insist that male-ness and femaleness is what sexual longing is fundamentally about' (273). An acceptance of our bodily state as male or as female, and hence as different from one another, corresponds, in the opinion of Seitz, with an acceptance of the human mortality that is also thematized in the story of Adam and Eve. The recognition of embodiment (as male over against female) and the inevitability of death marks the distinction between 'infantile' and 'adult' accounts of the human condition. Seitz therefore counsels his reader:

> To confront the other sexually, and not the same, is to comprehend this bodily otherness in a way for which homosexual acts have absolutely no analogy. Here stands the only possibility of becoming one flesh, which is what the reality of being a man and being a woman was originally about, for its own sake and in order to overcome individual isolation and restlessness and lack of purpose (Gen 2:18–24). For the complex package of human longing, a legacy of the fall, to be trumped, there must be a recognition of our own bodily state as men and as women, and with that comes the acceptance of our mortality. (274)

Now, if I choose to begin this chapter by calling attention to the discussion of Seitz, it is hardly because I imagine that he has much to tell us that has not been heard before about the Bible, the human condition, or sexuality. What interests me about his discussion is rather its typicality, and in particular the fact that it seems self-evident to Seitz that theological reflection on human sexuality carried out in dialogue with the Bible should proceed by way of the Genesis creation accounts. The rationale for such a conclusion is apparently found in the contents of the accounts themselves; these narratives are 'important stories *about* being *sexual* human creatures' (273, my emphasis). By asserting that the Genesis stories are 'about' 'sexual' issues, Seitz makes a move with many precedents in the history of biblical interpretation. Across the histories of Judaism and Christianity, readers of the Bible have often read the Genesis creation accounts – and especially the second, so-called 'Yahwist' account, beginning in Genesis 2.4 – as stories that are, at least in part, 'about' sexual matters.

What sorts of reading strategies are deployed when we conclude that a text is 'about' sexual questions? How do we decide (as Seitz has decided) that a particular biblical text sheds light on the decisions that individuals and communities have to make 'about' 'human sexuality' today? One goal of this chapter will be to reflect on these issues. I will not proceed by arguing that the story to which Seitz appeals is not *really* 'about' sexual matters. Rather, I want to point out, among other things, how flexible the process of determining what a biblical text is 'about' can be, so that the Yahwist creation story can be read as being 'about' not only sexual things but other things as well. The story can also be read, for example, and has been read in the past, as a story that is 'about' food and our relation to it.

My motivation for making this point, toward the beginning of a book on food, sex and biblical interpretation, lies in part in my suspicion that many readers simply assume that the potential relevance of the Bible for questions about sex is greater than its relevance for questions about food. I will *not,* however, be trying to argue that the Bible presents us with clear mandates for contemporary food practices in any way parallel to the sense in which Seitz imagines it to hold mandates for sexual activity. My aim is rather different: I wish to suggest, among other things, that our decisions as to what the Bible is 'about' – not only in terms of content, but also in terms of contemporary relevance – have at least as much to do with our own preoccupations and questions as readers, brought to the Bible and not simply extracted from it, as they do with 'the texts themselves'. Any conclusion as to what this story or any other biblical text is 'about', has a great deal to do with the tendency of readers to privilege certain elements of the story, and to draw conclusions about the story's relevance from those elements rather than others. Seitz has chosen to emphasize precisely those elements of the text that he believes pertain to sexuality, and these elements have been selected for attention because of our own contemporary preoccupations with sexual matters, preoccupations epitomized by Seitz's worries over homosexuality. Should we privilege other elements of the text – say, those having to do with food – we might draw rather different conclusions as to what the story is 'about'.

As numerous observers of biblical interpretation now point out, the 'meaning' of a text cannot be reduced to a single, easily delimited 'content', which is simply extracted from the text. On the contrary, readers of the Bible, asking different sorts of questions, working under the influence of diverse conventions of reading, and shaped by the interaction of such variables as religious tradition, cultural and historical context, gender, national origin, race and ethnicity, socio-economic class, political affiliation and a host of comparable factors, inevitably attribute multiple and even contradictory meanings to the 'same' biblical text.[1] As a consequence of recognition of this fact, studies of biblical interpretation now often focus not only upon the linguistic and literary structures of the biblical texts (as important as such structures are for textual meaning), nor exclusively upon the ancient contexts in which they were produced (although a thorough knowledge of such contexts is clearly a valuable component of biblical interpretation), but also upon the particular ways in which concrete readers can or do interpret those texts rhetorically for themselves and for specific 'interpretive communities'.

This latter notion of 'interpretive communities' is especially associated with a famous discussion of reading by Stanley Fish. In the course of putting forward his argument that the conventions of 'interpretive communities' direct our interpretations of texts, Fish suggests that disagreements over interpretation cannot be resolved by appeals to objective features of texts, as relevant 'facts' about the text are produced in the context of some interpretive perspective: 'text, context, and interpretation all emerge together' (Fish 1980: 340). However, this does not lead Fish to conclude that we are ever in a situation in which all interpretations are equally acceptable. Quite the contrary: at any time and place the conventions of interpretation at work in particular 'interpretive communities' rule out certain interpretations and allow other interpretations to be deemed plausible. Such constraints on interpretation do, however, vary from location to location, and they shift over time as well. As a result, 'within any community the boundaries of the acceptable are continually being redrawn' (343). As Fish recognizes, the implications of this continual redrawing are easily missed if we focus our attention on supposedly outlandish interpretations that are sometimes used as scare tactics by advocates of determinate meaning, advocates who wish to claim that there must be limits to the possible interpretations of a text: this text, after all, surely couldn't be made to mean *that*! Fish argues that such interpretations seem outlandish precisely because the institutional rules and protocols that might allow these interpretations to be deemed plausible are not now in existence. What one needs to do is look instead to the past and note the striking degree to which interpretations that seem 'alien and strange sounding' (345) in one context are deemed plausible or compelling in other contexts.

Here I want to underscore Fish's recognition of the importance, for his theory, of 'alien and strange sounding' readings of a text, taken from the history of interpretation. In order to interrogate the manner in which readers such as Seitz conclude that the story of Adam and Eve is 'about' 'human sexuality,' I will not begin with my own reading of the Genesis story (although I will turn to such a reading later in this chapter), but rather with some of the ways in which that story was read

1. Discussions of biblical interpretation that I find helpful on this point include Schüssler Fiorenza 1984, 1999; Bal 1988a; Moore 1989; Tolbert 1990, 1998; Weems 1991; Sugirtharajah, ed., 1991; Segovia and Tolbert, eds., 1995a, 1995b; Bible and Culture Collective 1995; Adam 1995; Fowl 1998; Fulkerson 1998; West 1999; Segovia 2000; Sherwood 2000.

in discussions of asceticism during Christianity's first half-millennium. We can discern in these discussions at least two emphases: the first emphasis understands the story to be 'about' sexual matters, not only in terms of plot but also in terms of implications for later readers; the second emphasis understands the tale to be 'about' food – again, not only in terms of plot but also in terms of implications for later readers. After showing, through this brief reflection on the story's reception, that the text and its implications can be understood in a rather different way if food matters are highlighted along with sexual matters, I will present my own re-reading of the story. This re-reading neither focuses solely on food matters nor ignores sexual matters, but pays greater attention to the presence of food within the story than do readings (such as that put forward by Seitz) which emphasize sex, but ignore questions about food.

II

Let us start, then, with the more obvious point that the Genesis creation accounts can indeed be read as 'stories about being human sexual creatures'. In the ancient world, these texts were often understood to shed light on the arrangements of sex, gender and kinship that God desires human beings to adopt. Within the Christian tradition one could even argue that the New Testament takes such an approach to the Genesis stories. Thus, in the Gospels of Matthew and Mark, Jesus is represented as quoting from both Genesis 1.27 ('And God created humankind in his image, in the image of God he created it, male and female he created them') and Genesis 2.24 ('Therefore a man leaves his father and his mother and clings to his woman, and they become one flesh') in order to question the practice of divorce (Matt. 19.3–9; Mk 10.2–9).[2] As both Jesus and his opponents note, divorce is sanctioned by the law attributed to Moses (cf. Deut. 24.1–4). Jesus, however, refers back to the moment of creation, prior to the giving of the law, in order to derive from the biblical account of creation some principle that will challenge the scriptural approach to divorce adopted among his contemporaries. He specifically appeals to biblical stories of creation in order to draw conclusions for his own time about sex and marriage. Other examples of such appeals to the creation accounts can be found elsewhere in the New Testament (e.g., 1 Cor. 6.16; 1 Tim. 2.11–15).

No later than the time of the writing of the New Testament itself, then, the creation narratives had already come to be understood (as they are still understood by Seitz) as 'important stories about being human sexual creatures'. It is therefore no surprise to find that, as studies of early Christianity emphasize, when early Christian writers attempted to work out a Christian approach to sexual desires and behaviors, they, too, frequently developed such an approach by interpreting the opening chapters of Genesis. As Elaine Pagels puts it, diverse Christian writers in the early centuries of the Common Era 'read the story of Adam and Eve, and often projected themselves into it, as a way of reflecting

---

2.   Throughout this volume, translations from the Hebrew Bible are my own except where otherwise indicated.

upon such matters as sexuality, human freedom, and human nature' (Pagels 1988: xx–xxi).[3]

For our purposes it is important to note that many of these ancient readers understood the story of Adam and Eve to have implications, not only for Christian approaches to sex, but also for Christian approaches to eating and food. After all, the first act of human disobedience, the one understood by Christian interpreters to have initiated the so-called 'fall', is a transgression of a food prohibition. Having been forbidden by God from eating the fruit of the tree of knowledge of good and evil (Gen. 2.17), Adam and Eve nevertheless proceed to do so. God explicitly asks Adam whether, 'from the tree which I commanded you not to eat, you have eaten' (3.11). Adam, while placing much of the blame for his actions on Eve, concedes that 'I ate' (3.12), and then Eve, in turn, after blaming the serpent, acknowledges also that 'I ate' (3.13). Immediately after this acknowledgment of eating, God decrees punishments for the serpent, Eve and Adam (3.14–19). Not only do these decrees respond to a transgressive act of eating; their contents touch upon food matters as well.

Should the fact that food and eating play an important role in this story be understood as relatively accidental? Do food and eating constitute nothing more than trivial means chosen to test the more important matter of obedience? Different readers of the story no doubt answer those questions in different ways, but for many early Christians the significant role of food and eating in the creation narratives was a reality to be taken seriously and handled by means of interpretation. Among other things, it illustrated the fact that food, like sex, was potentially dangerous for the Christian who understood properly that certain desires of the flesh needed to be resisted. The inability of Adam and Eve to withstand the carnal temptation of food served as a negative example for readers who might also be tempted by food. Thus, Basil of Caesarea, in the course of arguing that caution must be taken with respect to food, agrees with many ancient commentators when he explains his concern by pointing out that 'it was gluttony that betrayed Adam to death and brought wickedness upon the world, thanks to the lust of the belly' (Basil of Caesarea, *Sermo de Renuntiatione Saeculi* (Clarke 1925: 67)). Basil goes on to list other examples of biblical characters brought low by food and drink (Noah, Ham, Esau, Lot, Israel in the wilderness, etc.) but the case of Adam stands out for early Christians precisely because, in the words of a fifth century text quoted by Herbert Musurillo, 'it was the desire of food that spawned disobedience; it was the pleasure of taste that drove us from Paradise' (Musurillo 1956: 16). As Musurillo goes on to note, we have here a motif that is 'not infrequent in the Fathers', an emphasis upon the fact 'that the sin of the first man was one of gluttony' (17). The story of Adam and Eve is thus, for these readers, a story 'about' the dangers of food.

Given this concern in early Christian writings about 'the lust of the belly', it is not surprising that we also find in some of those texts an association between

---

3. In addition to Pagels see, for discussion of this trend in early Christian biblical interpretation, Brown 1985, 1988; Clark 1986, 1989, 1999; Shaw 1998: 161–219. Jewish discussions of sexual matters also frequently involved readings of Genesis, but they went in directions that were in many ways distinct from those chosen by their Christian counterparts (cf. Boyarin 1993).

chastity and fasting. Fasting is, to be sure, a complex phenomenon, which is surrounded by a wide range of motivations and explanations (cf. Arbesmann 1949–51; Musurillo 1956; Bell 1985; Bynum 1987; Grimm 1996). Certainly it is not always associated with sexual matters, and even when early Christian literature does link fasting to sex, the link is often made under the influence of ideas that have little to do with Genesis. Patristic thinkers who wrote about fasting had access, after all, to Greco-Roman texts that already contained associations between food and sex. As a number of scholars point out (e.g. Shaw 1998; Rousselle 1988; Elm 1994: 114–16; Martin 1995b: 198–228), early Christian discussions of food and sex were heirs to Greco-Roman traditions of thought about the body and desire which argued that sexual desires could be increased or decreased on the basis of, among other things, the type or amount of food and drink consumed. Consequently, Christian writings sometimes promote dietary changes, including fasting, as means for increasing or encouraging sexual purity. As gluttony leads to fornication, so fasting leads to abstinence. Even the troubling phenomenon of nocturnal emissions could be addressed in part through dietary manipulation (Brakke 1995). Moreover, empirical observation of the human body seemed to reinforce the associations between sex and eating that influenced discussions of fasting. Tertullian, for example, suggests in his treatise on fasting that the genitals are placed close to the belly because lust and gluttony 'are so united' (Tertullian, *On Fasting* I (ANF IV: 102)). The proximity of these body parts may also influence Clement of Alexandria when, in the middle of a discussion of procreation and sexual intercourse, he suddenly states (as if the connection is obvious) that 'We must keep a firm control over the pleasures of the stomach, and an absolutely uncompromising control over the organs beneath the stomach' (Clement of Alexandria, *Christ the Educator* 10.10.90 (Wood 1954: 169)). The link between fasting and chastity in early Christian literature has, then, a wide range of influences and associations.

Nevertheless, some early Christian discussions of the relationship between fasting and sexual chastity were worked out specifically through readings of Genesis. In order to understand the assumptions behind these readings we need to recall specific ways in which the story of Adam and Eve was appropriated in ancient discussions of sexual matters. Many Christian writers believed Adam and Eve to have been sexually chaste in the Garden of Eden. Chrysostom, for example, interprets the original situation of Adam and Eve as follows:

> After being fashioned, man remained in paradise and there was no reason for marriage. Man did need a helper, and she came into being; not even then did marriage seem necessary. It did not yet appear anywhere but they remained as they were without it. They lived in paradise as in heaven and they enjoyed God's company. Desire for sexual intercourse, conception, labor, childbirth, and every form of corruption had been banished from their souls. As a clear river shooting forth from a pure source, so were they in that place adorned by virginity. (Chrysostom, *On Virginity* XIV.3 (Shore 1983: 21))

Adam and Eve were virgins in the Garden, and there was no reason for sexual intercourse. It is not difficult to imagine how Christian readers of Genesis could reach this conclusion. The clearest references to sexual desire and childbirth in the story of the Garden of Eden appear, after all, in the punishments announced by

God in 3.14–19. Prior to that point we are told that men and women 'cling' to one another and become 'one flesh' (Gen. 2.24), but this statement (with its reference to the mother and father of the man in question) is clearly a description of life at the time of the story's writer, and its implications for Adam (who has no mother and father) and Eve remain vague. The text is simply silent about sexual relations in the Garden. The narrative may have been written by someone who assumed that Adam and Eve participated in sexual activity in the Garden (so Barr 1992: 66), but as the text nowhere explicitly states this, many Christian readers of Genesis assumed otherwise. Thus, Jerome asserts, 'What really happened is plain enough – that they who in Paradise remained in perpetual virginity, when they were expelled from Paradise were joined together' (Jerome, *Against Jovinianus* I:29 (NPNF VI: 368)). For such Christian readers as Jerome and Chrysostom, sexual activity distinguished the human condition after Adam and Eve were cast from the Garden from the human condition before Adam and Eve were cast from the Garden. The latter condition was understood as having been closer to the condition of the angels who, according to the gospels, do not participate in marriage (Mt. 22.30; Mk 12.25; Lk. 20.36).

It seems, then, that sexual intercourse, like death, was assumed to be characteristic of our current, cursed experience of humanity, but not intrinsic to the original divine intentions for humanity. This association between heterosexual intercourse and death, both of which were understood to be products of disobedience, appears clearly in the following comment by Chrysostom:

> Do you perceive the origin of marriage? why it seems to be necessary? It springs from disobedience, from a curse, from death. For where death is, there is marriage. When one does not exist, the other is not about. (Chysostom, *On Virginity* XIV:6 (Shore 1983: 22))

Such an association between marriage and death may seem odd to modern readers, but for Chrysostom, as for other Christian writers, sexual intercourse and the offspring that result from it were seen as something like consolation for death and a way to maintain human existence on the earth once immortality had been lost. In that respect, at least, the association that Seitz makes between heterosexuality and mortality stands in an odd sort of continuity with ancient sources.

However, advocates of Christian virginity drew from this link between mortality and heterosexual intercourse a rather different conclusion than the one Seitz draws, suggesting instead, in Peter Brown's words, that 'to abandon marriage was to face down death. It was to deliver no further hostages to death in the form of children' (Brown 1988: 298; cf. Brown 1985; Van Eijk 1972; Shaw 1998: 187–96). Advocates of virginity pointed out that the production of children resulting from heterosexual intercourse perpetuates the endless cycle of birth and death set in motion by the fall into sin. To live in chastity, however, was to participate in that overcoming of humanity's sinful condition which was initiated by Christ, and to abstain from the present sinful order in anticipation of that eschatological future in which those who are resurrected 'neither marry nor are given in marriage, but are like angels in heaven' (Mark 12.25, NRSV). In a sense, sexual abstinence returned one to the virginal state of humanity found in the Garden, allowing one to participate in, and to signify in one's body, the restoration of humanity made possible by Christ's overcoming of sin and death. Thus, Chrysostom urges his reader: 'Let us not think, therefore, that the power to marry, which arose in the beginning, is binding upon us for the future and keeps us from withdrawing from marriage. God wants us to leave it behind' (Chrysostom, On Virginity XVII:3 (Shore 1983: 25)).

Importantly, it was not only sexual matters that were understood through a reading of the Genesis story in terms of sin, death and redemption; so also matters of food and eating could be interpreted in this light. Thus Tertullian, in his treatise on fasting, emphasizes the importance of Christian fasting by contrasting it with Adam's sin of eating. As death came into the world through Adam's disobedient eating, Tertullian suggests, 'a renewed interdiction of food' is now required if 'the primordial sin' is going to be 'expiated' (Tertullian, *On Fasting* III (ANF IV: 103–4)); for that reason the Christian fasts. As Brown puts it in his discussion of the Egyptian desert fathers, 'to fast heroically, by living in the desert, the land without food, was to relive Adam's first and most fatal temptation, and to overcome it, as Adam had not done' (Brown 1988: 220–1). A more moderate Basil of Caesarea makes similar assumptions about the Christian's relation to Adam's 'fatal temptation' when he concludes: 'To sum it all up, if you gain the mastery over your appetite, you will dwell in paradise; if you do not, you will die the death' (Basil of Caesarea, *Sermo de Renuntiatione Saeculi* (Wagner 1950: 26)). Or, in the words of Gregory Nazianzen, 'We fast now, because we did not fast then, conquered by the tree of knowledge' (Oration 45 (as translated by Musurillo 1956: 23)).

In his treatise on fasting, Tertullian also points to another fact about eating that caught the attention of early Christian readers of Genesis: the first humans were vegetarians. While the first human is told by God that, with the exception of the tree of knowledge of good and evil, 'from every tree of the garden you can certainly eat' (2.16), the story of the Garden says nothing about meat. In fact, God only allows humans to eat meat at a later point in Genesis, after the fall and, indeed, after the flood, and a comparison is made at that point with the vegetation that God had allowed for human consumption from the beginning (Gen. 9.3). Thus, not only Tertullian but also such thinkers as Basil and Jerome could point out that meat was not part of the human diet in paradise (Shaw 1998: 177). One of the places in which Jerome calls attention to Adam's vegetarian diet is an interesting passage that brings together themes of fasting, vegetarianism, virginity and marriage:

> I will first point out that Adam received a command in paradise to abstain from one tree though he might eat the other fruit. The blessedness of paradise could not be consecrated without abstinence from food. So long as he fasted, he remained in paradise; he ate, and was cast out; he was no sooner cast out than he married a wife. While he fasted in paradise he continued a virgin: when he filled himself with food in the earth, he bound himself with the tie of marriage. And yet though cast out he did not immediately receive permission to eat flesh; but only the fruits of trees and the produce of the crops, and herbs, and vegetables were given him for food, that even when an exile from paradise he might feed not upon flesh which was not to be found in paradise, but upon grain and fruit like that of paradise. But afterwards when God saw that the heart of man from his youth was set on wickedness continually, and that His Spirit could not remain in them because they were flesh, He by the deluge passed sentence on the

works of the flesh, and, taking note of the extreme greediness of men, gave them liberty to eat flesh. (Jerome, *Against Jovinianus* II:15 (NPNF VI: 398))

For Jerome, Genesis shows us that God created humans to be vegetarians, and only allowed humankind to eat meat as a concession after the flood. However, Jerome also seems to believe that the Christian, by avoiding meat and wine now, can live in a redeemed state that reproduces the eating habits of paradise (see, e.g., *Against Jovinianus* 1:18 (NPNF VI: 360)).

Since Christ has come, Christians should live in the end as humans were to live in the beginning: hence, meat and wine are to be avoided. While Jerome may be an extreme case with respect to asceticism, Teresa Shaw puts forward a compelling argument, in her discussion 'Fasting and the Return to Paradise' (Shaw 1998: 161–219), that other early Christians also derived from Genesis a similar conclusion: 'Fasting and chastity symbolize and actualize the remaking of the present self and body according to an ancient and yet future ideal' (Shaw 1998: 219).

With respect to both food *and* sex, then, the stories of Genesis were read as accounts of the origins of our current sinful condition, but a condition that stood in contrast to both the original intentions of the creator and the ideal life of the person who lives in Christ. The story of the Garden of Eden, while certainly understood to be 'about' sex, was understood to be 'about' food as well. Christians appealed to the Yahwist creation account to give biblical support for both fasting and vegetarianism.

It is not my intention to determine how widespread this reading of Genesis as a text 'about' food as well as sex might have been during the first half-millennium of Christianity. Nor do I wish to be understood as attempting to distinguish orthodox positions or correct readings from heterodox positions or incorrect readings. My primary goal is simply to underscore the fact that, while a modern reader such as Seitz can, like many other modern readers, characterize these narratives as 'important stories about being human sexual creatures' without ever so much as mentioning food, early Christian readers were more inclined to think about these stories in terms of their relevance for food matters as well. We might borrow Seitz's own language and say that these Christian interpreters understood the early chapters of Genesis as 'important stories about being human *eating* creatures'.

Should we conclude from this distinction that the early Christians were better, or worse, readers of Genesis than Seitz? While ancient readers made use of elements of the text that Seitz and many other modern readers largely ignore, I am less inclined to characterize this distinction as a difference between more and less adequate readings, and more inclined to characterize it as a difference in interpretive situation. That is, such readers as Basil, Chrysostom and Jerome read Genesis in a situation in which not only sex but also food and eating were topics for serious ethical and theological debate among Christians. In this interpretive context, both 'food practices and sexual behavior were often singled out as a means of distancing the heretics from the true believers' (Grimm 1996: 93). Even questions about table etiquette, which many of us would be inclined to dismiss as having no religious significance whatsoever, were occasionally understood to have moral and political import (Leyerle 1995; Grimm 1996: 90–113). This interpretive situation to some extent 'produced' the biblical text that the early Christians saw, by directing them to put particular questions to the text and to pay careful attention to certain elements of the text rather than others.

Seitz, on the other hand, is reading the text of Genesis in a situation – the modern West – in which relatively few Christians worry about food *as a specifically Christian issue*, but in which the validity of homosexuality as a Christian practice is hotly debated. In this context food pluralism is accepted among Christians as a matter of course, and virginity as a lifelong vocation is no longer widely promoted; but approaches to homosexuality are 'singled out as a means of distancing the heretics from the true believers' (to borrow Grimm's words about food, quoted above). This interpretive situation to some extent produces the text of Genesis for Seitz and others like him (e.g. Gagnon 2001) as a story that is not necessarily about food but is certainly about sex; and not simply about sexual matters in general (Seitz is not explicitly worried about virginity, for example, as were so many of the fathers) but specifically about heterosexuality and homosexuality.

Whereas the first group of readers is preoccupied with food and virginity and reads – that is, produces – the text of Genesis accordingly, the second group of readers is preoccupied with the need to demonstrate the divine preference for heterosexuality over homosexuality and so reads – that is, produces – the text of Genesis accordingly. To return to Fish's language, it is precisely when we contrast the reading of Seitz (which no doubt seems like so much common sense to members of his own interpretive communities) with the 'alien and strange sounding' readings of the early fathers (which no doubt also seemed like so much common sense to members of their own interpretive communities) that we recognize a crucial point. It is not the case that the tendency of modern readers of the Bible to emphasize the importance of sex while ignoring food is in any way an obvious, inevitable outcome of careful attention to the biblical text. Rather, it is the tendency of modern religious interpretive communities to problematize sex far more than they problematize food, which directs modern readers to emphasize exactly those biblical texts that are thought to be most easily appropriated for sexual disputes (and especially disputes over homosexuality), while largely ignoring the many ways in which the Bible can be read as a book 'about' food.

III

One of the conventions of modern biblical scholarship is the supposition that it is useful to attempt, so far as one is able, to reconstruct the range of meanings a text can plausibly be said to have carried in the ancient contexts in which that text was written. Thus, having called attention to certain ways in which Genesis 2–3 was read by early Christians who understood those chapters to be 'about' food as well as sex, I now turn to a reading of that story which follows the modern convention of placing the text in its ancient context. My goal will be to consider whether, or in what ways, such a 'historical' reading accounts for elements of the text that early Christian writers related to the food and sex controversies of their own day.

First, however, a caveat is in order. It is not part of my claim here, or in later chapters, that by attempting to reconstruct plausible meanings for a biblical text in relation to its ancient contexts I will thereby have produced *the* 'correct' or 'true' meaning, over against which all other meanings (such as those produced by the Christian fathers or, for that matter, by Seitz) could be considered so many errors. Such a claim would indeed be compatible with the assumptions underlying much modern scholarship; as Tolbert points out, many scholars have assumed that 'the "right" interpretation was the most historically probable one, as argued through the reason-based premises of historical criticism and as judged by one's scholarly peers; "true" and "historically original" became steadfastly linked' (Tolbert 1995b: 340). Against this assumption, Tolbert mounts a compelling argument for using ethical rather than historical criteria when adjudicating among multiple readings of a text. For our purposes it is sufficient to note, as Tolbert does, that one can acknowledge the value of an interpretation of an ancient text 'within the context of its original historical production' (341) without subscribing to the view that this interpretation is the only, or most, legitimate interpretation of the text in question. Such a historical reading is, rather, one of a number of ways in which a text can be 'contextualized' for purposes of interpretation.

An initial step in formulating such an interpretation is to note the extent to which agricultural concerns dominated the lives of those responsible for writing the biblical texts. While the texts of the Hebrew Bible reflect a range of different time periods and social situations, the provenance of all of these texts in an 'agrarian' world needs to be underscored; this context had a significant impact on the nature, extent and purposes of biblical representations of food. Ancient Israel and Judah, like their ancient Near Eastern neighbors, were thoroughly agrarian societies, in which the majority of the population was probably rural, and many individuals living in 'urban' situations (as the writers of the biblical texts arguably did) are thought to have engaged in some sort of farming from time to time (cf. McNutt 1999: 195). Not so long ago, scholars living in an industrialized world and focused more upon theological ideas than material realities sometimes failed to stress the Bible's agricultural context sufficiently. Today, scholars rightly emphasize the importance of agricultural concerns for the Israelites.[4] Consequently, the centrality of agricultural concerns in numerous biblical texts has become easier to recognize and interpret. For example, awareness of the importance of the cultivation of grains, grape vines and olive trees in the lives and economies of the Israelites helps us both to recognize and explain the fact that images of grain, wine and oil play such a large and recurring role in the biblical texts (as they do in other texts from the ancient Mediterranean). Awareness of the fact that agriculture in ancient Israel was dependent on seasonal rainfall, and could not rely (as did agriculture in Egypt and Mesopotamia) on great river systems, helps us both to notice and understand the importance of rain imagery throughout biblical literature. Moreover, such agricultural concerns are not peripheral matters but stand at the very center of the Israelite covenant with Israel's god, Yhwh. This centrality is clear in, for example, Deuteronomy 11:

> So keep all the commandment that I am commanding you today, so that you
> may have strength to go in and take possession of the land that you are crossing

4.　See Stager 1985; Hopkins 1985; Borowski 1987, 1992; Meyers 1988; Hiebert 1996; Westenholz, ed., 1998; McNutt 1999; Walsh 2000a; King and Stager 2001; Yee 2003.

over to possess, and so that you may live for a long time on the soil that Yhwh
swore to your fathers to give them and to their seed, a land flowing with milk
and honey. For the land that you are about to enter to possess is not like the land
of Egypt, from which you have come, where you sow your seed and irrigate with
your foot like a vegetable garden. The land that you are crossing over to possess
is a land of hills and valleys. From the rain of the sky it soaks up water. It is a
land that Yhwh your God looks after. The eyes of Yhwh your God are always
on it, from the beginning of the year to the end of the year. And so if you will
keep his commandments that I am commanding you today, loving Yhwh your
God, and serving him with all your heart and with all your soul, then he will
give the rain for your land in its season, the early rain and the later rain, and you
will gather in your grain, your wine, and your oil. And he will give grass in your
fields for your cattle and you will eat your fill. Take care lest you are seduced to
turn away, to serve other gods and to worship them. For the anger of Yhwh will
burn against you and he will shut up the skies, so that there will be no rain and
the soil will not give its produce. And you will soon perish from the good land
that Yhwh is giving you. (Deut 11.8–17)

The result of obeying God's commandments is understood here precisely as
agricultural success, and hence life, in a particular geographical location with a
distinct terrain and ecology. Food concerns are central to this understanding of
Israel's relations with God. Whereas modern readers frequently recall the importance for biblical religion of keeping God's commandments and 'loving Yhwh
your God, and serving him with all your heart and with all your soul' (11.13), too
often those same readers neglect to notice that these familiar injunctions are tied
in passages like this one to rain, agriculture, food provision and eating, not only
throughout Deuteronomy, but elsewhere in the Bible.

Given the importance of agricultural matters for the Israelites and biblical
religion, it is not surprising that such matters play a prominent role in the story of
Adam and Eve. Indeed, an agricultural interest is apparent from the beginning of
the story, which opens as follows:

> On the day when Yhwh God made the earth and the heavens, before any plant
> of the field was on the earth and any vegetation of the field had sprung up, for
> Yhwh God had not sent rain upon the earth, and there was no human to work
> the ground, but a mist would rise from the earth and water all the face of the
> ground (Gen. 2.4b–6)

In his study of the 'Yahwist' writer who gave us this story, Theodore Hiebert
suggests that the two phrases which I have translated generically as 'plant of the
field' and 'vegetation of the field' had more specific meanings in the text's original
context, rendered idiomatically by Hiebert as, respectively, 'pasturage' and 'field
crops' (Hiebert 1996: 37). Hiebert argues that the two types of vegetation are best
understood as, first, shrubbery that is useful for grazing and, second and more
importantly, agricultural produce, or more specifically (given the parallel between
this term and the word 'bread' in 3.18–19) some sort of grain. In other words, in
Genesis 2.5 we have references to plants that served as food for domestic animals
and humans. Trying to imagine a situation prior to, and outside of, the Garden of
Eden, the Yahwist is not simply characterizing this moment in terms of a lack of

vegetation *in general*, but more specifically in terms of the absence of those particular types of vegetation that the Israelites and their animals relied upon *for food*.
So, too, the passage calls attention to the absence of rain and agricultural laborers.
The narrator is noting that the story opens at a moment prior to the existence of
those agricultural realities with which the story's ancient audience would have
been readily familiar. Food matters, then, structure the story of the Garden of
Eden from the beginning, if only (at first) by specification of their absence.

Once Yhwh begins the process of creation, however, Yhwh does not immediately bring into existence the agricultural world of the Israelites. In a frequently
noted play on words, Yhwh creates an *'adam* from the *'adama*. Modern scholars
have attempted to capture the Hebrew wordplay in English translation – for
example, an 'earth creature' from the 'earth' (Trible 1978: 76–7) or a 'human'
from the 'humus' (Meyers 1988: 82; Batto 1992: 50) – but the important point to
note is that the *'adama* is not simply dirt but rather soil that is good for cultivation,
'arable soil' as Hiebert puts it (Hiebert 1996: 62; cf. Meyers 1988: 82). Right from
the beginning of the creation process, then, the language of agriculture is closely
linked to humanity. The human creature is produced from precisely that substance
without which other forms of produce cannot grow. It is a 'clod' (Bal 1987: 113) of
the cultivable soil.

Even after forming this earth creature, however, Yhwh does not immediately
produce 'field crops'. The 'field crops' are linguistically distinct from the 'trees',
described as 'pleasant to see and good to eat', that God causes to grow in the
Garden in 2.9 and allows the human to eat in 2.16. While the fruit-bearing trees
play an important role in the events that subsequently take place inside the Garden,
the 'field crops', referred to in their absence at the beginning of the story, only
reappear in 3.18. At that point God does refer to those crops as food for humans,
but specifically in the context of the curse that God places on the soil from which
Adam was taken:

> Because you listened to the voice of your woman and ate from the tree about
> which I commanded you, saying 'You will not eat from it', cursed is the ground
> because of you. By toil you will eat from it all the days of your life. Thorns and
> thistles it will put forth for you, and you will eat the field crops. By the sweat of
> your face you will eat bread until you return to the ground, for out of it you were
> taken. For dust you are, and to dust you will return. (Gen. 3.17b–19)

This grim picture of the difficulties involved in obtaining food reflects the writer's
understanding of agricultural realities prevalent in that writer's own time and
place. Although the precise date and location for the writing of this story remain
matters of dispute, the curse on the soil can plausibly be construed as an etiology,
a sort-of 'just-so' story, for the intensive labor necessary for agriculture in the
Mediterranean highlands environment of ancient Israel (cf. Meyers 1988: 83–4,
92–4). The narrator tells us how these agricultural realities initially came into
existence. Thus, a contrast is made in this story between, on the one hand, the
situation at the time of the story's telling, a situation reflected in the message to
Adam in chapter 3 which understands that food can normally be secured only
through laborious agricultural practices; and, on the other hand, a more idealized

situation, projected back into the mythical Garden of Eden, in which good food is said to have been more easily obtainable. If humans now have to struggle constantly with the soil, and against thorns and thistles in order to produce the field crops necessary for sustenance, at one time it was not so. Our first ancestors enjoyed a situation in which God rather than humans initially planted gardens (Gen. 2.8–9), in which humans did not have to wrestle with the soil from which they were taken, in which flowing rivers rather than seasonal rains irrigated the soil (2.10), and in which fruit was available that was both visually attractive and 'good to eat' (2.9). Through a series of events, however, those ancestors lost access to that happy situation and now we – that is, the Yahwist and the Yahwist's ancient audience – toil endlessly for food under difficult circumstances. The difference between paradise and the present is to a significant degree a difference between two situations – one real and one imagined – with respect to the production of food.

But perhaps the word 'paradise' misconstrues the story's characterization of life inside the Garden. Even though the story draws a contrast between the realities of life with which the writer was familiar, and the life imagined for the first humans inside the Garden, still the writer understands the human creature to have been created from the beginning to work. Human life inside the Garden was not entirely a life of leisure. On this point as on several others, the story of Adam and Eve stands in cultural continuity with stories told elsewhere in the ancient Near East. A number of those stories claim that humans were created as something quite close to slaves for the gods. So, for example, in the *Atrahasis* myth a goddess brings humans into existence to 'bear the load of the gods' (trans. Dalley 1989: 14, 15). In a similar fashion, in Genesis 2, God initially places the human in the Garden precisely 'to work it and keep it' (Gen. 2.15). While the second task here, commonly translated 'keep', can sometimes mean something like 'guard', the first term is certainly a word for 'work', indeed a word with a semantic field that elsewhere in the Bible is used numerous times in connection with slavery. NRSV and other translations plausibly render the word 'till' in Genesis 2.15, and later in the story – after the humans have been cast out of the Garden – the same term is used when the narrator notes that they were sent out 'to work the soil from which they were taken' (Gen. 3.23). It appears, then, that with respect to the vocation of the first humans, the *Atrahasis* myth stands as a sort of parallel to the Yahwist creation account (Batto 1992: 50–1). At the beginning of the *Atrahasis* myth, the gods carry out tasks that are later taken over by humans. So, too, the Yahwist understands the first human to have been created to work for Yhwh, who otherwise may have to do the work in question himself and who, indeed, at first causes vegetation to grow (Gen. 2.8–9). The Yahwist appears to assume, in Hiebert's words, that 'from its very inception, even in Eden, human life is equated with farming' (Hiebert 1996: 59). The difference between life in the Garden and life outside the Garden is therefore not a difference between a situation in which agricultural work is unnecessary and a situation in which such work is required. Agricultural or horticultural work is assumed to be part of the human vocation both before and after the expulsion of the humans from the Garden. What changes over the course of the story is the nature of the work in question. Cultivation of a lush garden in which food was relatively easy to secure is exchanged for brutal labor in a harsh and hostile environment.

For the Christian reader, it will be tempting to discuss this change in the traditional theological terminology of a 'fall'. However, the theological idea of a 'fall' into sin and death, while helpful as a way of characterizing interpretations of Genesis made by Christian readers, is probably a misleading characterization of the significance of the story (which never uses the word 'fall' or any of the biblical vocabulary for 'sin') in its original context (see Westermann 1984: 275–7; Meyers 1988: 76–7, 86–8; Batto 1992: 45–6; Simkins 1994: 184–5). James Barr argues that 'the main emphasis' of the story falls 'not on the origin of sin or evil, and not upon the entry of death into a world where there had been no death, but upon the loss of a chance of immortality which might conceivably have been seized by humanity' (Barr 1992: 57). Here Barr broaches the topic of death that played an important role in the early Christian interpretations of this story. In distinction from most of those interpreters, however, Barr is not convinced that the narrative assumes that Adam and Eve would have lived forever had they not eaten fruit from the forbidden tree. Neither the narrator nor God ever says, after all, that humans were created to be immortal. To be sure, God does state, after forbidding the consumption of fruit from the tree of knowledge of good and evil, that 'on the day you eat from it you will certainly die' (Gen. 2.17b). However, the Snake contests the truth of this threat, retorting, 'You will not certainly die, for God knows that on the day you eat from it, your eyes will be opened, and you will be like gods, knowing good and evil' (Gen. 3.4b–5). And it turns out that Adam and Eve do not die 'on the day' they eat the fruit. To the contrary, Adam lives for nearly another millennium (Gen. 5.4–5). Thus, Barr concludes that the Snake rather than God is the one who is telling the truth in this story: 'They ate of the fruit; their eyes were opened; they found that they knew good and evil; and they did *not* die. The serpent was the one who was right in such matters. They did not die' (Barr 1992: 8, original emphasis).

Many readers of Genesis, reading the Bible out of religious motives, may find it doubtful that the Snake rather than God could be understood as telling the truth here, and will perhaps be dismayed to find biblical scholars arguing over whether God was lying (cf. Moberly 1988) or was only 'innocently mistaken' (Batto 1992: 61). As Adam and Eve do not immediately die, and yet God by virtue of being God is assumed by many religious readers to have spoken truthfully about the consequences of eating, such readers probably conclude that the threat of death must be a threat to remove an immortality that, while perhaps never explicitly narrated, is surely implied.

However, if we are trying to read the story in the context of its ancient setting, there are several considerations that work against this popular conclusion. In the first place, on occasion the Hebrew Bible certainly does associate Israel's god with deceptive communication, as, for example, in those instances in which Yhwh puts a lying spirit in the mouths of prophets in order to deceive a king (1 Kings 22.19–23) or is understood to have given to the Israelites 'statutes that were not good and commandments by which they could not live' (Ezek. 20.25) in order, apparently, to show that the Israelites would follow laws that were self-evidently horrifying. However shocking such representations of God might be from the point of view of later religious orthodoxies, these representations are actually quite mild in an ancient world where mythological traditions assumed, as a matter of course, that divine beings, like human beings, would practice deception to achieve particular goals.

We must underscore the fact, moreover, that in matters other than the question of death the Snake tells Eve the truth. It is the Snake who points out to Eve that God is actually concerned that Adam and Eve will, by obtaining knowledge of good and evil, become 'like gods' (3.5). Certainly the human pair obtain, as a result of their eating, knowledge they did not previously have. This increase in knowledge is signified by the narrator with the very idiom previously used by the Snake: 'the eyes of the two of them were opened' (3.7). At a later point in the story, moreover, God's own words betray exactly that insecurity about the distinction between divinity and humanity which the Snake has shrewdly noted:

> Then Yhwh God said, 'Look, the human creature has become like one of us, knowing good and evil. Now he might reach out his hand and take also from the tree of life, and eat, and live forever.' So Yhwh God sent him out from the garden of Eden, to till the ground from which he was taken. (Gen. 3.22–3)

Yhwh acknowledges that in the matter of knowledge of good and evil the humans have become like gods, just as the Snake pointed out; clearly, Yhwh is worried here about the possibility that the humans, having already taken one step toward divine status, will now take another. All of this coheres with the Snake's words to Eve. It is quite logical to conclude, therefore, that in the matter of death as well it is the Snake who is telling Eve the truth. Nothing in the language of the narrative prevents one from reaching this conclusion. As one scholar puts it, 'As much as we might wish it otherwise … in basic ways the Snake was right. The result of eating is knowing good and evil, being like God/gods ("one of us"), and not dying on the day they eat. The Snake is correct in what he suggested was really on Yahweh God's mind' (Humphreys 2001: 49).

So Yhwh has made a threat of immediate death, but in the event of disobedience that threat is not carried out. The purpose of the threat, as the Snake suggests, is to protect a divine prerogative to the knowledge of good and evil, which prerogative is supposed to maintain the distinction between god and human. A narrative working out of the distinctions between humankind and the divine, in such matters as immortality and the knowledge of good and evil, seems to be one of the underlying motives behind the story (cf. Batto 1992: 54–62). One can, therefore, quite plausibly read the narrative as assuming at the beginning of chapter 3 that the humans, having eaten from neither tree, were, in distinction from God, characterized by neither immortality nor the knowledge of good and evil. By the end of the chapter they have obtained one divine prerogative (the knowledge of good and evil) by the consumption of forbidden food but have missed their chance to obtain another divine prerogative (immortality) by the consumption of forbidden food. Food, then, plays a crucial role in this story as a potential path toward the erasure of distinctions between human and divine.

Yhwh's worries about transgression of this boundary between human and divine revolve, in the early chapters of Genesis, not only around food, but also around sex. In Genesis 6 we find the following passage:

> When humans began to increase on the face of the ground, and daughters were born to them, the sons of God saw that the human daughters were attractive, and they took for themselves women, from all that they chose. Then Yhwh said,

'My spirit will not remain with human beings forever, inasmuch as they also are flesh. Their days will be one hundred and twenty years.' The Nephilim were on the earth in those days and also afterward, when the sons of God went in to the human daughters, who bore offspring for them. (Gen. 6.1–4a)

In the ancient world this obscure passage, difficult to translate and difficult to interpret, sparked a great deal of interest and commentary; the story was widely understood as an account of sexual relations between angels and human women. Modern readers often ignore or downplay the story, perhaps because of its frank incorporation of mythological concerns that are difficult to integrate with modern theological notions about the Bible (cf. Barr 1992: 84). Biblical scholars, however, generally assume that the story refers to sexual intercourse between human women and divine or semi-divine males (see Westermann 1984: 371–3). Such couplings appear to lead Yhwh to restrict further the human lifespan, which, in the previous chapter of Genesis, has been represented in many cases as nearing a millennium. The incident takes place just before the flood, and is narrated as part of the recounting of circumstances that cause Yhwh to regret having created human beings. The text thus serves as another example of the Yahwist's characterization of Yhwh as a god anxious to maintain distinctions between human beings and heavenly beings, and of the Yahwist's linking of such concerns to questions about the duration of human life. But, whereas in chapter 6 the blurring of boundaries between human and divine involves sexual transgression, in the creation story the blurring of boundaries between human and divine involves food transgressions.

Genesis is not the only ancient text that links food to a close brush with immortality. In at least two surviving Near Eastern myths, a human also comes close to obtaining immortality by eating a particular substance. One of these stories describes interactions between several deities and a sage named Adapa. While the beginning and end of Adapa's narrative are unfortunately missing, it is clear that Adapa has an opportunity to achieve immortality by ingesting 'bread of life' and 'water of life'. For reasons that are difficult to discern from the fragmentary text, however, Adapa does not partake of this bread and water and has to return to the earth (Dalley 1989: 184–7; cf. Walls 2001: 138–40).

More relevant, because better-known and better-preserved, is the Epic of Gilgamesh. The Gilgamesh Epic is, for several reasons, important for any study of food and sex in the ancient Near East. A key component of the story is the way in which sexual relations with the prostitute, Shamhat, effect the transition of Enkidu from beast to human. This transition is marked, however, by practices of eating and drinking. Before he has sexual relations with Shamhat, Enkidu eats with, and like, the animals. After having sexual relations with her, Enkidu is given bread and beer by Shamhat; it is only after eating the bread and drinking the beer that Enkidu 'became like any man' (Dalley 1989: 138), putting on clothes, anointing himself with oil and so forth. It is clearly the case, as Tikva Frymer-Kensky notes, that this story 'shows how essential food, beer, and clothing were to the Mesopotamian definition of humanity' (1992: 33; cf. Foster 1989: 29; Leick 1994: 255; Walls 2001: 28–9, *passim*); but the process by which Enkidu learns these essentials revolves around his sexual intercourse with Shamhat. Food and sex are thus closely intertwined.

For our purposes here, a more relevant section of the story occurs when a character named Utnapishtim tells Gilgamesh about a plant that is 'the secret of the gods'. This plant provides the one who eats it with immortality, or at least with a regenerating return to youthfulness. Gilgamesh manages to secure the plant, and with anticipation speaks to Ur-shanabi the boatman as follows:

> Ur-shanabi, this plant is a plant to cure a crisis!
> With it a man may win the breath of life.
> I shall take it back to Uruk the Sheepfold; I shall give it to an elder to eat, and
>   so try out the plant.
> Its name (shall be): 'An old man grows into a young man'.
> I too shall eat (it) and turn into the young man that I once was.
>
> (Dalley 1989: 119)

Unfortunately, things do not turn out quite as Gilgamesh has planned. While Gilgamesh is washing, a snake, smelling the plant's fragrance, carries it away. As the snake goes away it sheds its skin, which no doubt signifies the sort of regeneration that Gilgamesh was hoping for ('An old man grows into a young man'), and probably explains why the snake, of all creatures, was associated with the possibility of immortality.

Such stories indicate that an ancient writer like our Yahwist could easily, and in accordance with ancient Near Eastern mythological tradition, assume that humans, though now mortal and probably created as such, once had a chance to obtain immortality by eating a food known to the gods. Unfortunately we missed our opportunity at such immortality, due in part (according to both Genesis and the story of Gilgamesh) to the actions of that crafty creature, the Snake. Thus, the ancient comparative evidence supports Barr's contention that the story of the Garden was not, in its original context, about a fall into sin and death but rather about a lost chance at an immortality we never had. The point to underscore here is that the route to eternal life is, in all three mythological cases, the ingestion of food. The attention to eating in the story of Adam and Eve is, therefore, not an accidental feature but rather an element shared with other ancient Near Eastern mythological reflections on immortality, all of which were shaped, no doubt, by an awareness of the necessity of food for life.

What about sex? Readers who understand the story of Adam and Eve to be a story 'about' sex emphasize Genesis 2.23–4:

> And the human said, 'This at last is bone of my bones and flesh of my flesh. This one will be called Woman, for out of Man was this one taken'. Therefore a man leaves his father and his mother and clings to his woman, and they become one flesh.

This passage, crucial for the position taken by Seitz, derives from the creation of a second human something like an etiology for the coupling of women and men. As we have seen, silence about sexual contact in the Garden allowed early Christian advocates of virginity to argue that Adam and Eve had no sexual relations prior to expulsion from that Garden. However, one can argue in the other direction and suggest that sexual relations between the pair are not specified simply because they are, like mortality, unproblematically assumed (Barr 1992: 66–70). Although the ambiguity of the text leaves room for both interpretations, the parallel between food and sex perhaps leads in the latter direction. After all, the statements in 2.23–4 reflecting an acceptance of intercourse ('they become one flesh') precede human disobedience in the narrative. They are most plausibly construed as a mythological explanation for the origins of a situation that the Yahwist and his audience could, at the time of the story's production, see everywhere around them. As in the case of agriculture, so also in the case of sexual coupling, certain realities were known to exist. That men and women commonly came together to form a kinship unit was just as apparent to the Yahwist as the fact that the successful cultivation of food sources formed the foundation for human life. The crucial issues that the narrative attempts to explain are how these phenomena first came into existence, and how they secondarily came to assume less idealized forms.

As in the case of food production, so too in the case of sexual reproduction, the narrative recognizes that current realities leave something to be desired. This recognition is most apparent in the punishments described in chapter 3. Just as God's decree to Adam about the difficulties of agricultural labor indicates an awareness that the quest for food now takes place under less idealized conditions than those that originally obtained, God's decree to Eve indicates an awareness that matters of sex and kinship are, for women in particular, now taking place under less idealized conditions than those that originally obtained:

> To the woman [God] said, 'I will greatly increase your pain and your pregnancies. In pain you will bear children, yet toward your man will be your desire, and he will rule over you.' (Gen. 3.16)

Much ink has been spilled over this verse in recent years as it can be, and has been, read as justification for the subordination of women to men. Certainly the verse does at a minimum recognize and attempt to explain the fact that, when it was written, men exercised some sort of dominion over their wives – just as the story recognizes that food was normally secured through arduous agricultural labor involving a struggle against thorns, thistles and recalcitrant soil. In a similar fashion the story acknowledges that the process of childbirth – another form of arduous labor – is for women painful. Yet the fact that these acknowledgments appear only in descriptions of consequences for disobedience and not in previous descriptions of the purposes for which humans were created, probably indicates that such phenomena as pain in childbirth, back-breaking agricultural labor, and the subordination of women to men – but not the cultivation of plants or sexual intercourse as such – are all to be read as alterations in, rather than realizations of, 'God's original intention for creation'. These consequences are all 'etiologies of life's hardships' (Bird 1997a: 190) that stand in contrast to a previous state of affairs in which such hardships were apparently absent.

In that light, one must underscore this passage's reference to the woman's desire for the man. It is a striking fact, too often ignored, that the first explicit reference to female heterosexual desire in the Bible appears in Yhwh's description of the *negative consequences* of Eve's food transgression. The positive evaluation of heterosexual intercourse in 2.23–4 is narrated in such a way as to incorporate only the man's point of view. Scholars have given far too little attention to the association, in 3.16, between the woman's desire for the man and the largely negative context in which that desire is mentioned, perhaps out of an urge to avoid the implication that female heterosexual desire is itself a negative consequence of disobedience. In one of the few discussions even to mention this possibility, Carol Mcyers appeals to the structure of the Hebrew sentence in order to argue instead that 'the "desire" that the woman has for her companion is an attraction that already exists and is no part of the divine prescription of the oracle' (Meyers 1988: 110). I am not convinced that the grammar and syntax of the Hebrew passage rule out the conclusion that the woman's desire is 'part of the divine prescription of the oracle',[5] and I cannot resist voicing the suspicion that, precisely by such foreclosures, does scholarship contribute, consciously or unconsciously, to the naturalization of heterosexuality. Even if one assumes with Meyers that the passage is more plausibly understood as simply accepting the prior existence of a woman's heterosexual desire and recontextualizing that desire in terms of the changed circumstance of increased pain in childbearing, Meyers' subsequent discussion leads to a provocative conclusion. Based on a combination of literary analysis, archaeology and comparative evidence, Meyers points out that ancient Israelite women would have had good reasons to wish to avoid childbirth. The combination of high rates of child mortality and the need – in the context of intensive subsistence agriculture – to have large families, contributed to a situation in which women almost certainly had lower life expectancies than men (112–13). Thus, we should not be surprised that

5. For those readers interested in the technicalities of the situation, the passage in question is, in Hebrew, a verbless or nominal clause. In the Hebrew text we simply have (to give a very literal English rendering) 'and to your man your desire'. Such clauses are common in biblical Hebrew and it is understood by all translators that English translation normally requires the insertion of some 'verb of being'. However, Meyers argues in addition that 'the clause lacks a verb and therefore expresses a stative, existing condition. The "desire" that the woman has for her companion is an attraction that already exists and is not part of the divine prescription of the oracle' (Meyers 1988: 110). This position has implication for her translation of the verse as a whole, which is as follows:

I will greatly increase your toil and your pregnancies;
(Along) with travail shall you beget children.
For to your man is your desire,
And he shall predominate over you (118).

The impact of her approach to the nominal clause is apparent if we contrast the translation of the third line with the translation of the first, second and fourth lines. The first, second and fourth lines, understood by Meyers to communicate consequences of the now-changed situation, are translated with an English future tense. The third line is translated with an English present tense.

I cannot here engage all of the technicalities of the Hebrew nominal clause, but suffice it to say that, while Meyers' statement would certainly hold true for most nominal clauses in biblical Hebrew, I do not see that the absence of a verb rules out the possibility of translating this passage as, e.g., Fewell and Gunn (1993: 35) do: 'but towards your man [husband] shall be your desire.' So also the influential grammar of Joüon, translated into English by T. Muraoka (himself an expert on nominal sentences), renders the passage 'it shall be your husband that you will yearn for' (Joüon 1991: 572). Whether such an understanding is thought to be logical from the point of view of normative heterosexuality is, of course, another matter. As I suggest elsewhere (Stone 2000), the story's support for the 'heterosexual contract' is much less secure than many readers suppose.

the oracle to the woman, who will shortly be named the 'mother' of all humans (Gen. 3.20), implies 'that women would just as soon not be expected to work so hard or to have so many children' (111). The woman's desire for the man is referred to in Genesis 3.16 because, in the specific context in which the text was put together, that desire encourages her to participate in an activity – heterosexual intercourse – which she might, on the basis of self-interest, prefer to avoid.

Thus, Genesis 3.16 can plausibly be read as acknowledging that the concrete hardships of life for women are exacerbated by the effects of heterosexual intercourse. Female desires for men are understood by the Yahwist as encouraging women to participate in such intercourse in spite of the fact that their own individual well-being might produce a 'female hesitation to beget many offspring' (112). If, therefore, the story of Adam and Eve can be read in its ancient context as a story 'about' sexual matters, the attitude taken toward such matters is hardly celebratory, especially in terms of the impact of heterosexual desire on the lives of ancient women.

In its original context, then, the Yahwist creation account was arguably a story that dealt with several different matters understood to be of great importance, including mortality and immortality, agricultural production and the securing of food, and sexual reproduction. These sets of concerns are not distinct but interrelated, for mortal human life as experienced by the Israelites was strongly determined by material realities involving both food and sex.

IV

It is obviously not part of my argument that readers such as Seitz are wrong to find stories 'about' sex in the Genesis creation accounts, for concerns about sexual reproduction clearly influenced the production of the text. Not only Seitz, but also early Christian readers of Genesis, have worked through their own sexual concerns by interpreting the story of Adam and Eve. However, the specific nature of sexual concerns changes drastically over time, in part because of radical changes in context. If, in ancient Israel, sexual anxieties centered around such issues as the need for numerous offspring in the face of high infant mortality rates and severe labor needs, among early Christian writers sexual anxieties had more to do with a suspicion of bodily desires and the relative merits of virginity and sexual intercourse. There is thus a real sense in which the text of Genesis read by, for example, Jerome, is actually a rather different text than the one that would have been read earlier by an Israelite or Judahite audience, for changes in interpretive context lead to very different sorts of interpretive attention and the posing of very different interpretive questions. To return to Fish's language, 'text, context, and interpretation all emerge together' (Fish 1980: 340).

So, too, particular concerns and assumptions about agricultural production influenced the ways in which these tales were put together. The struggle for food was no easy task in the ancient Mediterranean and Near Eastern world, and it is no surprise that food matters play a significant role in the story told by the Yahwist about the origins of that world. At a later point, early Christian readers were also much concerned with questions about food, and the interpretation of biblical creation accounts became a convenient forum in which to work through these concerns, in part because the earlier texts had indeed been written in such a way that food matters were easily noticed and could be emphasized for particular interpretive purposes. As with sex, so also with food, early Christian readers approached the Genesis narratives with very different assumptions and needs than those which were most pressing for biblical writers. If, for the Yahwist, food concerns centered around the realities of agricultural production in ancient Israel, for the early Christian readers food concerns more often involved the attempt to come to terms with those bodily appetites that also influenced their worries about sex. For both the Yahwist and the early Christian readers, then, the story of Adam and Eve was a story 'about' *both* food *and* sex (and other things as well, including immortality). Nevertheless, the story in general, and its implications for both food and sex in particular, were understood in quite different ways.

Modern readers such as Seitz are frequently inclined to find in the creation accounts stories 'about' sex, but the specific sexual concerns raised in relation to the stories are often quite different from the matters that seem to have concerned either the Israelites or the early Christians. Now, for example, it is frequently homosexuality that is debated in relation to the story of Adam and Eve, not because that story anywhere refers to homosexuality, but rather because homosexuality has become a matter of great concern in religious communities and there are few biblical texts that discuss it. It is striking, however, that few modern readers find in the tale of Adam and Eve a story that sheds light on contemporary questions about food.[6] The food concerns that seem to have motivated not only the Yahwist writer, but also many early Christian readers, appear much less frequently in modern interpretations of Genesis, including those put forward by readers such as Seitz who assert strenuously that communities of faith ought to make decisions on the basis of attention to what the texts are 'about'. The texts – that is, the actual letters, words and sentences laid out on the page – have not changed in any way significant enough to account for this tendency to understand them as stories 'about' sex but not 'about' food. Rather, it is the central questions and obsessions of readers that have changed, and that lead to particular rhetorical arguments (such as those put forward by Seitz) which claim to tell us what the biblical texts are 'about'.

If it seems strange to imagine that one could think about food, sex and biblical interpretation in relation to one another, we should not conclude that this has anything to do with the actual foci of the biblical texts. We may be inclined to imagine that the Bible tells us a great deal 'about' sex but relatively little 'about' food, or that the two are in any case not linked to one another in the Bible. However, our own prior disposition as readers to place more emphasis on sex than on food, and our own failure to ask about the frequency with which food and sex are associated with one another in the Bible, lead us to construct a particular picture of supposed biblical concerns when other conclusions might plausibly be reached. What we

---

6.   Such readers do exist. Stephen Webb, for example, arguing for a Christian vegetarianism, calls attention to the early chapters of Genesis in a discussion of 'the first vegetarians' (Webb 2001: 62–6). Webb's own discussion acknowledges, however, that his food-oriented readings 'talk about the Bible in ways that surprise even the most dedicated Christians' (12).

must do, then, is look intentionally for biblical passages in which food and sex appear in close conjunction with one another. Should we find such passages, we must ask whether this conjunction is more than accidental. We must be prepared to interrogate the biblical texts dealing with food and sex precisely by asking, on the one hand, just as early Christian readers did, whether, or how, those texts can be read when they are brought into relationship with our own concerns about food and sex, and, on the other hand, whether, or how, those texts appear in yet another light when they are read with an eye toward their contexts of production. Such tasks are among those which face us in the pages that follow.

CHAPTER 2

BORDER ANXIETY:

FOOD, SEX AND THE BOUNDARIES OF IDENTITY

I

When readers develop an appetite for the study of biblical perspectives on food, they are drawn almost inevitably to the biblical legal texts. In the ancient world the *Letter of Aristeas*, probably written before the birth of Christianity, discussed biblical laws by pondering 'why, since there is one creation only, some things are considered unclean for eating' (129 [Shutt 1985: 21]). Roughly two millennia later, reflection upon this fact that 'some things are considered unclean for eating' in the laws played a major role in Mary Douglas's anthropological classic, *Purity and Danger* (Douglas 1966).

It is difficult to overstate the influence of Douglas on modern readings of biblical food laws, which nearly always engage Douglas's work to some degree.[1] *Purity and Danger* is concerned first of all, however, with the classification systems by which human beings strive to make sense of our world. These classification systems serve as interpretive frameworks that impose order on the flux of experience by attempting to fit objects of perception into patterns and categories. Inevitably, though, phenomena are encountered that are either 'anomalous' or 'ambiguous' with respect to the classification systems in question. Such phenomena are frequently singled out for special treatment, often being understood as dirty, unclean or polluting. In order to interpret views about pollution and dirt in a particular society, one must, in Douglas's opinion, know something about the classification systems that produce those views as a byproduct. Douglas's interpretation of the biblical dietary laws serves as one example of an analysis of pollution rules in terms of such a broader system of cultural classifications.

Douglas rejects a number of arguments that purport to explain why particular animals are forbidden in Leviticus and Deuteronomy, such as the argument that proscribed animals are less healthy to eat. It is a mistake however, in Douglas's opinion, to dismiss prohibitions on particular animals as illogical or 'primitive'.

---

1.   Cf., e.g., Alter 1979; Carroll 1985; Firmage 1990; Milgrom 1991: 643–742; Houston 1993; Feeley-Harnik 1994; Sawyer, ed., 1996; Harrington 2001. These studies agree or disagree with Douglas to greater and lesser degrees, but they are all compelled to interact with her arguments. On *Purity and Danger*'s wider influence see Fardon 1999: 80, *passim*.

What we must do instead is work out the logic that led to the proscription of precisely those animals that in some way troubled the classifications presupposed by the Israelites. This Douglas attempts to do, in part, by explicating formulations found in the biblical texts themselves. Thus, Douglas notes the explicit statement in Leviticus 11.3 that the Israelites may eat 'any animal that has divided hoofs and is cleft-footed and chews the cud' and compares that statement with the reasons given in the text for prohibiting four mammals: the camel, rock badger and hare because, though understood to 'chew the cud', they are not thought to have 'divided hoofs' (7.4–6); and the pig which, though it has divided hoofs and is cleft-footed, 'does not chew the cud' (7.7). As Douglas sees it, these animals are 'unclean' (7.8) because they fail to conform to the class of edible animals as 'cloven-hoofed, cud-chewing ungulates' (54). They are, therefore, 'anomalous' with respect to Israelite classifications. Douglas goes on to extend the general principles behind this analysis to other groups of animals forbidden in the texts. Though the rationales given in the texts for proscribing some of these animals are less explicit than those given for the mammals, Douglas argues that 'in general the underlying principle of cleanness in animals is that they shall conform fully to their class. Those species are unclean which are imperfect members of their class, or whose class itself confounds the general scheme of the world' (Douglas 1966: 55).

An important component of Douglas's argument, for my purposes, is her supposition that biblical dietary laws are related to other biblical stipulations; they all rest upon a common set of assumptions about purity, pollution, holiness and classification which, though often implicit, can be teased out and elaborated by the analyst. As Douglas points out, not only potential food animals but also other phenomena that blur the boundaries between cultural classifications are condemned. Thus, the interbreeding of two kinds of cattle, the sowing of two kinds of seed in the same field, and the creation of a garment out of two kinds of material are all forbidden (Lev. 19.19). Such prohibitions, which are often ignored by modern readers, rest in Douglas's view upon the notion that 'holiness requires that different classes of things shall not be confused' (1966: 53). Although Douglas does not note this, similar sorts of proscriptions are found in Deuteronomy 22, where prohibitions against sowing a field with two kinds of seed (Deut. 22.9) and wearing a garment made of both wool and linen (Deut. 22.11) are joined by a prohibition against yoking a donkey and an ox together (Deut. 22.10) and a prohibition of cross-dressing: 'The garments of a man should not go on a woman, and a man should not put on the clothes of a woman, for everyone who does these things is an abomination to Yhwh your god' (Deut. 22.5). As Douglas states elsewhere, 'there are obviously as many kinds of anomaly as there are criteria for classifying' (Douglas 1975: 282); and, applying Douglas's notions of holiness, confusion and anomaly to Deuteronomy 22.5, we could conclude that Deuteronomy forbids cross-dressing because it is understood to be anomalous with respect to, and so threatens to confuse, the classes 'male' and 'female'. We could argue as well that the prohibition of male homosexual intercourse in Leviticus 18 and 20 is grounded in concern about the confusion of these same classes, 'male' and 'female', as the linguistic form of the prohibition itself indicates.[2] Although Douglas does not address homosexuality, she does note an example of the condemnation of the *sexual* confusion of categories in Leviticus 18.23: 'You should not put your penis in any animal to defile yourself with it, and a woman should not place herself before an animal to mate with it. It is perversion.'[3] As Douglas recognizes, the word translated here as 'perversion' refers to a sort of confusion brought about by mixing or mingling. We see in the proscription of bestiality, then, as in the proscription of certain kinds of animals as food sources, that phenomena which are ambiguous or anomalous with respect to, and so threaten to confuse, cultural classifications are forbidden.

Thus, a similar logic, having to do with a concern for boundaries and systems of classification, underlies both the prohibition of certain kinds of food and the prohibition of certain kinds of sex in the biblical laws. No doubt such fear of the sexual confusion of classes also motivates the horror with which Genesis 6 views sexual intercourse between divine and human beings.

Although *Purity and Danger* provides an opening for thinking about biblical food notions and biblical sex notions in relation to one another, analogies between food and sex did not play a major role in Douglas's own initial analysis. Indeed, Douglas recognized this fact when, several years later, she returned to the topic of food in two essays included in her volume *Implicit Meanings* (1975: 249–318). In the intervening years, several anthropological analyses of animal classifications in non-Israelite cultures had appeared, and at least some of these studies (e.g., Bulmer 1967; Tambiah 1969) argued for closer links – in the cultures with which they were concerned – between taxonomies of edible and inedible animals, and categories of permitted and forbidden marriage partners. In the words of Edmund Leach, such studies uncovered a 'correspondence between the categories of sexual accessibility and the categories of edibility' (Leach 1964: 44). Responding to such arguments, Douglas acknowledges in *Implicit Meanings* that she perhaps paid insufficient attention in *Purity and Danger* to the interrelations between the biblical system of classifying edible animals and the larger social context of this system (a context that included patterns of marriage). Yet she also suggests that the 'strong analogy between bed and board' discernible in some cultures is not so apparent in the Bible. Whereas certain societies draw a parallel between classifications of animals and 'categories of marriageable persons', when one turns to 'Leviticus we seek in vain a statement, however oblique, of a similar association between eating and sex. Only a very strong analogy between table and altar stares us in the face' (Douglas 1975: 262).

Now I will suggest below that this last assertion is overstated, for a particular 'association between eating and sex' does in fact exist in Leviticus. Even Douglas does not conclude, however, that food classification and the marriage system are entirely unrelated in the biblical worldview. What one must discern is rather the nature of the relations in question, and the nature of the system that these relations

---

2. Versions of such an argument, written in dialogue with Douglas, appear in Thurston 1990; Fewell and Gunn 1993: 107–8; Stone 1996: 77–8. But cf. the reservations in Olyan 1994: 109.

3. For the translation 'penis' see Milgrom 2000: 1550, 1570.

constitute. In that regard, Douglas finds it significant that several biblical texts – for example, the principle of giving the firstborn to God (Exod. 22.29–30) and the rule of Sabbath observance (Exod. 20.10) – seem to include Israelite animals within stipulations of the covenant between God and Israel. Thus, in Douglas's opinion, Israel's relations with its animals, as articulated by the Pentateuch, fit into a larger system of relations, patterns and boundaries that demarcate Israelites, with whom God has made a covenant, from non-Israelites. This system of demarcation also includes a largely negative outlook on intermarriage between Israelites and non-Israelites, and an encouragement of endogamy. Douglas recognizes that the negative attitude toward intermarriage between Israelites and foreigners is not uniform even within the Pentateuch. Nevertheless, when she compares Pentateuchal guidelines for sex and marriage with those of other cultures, Douglas discerns a contrast between cultures that promote or tolerate exogamy and cultures such as that represented in the biblical texts, which do not promote exogamy and even, sometimes, discourage it. Douglas correlates this contrast with another contrast between, on the one hand, cultures that adopt an ambivalent or even positive attitude toward animals which are anomalous with respect to cultural classifications; and, on the other hand, cultures such as that represented in the biblical texts which adopt a more negative attitude toward anomalous animals. In short, Douglas discerns in the Pentateuch a sort of parallel between a negative attitude toward marriage with foreigners and a negative attitude toward anomalous animals. These attitudes are for Douglas evidence of a group of people who 'cherish their boundaries and want nothing better than to keep them strong and high' (1975: 304). Such biblical concerns about boundaries are easily contextualized in the exilic and/or post-exilic periods (when most biblical scholars believe the Pentateuch reached its final form), for 'a people whose experience of foreigners is disastrous will cherish perfect categories' and 'reject exchange' (307).

Thus, distinctions between clean and unclean, between permitted and forbidden food and sacrificial animals, and between permitted and forbidden marriage partners all reinforce one another in such a way that a particular message about Israelite identity is transmitted. By comparing biblical precepts concerning purity, food and marriage, Douglas is able to conclude that 'Israel is the boundary that all the other boundaries celebrate and that gives them their historic load of meaning' (Douglas 1975: 269). Guidelines for practices associated with animals and food, and guidelines for practices associated with marriage and sex, all contribute to the creation and maintenance of the boundary that demarcates Israelite identity.

Douglas's argument about boundary maintenance, then, is especially important for understanding relations between food and sex in biblical law, and it sheds light on texts that she does not herself discuss.[4] The importance of the boundary between Israelite and non-Israelite is stated clearly in Leviticus 20, a chapter that is

---

4.   This is a convenient place to note that Douglas has subsequently written several works on biblical literature that reexamine or move beyond the biblical food laws with which she initially started (see, e.g., Douglas 1993, 1996a, 1996b, 1999). In several of these texts, Douglas modifies her earlier arguments in the context of rather different interpretations of the Pentateuch. For my purposes, however, the earlier formulations (1966, 1975) are more useful.

concerned explicitly with sexual behavior but also touches upon diet. At the end of a series of proscriptions of forbidden forms of sexual contact, we find the following comments:

> You will keep all my statutes and all my commandments, and do them, so that the land into which I bring you to dwell does not vomit you out. You will not walk according to the statutes of the nations that I am driving out before you, for they did all these things and I loathed them and said to you: You will possess their land, and I will give it to you to possess, a land flowing with milk and honey. I am Yhwh your god, who separated you from the peoples. You will therefore separate the clean animal from the unclean, and the unclean bird from the clean. You will not make your throat[5] detestable with an animal or with a bird or with anything swarming on the ground, which I separated from you as unclean. You will be holy to me, for I, Yhwh, am holy, and I set you apart from the other peoples to be mine. (Lev. 20.22–6)

This passage, curiously not discussed by Douglas, links biblical sex laws with biblical food laws by way of references to clean and unclean animals in a chapter otherwise devoted to sexual proscriptions. It does so, moreover, in a way that suggests the importance of both sex and food for marking the supposed distinction between the holiness that God requires of the Israelites and the abominable behavior of people previously cast out of the land. Here we have, in other words, precisely that 'association between eating and sex' that Douglas claimed to have had some difficulty finding in Leviticus. God's 'separation' of the Israelites from other peoples is made manifest by, among other things, particular food practices and particular sexual practices. Food and sex are singled out in Leviticus 20 as making a contribution to that 'boundary' which demarcates the Israelites as a holy people and identifies them as a specific people.

II

The fact that food and sex in particular are used in Leviticus 20 to differentiate the Israelites as a people is hardly surprising. As Douglas notes, the human body often symbolizes the larger social body, and 'the orifices of the body ... symbolize its specially vulnerable points' (1966: 121; cf. Berquist 2002; Aho 2002). As eating and sexual intercourse involve the transgression of the body's boundaries, and the incorporation by the body of foreign substances, food and sex function as powerful symbolic markers of the boundaries between social units.

With respect to food, for example, distinctions are frequently made between groups of people on the basis of differences (real or perceived) in preferred foodstuffs, modes of food preparation, or practices of eating. Food often serves to mark, negotiate, and sometimes transform ethnic or national boundaries.[6] As we shall discuss in more detail in chapters 4 and 5, gender differences are associated with food as well. So, too, differences in class and status are determined and

---

5. On the translation 'throat' see Milgrom 1991: 684–5; 2000: 1763.
6. See, e.g., Ohnuki-Tierney 1993; Pilcher 1998; Gabaccia 1998; Pillsbury 1998; Witt 1999; Longo 1999; Diner 2001; Inness 2001: 88–108; Inness, ed., 2001b.

negotiated through food selection, preparation and consumption, as can be seen from such diverse phenomena as, e.g., the 'civilising of appetite' by which 'taste' is linked to social prestige; the history of the development of *haute cuisine*; the use of particular types of kitchen spaces or cooking appliances to signify style or economic purchasing power; the use of table etiquette to mark class distinctions; the relationship between socio-economic class and nutrition; the food rules regulating distinctions among the castes in Hinduism, and so forth.[7]

Associations between food and status are ancient; and within the Bible itself, as Saul Olyan (2000) points out, distinctions of rank and prestige emerge from a complex network of regulations that include specifications of the particular persons who had access to particular types of food offering. Today, in the West, distinctions of social status still take food-related forms, some of which are specific to conditions of globalization. Thus, Lisa Heldke (2003) has recently called attention to implicit functions of the pursuit of 'exotic' cuisines. Among educated, and often quite liberal persons in the United States, one's location on the scale of prestige may be marked by one's supposed ability to distinguish 'authentic' versions of the cuisines of other cultures from the mongrelized products of global mass culture, as well as by one's ability to recognize and purchase the exotic foodstuff, wine, or restaurant experience in question before they become widely known or accessible to the local masses. Although the underlying notion of 'authenticity' is, as Heldke shows, riddled with problematic and often colonialist assumptions, the appeal to it has now become a means with which Western 'foodies' generate 'cultural capital' for themselves by appropriating the foodways of others.[8]

This use of food as boundary marker does not, however, always rest upon an appreciative perception of the food practices of those existing on the far side of the boundary. Descriptions of 'the food of Others' (Longo 1999) sometimes take on a polemical quality, becoming 'a prominent feature of ethnic slurs' (Rappoport 2003: 72). Such slurs perhaps achieve their most extreme form in the tendency to accuse stigmatized Others of cannibalism (cf. Arens 1979).

Such polemics are even more apparent in the widespread appeal to sexual practices, or beliefs about them, as markers of boundaries between supposedly distinct groups of people. Certainly in the United States, beliefs or claims about sexual practice have played a crucial role in consolidating the 'color line' between black and white (cf. Somerville 2000). One must be cautious, however, about assuming too close a correspondence between the rhetoric deployed in the construction of such boundaries, and the actual practices of the people concerned. As the anthropologist Lila Abu-Lughod points out, beliefs about the shameless sexual behaviors of others are put forward even when opportunities for the actual observation of such persons and practices are absent (Abu-Lughod 1986: 48). If members of one social group view members of another social group with suspicion or hostility, they

7.   See Dumont 1980: 130–51; Goody 1982; Bourdieu 1984: 177–200; Mennell 1985; DeVault 1991: 167–226; Visser 1991; Wiessner and Schiefenhövel, eds., 1996; Beardsworth and Keil 1997: 87–99; Trubek 2000; Inness 2001: 82–5; Diner 2001; Fernández-Armesto 2002; Rappoport 2003.

8.   Both the notion of 'cultural capital' and its link with food are discussed by Bourdieu (1984), upon whom Heldke partly relies.

are more likely to credit or generate rhetoric about the supposed sexual misconduct of those positioned on the far side of the symbolic boundary distinguishing one group from another; such sexual rhetoric contributes to a strengthening of the boundary in question, irrespective of empirical evidence (or the lack thereof) for sexual activities used to mark the boundary. Indeed, such rhetoric itself comes to serve as evidence for the debased nature of those on the other side of the boundary, and so as justification for maintaining the boundary in question.

Exactly this sort of dynamic may, in fact, be at work in biblical texts that appeal to sex as part of the project of Israelite boundary definition. In an essay that emphasizes this phenomenon, Randall Bailey argues that not only laws but also narratives are sometimes structured in such a way that, in Bailey's words, the 'use of sexuality by either innuendo or graphic detail functions literarily as part of an agenda of discrediting … individuals and nations and thereby sanctioning, or sanctifying, Israelite hatred and oppression of these people' (Bailey 1995: 124). Although Bailey focuses upon sex but not food, some of the texts analyzed by Bailey are also relevant for our attempt, to 'think' food and sex together.

In Genesis 19, for example, just after the story of Sodom, we encounter the following scene:

> And Lot went up from Zoar and lived in the hill country, and his two daughters were with him. Because he was afraid to live in Zoar, he and his two daughters lived in a cave. Then the older daughter said to the younger, 'Our father is old, and there is not a man in the world to come in to us according to the way of all the world. Come, let us make our father drink wine, and let us lie with him, and from our father we will keep seed alive.' So they made their father drink wine that night, and the elder went in and lay with her father, and he did not know when she lay down or when she got up. The next day, the elder said to the younger, 'Look, I lay with Father last night. Let us make him drink wine also tonight, and you will go in and lie with him, and from our father we will keep seed alive.' So also that night they caused their father to drink wine, and the younger one got up and lay with him, and he did not know when she lay down or when she got up. Then the two daughters of Lot became pregnant by their father. The elder gave birth to a son and named him Moab, he is the father of the Moabites until today. And the younger also gave birth to a son and named him Ben-Ammi, he is the father of the Ammonites until today. (Gen. 19.30–8)

Technically, drinking rather than eating is narrated here. However, wine was a 'staple food' in ancient Israel (Walsh 2000a: 210–19); and, in this story, the ingestion of wine leads to a sexual encounter. Because Lot is drunk, his daughters are able to initiate and consummate sexual relations with him, and to bear children as a result.

Since this story, like many biblical stories, is told with a minimal amount of explicit evaluative discourse, commentators disagree over whether the actions narrated are best understood in a negative, a positive, or simply a neutral light. Readers disposed toward a more positive interpretation emphasize the importance of procreation and lineage in biblical literature and see here 'the rising again of new life, or of a new generation after an annihilation' (Westermann 1985: 315). Variations of such a reading have been put forward by some feminist interpreters, who wish to cast in a positive light the steps taken by Lot's daughters to insure the continuation of their father's line. Lot's daughters find themselves in especially dire circumstances, after all, and so take the initiative to ensure that their father's lineage continues. By highlighting the point of view communicated in the words of the elder sister, and the agency assumed by two women in a chapter that earlier grants control over their sexuality entirely to their father (cf. Gen. 19.8), one can generate an interpretation that may have strategic value for readers hoping to find active female characters in the Bible (e.g., Frymer-Kensky 2002: 258–63; cf. Brett 2000: 68–9).

If, however, we wish to assess the likely connotations of the story in its ancient Israelite context, we must consider the Bible's attitude toward the peoples for whom this story serves as an etiology: the Moabites and Ammonites. Elsewhere in the Pentateuch, Ammonites and especially Moabites are viewed quite negatively. In Deuteronomy 23, for example, we read the following:

> No Ammonite or Moabite can enter the congregation of Yhwh. Even to the tenth generation, none of their descendants can enter the congregation of Yhwh, because they did not meet you with food and water on your journey out of Egypt, and because they hired against you Balaam … to curse you. …You will never seek their welfare or benefit for as long as you live. (Deut. 23.4–5, 7)

This text is hardly neutral in its attitude toward Ammonites and Moabites. The Israelites are explicitly admonished not to promote the well-being of these two peoples, who are identified, among other things, by their refusal to give food and water to the Israelites. Moreover, this passage appears in Deuteronomy just after the following stipulation:

> No bastard will be admitted into the congregation of Yhwh, even the tenth generation will not be admitted into the congregation of Yhwh. (Deut. 23.3)

Although the word that I have translated (following Bailey) as 'bastard' is admittedly obscure, its reference to the offspring of some reprehensible form of intercourse is widely accepted. NRSV, for example, translates as 'those born of an illicit union'. The placement of this verse just before a specification that Ammonites and Moabites are not to be admitted to the 'congregation of Yhwh' can hardly be accidental. As Bailey recognizes, verses 4–7 probably function as an example of those 'bastards' who, according to verse 3, must be kept out of the congregation of Yhwh. Deuteronomy 23 arguably presupposes some knowledge of the tradition about Ammonites and Moabites found in Genesis 19, and indicates that events recounted in Genesis were viewed with suspicion.

Moreover, Moabites in particular are associated with detestable sexual liaisons and suspicious food practices elsewhere in the Pentateuch. In Numbers 25, just after the story about Balaam referred to in Deuteronomy 23, we encounter the following note:

> Israel was dwelling at Shittim, and the people defiled themselves by whoring after the daughters of Moab, who invited the people to the sacrifices of their gods. The people ate and bowed down to their gods. Israel attached itself to Baal of Peor, and Yhwh became angry with Israel. (Num. 25.1–3)

These verses refer not only to transgressive sexual relations but also to transgressive eating. Like their ancestress the daughter of Lot, Moabite women cause others to ingest food, and the men who ingest food have sexual relations with the women who lead them to that food, just as Lot has sexual relations with the daughters who give him wine. When this story is retold in Psalm 106, detestable eating is highlighted ('And they attached themselves to Baal of Peor, and ate sacrifices of the dead' [Ps. 106.28]). Moabites, then, are said to have led Israelites into both sexual and eating practices that stir up Yhwh's anger. Moabites and Ammonites are also viewed negatively elsewhere, for intermarriage with them horrifies both Ezra (9.1–3) and Nehemiah (13.23–7).

It is difficult to escape the impression that Israelite readers would have interpreted the actions of Lot's daughters negatively. These actions result in the origin of two peoples despised by the Israelites and associated with both detestable practices of sex and negative uses of food; Ammonites and Moabites either refuse to give food to the Israelites when it is needed, or cause the Israelites to eat food that should not be eaten. Lot's daughters act in accordance with just such an association with food and sex. By causing their father to drink too much wine, Lot's daughters make of him a sexual object, thereby reversing the roles of subject and object normally allotted to males and females (cf. Stone 1996) and shaming Lot in the process. Only at the end of the narration of this incident does the narrator state explicitly, and almost as a punch line, that these shameful unions produced the Moabites and Ammonites. Such knowledge must have caused no little satisfaction for the Israelites. Wine and sex are combined in the story to produce a 'derisive critique' of the ethnic origins of their enemies (Fuchs 2000: 69; cf. Coats 1983: 147).

Against this sort of polemical interpretation, some scholars attempt to cast Lot's daughters in a more positive light by calling attention to possible links between their story and the story of one of Lot's female descendants, Ruth (e.g., Frymer-Kensky 2002: 257–63). At first glance this comparison has much to commend it, especially as the book of Ruth brings together themes of food and sex. Images of food and agriculture are abundant in the book of Ruth from the opening chapter. There, famine and death in the land of Moab lead Naomi and Ruth to return to Bethlehem, the 'house of bread/food' in Judah, from which Naomi and her family traveled previously because of another famine. While chapter 2 focuses on events whereby Ruth, having journeyed to the house of food, is able to secure food from the field of Boaz, chapter 3 contains a scene with widely acknowledged sexual connotations. One night when Boaz has been winnowing barley, he eats, drinks, and lies down beside a heap of grain. Once Boaz has ingested food and drink, his contentment is described by specifying that his 'heart was good' (Ruth 3.7). The language is reminiscent of other biblical passages in which a merry heart is associated with wine (e.g., 1 Sam. 25.36; 2 Sam. 13.28; Est. 1.10), perhaps indicating that Boaz, like Lot, is inebriated. Only at that point, moreover, does Ruth, like Lot's daughters, go and lie with the sleeping man; the verbal root used to describe the lying down of the women is identical in both stories. In addition, Ruth's act of 'uncovering his feet' is sexually suggestive, as 'feet' can function in biblical Hebrew as a euphemism for the genitals (Campbell 1975: 121; Linafelt 1999: 49).

While sexual intercourse is not explicitly reported, it is, as Phyllis Trible rightly notes, 'patently certain' that 'sexual overtones are present' (Trible 1978: 182). This scene of seduction at the threshing floor (where food is produced) sets in motion events that result (as did sexual relations between Lot and his daughters) in the birth of a son. Moreover, the narrator notes at the end of Ruth (4.17–22), just as the narrator notes in Genesis 19.37–8, whose ancestor this son turns out to be. If Ruth's actions, though unconventional and almost certainly narrated in such a way as to raise eyebrows, are nevertheless presented positively as clever actions that secure lineage and plenitude in the face of possible barrenness, why should the same not be said of the actions of Lot's daughters?

Although the question is a valid one, a major difference between the likely connotations of the stories in their ancient context results from an important distinction between the male descendants traced to each of these unions. Ruth's sexual intercourse with Boaz eventually produces David, the founder of Judah's ruling dynasty and a figure likely to have been revered among those telling the story. The revelation that David's ancestress was a Moabitess – moreover, a Moabitess who lived up to the reputation of Moabite women as sexual seductresses – would be unsettling to Judahites who abhorred intermarriage with Moabites. It is arguable that the book of Ruth was originally a 'politically subversive pamphlet' written in the Persian period to undermine the views of such Judahites (LaCocque 1990: 100, *passim*). The subversive impact of the story depends, however, on the juxtaposition of a positive attitude toward David with the negative reputation of the Moabites. The revelation that David's ancestry includes a Moabite woman is most surprising precisely to those who held David and his dynasty in high regard. Lot's daughters, by contrast, are not linked in Genesis to any Israelite or Judahite, but only to the hated Moabites and Ammonites.

A closer parallel to the story of Lot and his daughters may be found elsewhere in Genesis. In chapter 9, we find the following passage:

> The sons of Noah who went out of the ark were Shem, Ham and Japheth; and Ham was the father of Canaan. These three were the sons of Noah, and from these was dispersed all [the peoples of] the earth. Noah, a man of the soil, was the first to plant a vineyard. He drank from the wine and became drunk, and he was uncovered in his tent. And Ham, the father of Canaan, saw the nakedness of his father and told his two brothers outside. So Shem and Japheth took a garment and placed it on both of their shoulders and walked backward, and they covered the nakedness of their father. Their faces were turned away, and the nakedness of their father they did not see. When Noah woke up from his wine and knew what his youngest son had done to him, he said, 'Cursed is Canaan. The lowest of slaves may he be for his brothers.' And he said, 'Blessed by Yhwh my God is Shem. May Canaan be his slave. May God enlarge Japheth, and let him live in the tents of Shem, and let Canaan be his slave.' (Gen. 9.18–27)

While this story may not impress the average reader as having much to do with Lot and his daughters, there are striking similarities between the two tales. Both stories take place after events of great destruction initiated by God in response to human wickedness. In both stories a father and children survive that great destruction through divine intervention. The plot of both stories involves the ingestion of a specific foodstuff – wine – which leads to the inebriation of the father. In both cases a child approaches that drunken father and does something of which the father is initially unaware. And, in each story, the child who approaches the drunken father turns out to parent the ancestor of people hated by the Israelites.

But what, exactly, is Ham here represented as doing? Although the text is replete with interpretive difficulties, at first glance the answer to this question seems simple enough. Taken literally, Ham 'sees' his father while his father is naked. While the severity of Noah's response may seem disproportionate to the offense, and while it may be difficult to understand as a matter of logic why Ham's son Canaan ought to be punished for Ham's offense, nevertheless other biblical texts allow us to construct a framework of cultural assumptions within which these features of the story might be explained. Certainly the exposure of nakedness is elsewhere seen as a source of shame in the Bible, and is even linked in some texts to drunkenness (e.g. Hab. 2.15; Lam. 4.21). The narrated actions of Ham's brothers do seem to indicate that a literal viewing of the father's nakedness is at issue in the story (Gen. 9.23). Moreover, the punishment of a child for the actions of a parent is hardly exceptional in the Hebrew Bible, however difficult it may be to under-stand in a modern individualistic context.[9] Thus, a literal understanding of Ham's offense as having seen his father's nakedness, and perhaps also as having failed to cover that nakedness, is certainly plausible.

Yet already in the distant past readers of the story wondered whether something else might be implied by this text. The Talmud, for example, indicates that certain rabbinic readers understood Ham to be guilty of either castration or homosexual incest (*b. Sanh. 70a*), and modern scholars also raise suspicions that Ham com-mitted some sort of sexual offense (cf. Bassett 1971; von Rad 1972: 137; Phillips 1980: 41; Brenner 1997: 107-9; Rashkow 2000: 93-113). This sexual interpreta-tion of Ham's misdeed is less far-fetched than many readers imagine, for the vocabulary of Genesis 9 has points of overlap with that of legal texts in which forms of intercourse are forbidden. Language about 'uncovering the nakedness' of some person or another is clearly, in Leviticus 18 and 20, an indication of sexual intercourse; Deuteronomy 23.1 uses very similar language about 'uncovering the skirt of one's father' to speak about sexual relations with one's father's wife. Thus, the language of Genesis 9 may cause the reader familiar with biblical registers of sexual intercourse and proscribed unions at least to wonder whether something sexual is taking place, even if the passage, read literally, can also be understood in a less sexual fashion. Bailey, therefore, concludes that 'sexual innuendo is used polemically' here (Bailey 1995: 133).

But Bailey, cognizant of later uses of the story of Ham to justify Euro-American enslavement of peoples of African descent (cf. Haynes 2002), also connects the use of sexual innuendo in this story to a wider biblical tendency to manipulate sexual rhetoric so as to stigmatize members of other ethnic groups. In that respect the story of Noah, Ham and Canaan is

9.   In a study concerned, in part, with food, it is worth noting that prophetic passages which *contest* the punishment of children for the misdeeds of parents (e.g., Jer. 31.29–30; Ezek. 18.2) use food imagery to do so.

remarkably similar to the story of Lot and his daughters. In both stories, the ethnic boundary between Israelites and non-Israelites (Canaanites, Moabites, Ammonites) is marked and solidified by the use of a narrative complex involving fathers, children, wine, drunkenness, and the transgression of sexual boundaries. As Bailey and others (e.g. Phillips 1980: 41) recognize, this particular narrative complex functions intertextually to reinforce the argument found in the Levitical legal texts that sexual misconduct was characteristic of Israel's neighbors and predecessors. It is significant that Ham's descendants include Egyptians and Canaanites, both of which are associated in Leviticus 18.3 with proscribed sexual activities, and it cannot be accidental that the story of Ham's offense results in a curse on Canaanites in particular. For, among the many instances of the widespread tendency to stigmatize other ethnic groups by attributing to them sexual misconduct, surely no instance is more relevant for biblical interpretation than the longstanding tradition, manifest in both biblical discourse and the discourse of biblical scholarship, of characterizing the Canaanites as sexual deviants.

III

It is probably safe to say that most Jews and Christians understand themselves to be related in some way to the Israelites represented in the Bible. However, whereas the structure of many biblical passages invites readers to identify *with* the Israelites, some of those same passages invite readers to identify themselves over *against* the peoples who dwell in the land of Canaan *prior* to the Israelites. Several such passages (e.g., Deut. 7.1–6; Josh. 3.10; 9.1; 24.11, etc.) refer to the non-Israelite peoples with a list of names, only one of which is 'Canaanites'. However, the same term, 'Canaanites', is also used in certain passages in a more general sense, referring collectively to various non-Israelites who are understood to have lived throughout the land (e.g., Judg. 1). This more general use of the term 'Canaanites', as a convenient way of referring collectively to inhabitants of the land entered by the Israelites, has been characteristic also of the term's deployment in modern scholarship (cf. Lemche 1991: 73–121).

It is possible that most readers imagine these Canaanites to be fairly easy to describe historically and to differentiate from Israelites. It may therefore come as some surprise when the reader learns, from a recent monograph on the Canaanites, that 'the Israelites were themselves Canaanites, and "historical", as opposed to "literary", Israel was, in reality, a sub-set of Canaanite culture' (Tubb 1998: 16). This statement reflects a major recent scholarly trend. All scholars recognize, of course, that the Bible draws a distinction between Israelites and Canaanites and locates that distinction far back in the genealogies of the two peoples (cf. Gen. 9.18–10.31). Nevertheless, most historians of Israel today argue that the ancestors of the Israelites, rather than entering the land of Canaan as a distinct group of people and confronting there radically 'other' groups of people such as Canaanites, were instead indigenous to that very land. The Israelites were not in their origins ethnically distinct from the Canaanite population, but became distinguishable from those Canaanites only over time. While the social and historical processes through which the Israelites emerged as a distinct group of people were complex, and the details of those processes remain greatly disputed, many scholars with otherwise divergent opinions about those processes would agree with two archaeologists who recently concluded that 'the early Israelites were – irony of ironies – themselves originally Canaanites' (Finkelstein and Silberman 2001: 118).[10]

It is not entirely clear to all scholars, moreover, that these Canaanites, from whom the historical Israelites are supposed to have emerged, can themselves be unambiguously identified. Niels Peter Lemche (1991) argues that an analysis of non-biblical ancient Near Eastern references to 'Canaan' and 'Canaanites' actually fails to produce a consistent picture either of a clearly bounded geographical territory known to all as 'Canaan' or of a clearly bounded group of people known to both others and themselves as 'Canaanites'. 'Canaan' does seem to have served as a general term for an area of western Asia close to the Mediterranean Sea, and persons from that area were called 'Canaanite' by others. Yet, on Lemche's reading, there is relatively little evidence that more precise understandings of the term were widely shared. 'Canaanite' seems to have been used most often to refer to some people other than one's own, and persons referred to as 'Canaanites' by others do not always seem to have understood themselves to be 'Canaanites'.

Now it may be objected that the relevant issue for readers of the Bible is not appellation, ethnicity, geography, or historical origins, but rather religion. Is it not on the basis of religion that 'Canaanite' and 'Israelite' ought to be distinguished? This solution, borrowed directly from the Bible, has often been adopted also by scholars. In more recent scholarship, however, the imprecision of the boundary between 'Canaanite' and 'Israelite' extends even to matters of religion. 'It is essential', Michael Coogan insists, 'to consider biblical religion as a subset of Israelite religion and Israelite religion as a subset of Canaanite religion' (Coogan 1987: 115). So, too, William Dever, right in the middle of arguing that remains found at a certain archaeological level are 'Israelite' or 'proto-Israelite', acknowledges that the few religious objects found at that level 'suggest connections with the old Canaanite cult of the male deity El'. If Dever's archaeological 'Israelites' are characterized in terms of religion, that religion must be described as 'still in the tradition of' the 'older Canaanite "fertility religions" that would have been well-suited to an agrarian lifestyle' (Dever 2001: 114; cf. 1990: 121–66; 1992: 34–5). Even with respect to religion, then, a clear boundary separating Israelites from Canaanites is, outside of the Bible at least, surprisingly elusive.

Given this ambiguity in the extra-biblical sources, one may wonder whether the distinction between 'Israelites' and 'Canaanites' in the biblical texts is as clear as it might first appear. The answer to this question depends a bit on which biblical texts one consults. The representations of Canaanites and other non-Israelite residents of Canaan in parts of the book of Genesis, for example, stand in some tension with representations of those peoples in such books as Deuteronomy and Joshua (cf.

---

10. Cf. the often otherwise divergent opinions of Ahlström 1986; Coote and Whitelam 1987; Coote 1990; Dever 1990: 39–84; 1992: 53; Lemche 1998; McNutt 1999: 33–63; Whitelam 2002.

Cohn 1994), and the relatively neat picture found in the latter two books stands in some contrast, again, with the more complicated picture found in Judges. So, too, the books of Chronicles arguably take a distinct approach to the question of Israel's origins which may not assume that the Israelites entered the land of Canaanites from the outside (cf. Japhet 1979). In an intriguing passage, Ezekiel is told to open an oracle to Jerusalem by saying, 'Thus says lord Yhwh to Jerusalem, "Your origin and your birth were in the land of the Canaanite. Your father was the Amorite, and your mother the Hittite"' (Ezek. 16.3).

Notwithstanding such differences of emphasis, however, much biblical literature does deploy the word 'Canaanite' and related terms largely to distinguish Israelites by way of contrast, especially with respect to religion. Whatever the historical realities in ancient Palestine might have been, the term 'Canaanite' is, in the Bible, frequently a relational term, assuming particular meanings within specific contexts by serving as a point of contrast to something else – the 'Israelite' – which, of course, it thereby helps to define. As Lemche puts it (1998: 129):

> The Canaan of the Old Testament, the archetypal enemy of ancient Israel, is therefore not an enigmatic old nation that once upon a time occupied Palestine. It is more of a literary device created in order to make a distinction between the heroes of the narrative, the biblical Israelites, and the villains, the Canaanites.

Rather than being a self-evident fact of ancient Palestinian history, the binary opposition between 'Israelite' and 'Canaanite' turns out, in large part, to be an effect of particular biblical discourses.

This biblical distinction between 'Israelites' and 'Canaanites' has not simply influenced readers of the Bible, however, but has been perpetuated by them in turn. Until recently, scholars were not content to accept the biblical representation of the Canaanites as a group of people who preceded the Israelites in the land of Canaan. They also accepted, and elaborated upon, the biblical representation of Canaanites as an especially wicked lot (cf. Hillers 1985; Whitelam 1996). This elaboration can be seen clearly in the long tradition of writing about 'Canaanite religion' as a 'fertility religion'. Such a phrase accurately recognizes that concerns about agricultural production and the generation of offspring were characteristic of most religions in the ancient Near East, including the religion of Israel (cf. Hackett 1989: 68). But throughout the twentieth century, scholars further associated the 'fertility religion' of the Canaanites with a supposed 'sex cult' (Wolff 1974: 14), so that influential writers discussing the Canaanites referred ominously to 'sexual abuses in the service of religion' (Albright 1968: 132). These characterizations of Canaanite religion functioned within the discourse of biblical scholarship to make moral distinctions between Israelite religion and Canaanite religion, which then served to justify the harsh condemnations and violent treatment of the Canaanites in biblical literature. Drastic measures were necessary, scholars were quick to assure us, to combat 'the inroads of a Canaanite sexual rite into Israel' (Wolff 1974: 14).

While these supposed 'sexual rites' were said to have been used by the Canaanites to promote agricultural fertility, evidence for such rites is very murky. Frequently, appeal has been made to scattered biblical references to *qedeshim* and *qedeshot*, often translated as 'cult prostitutes', 'temple prostitutes' or 'sacred prostitutes'. These references will be known to many participants in the debates over religion and homosexuality, for it has sometimes been argued that Levitical references to male homosexual intercourse are actually references to cultic intercourse supposedly practiced by *qedeshim*. Nevertheless, while male *qedeshim* and female *qedeshot* are certainly religious functionaries looked upon negatively by the biblical texts, their actual function is extremely ambiguous and has been the subject of much reassessment of late on the part of biblical scholars and scholars of ancient literature.[11] Cognate terms outside the Bible, while also somewhat obscure, are not used in such a way as to support a sexual interpretation. The occasional appearance of these figures in the Bible in close textual proximity to prostitutes and harlots (in, e.g., Deut. 23.17–18 and Hosea 4.14) is probably not an indication of their function but a product of the rhetorical association made in biblical literature between sexual promiscuity and forms of religious practice that were distasteful to the biblical writers. A more complex interpretive puzzle surrounds the use of the term *qedeshah* in the story of Tamar in Genesis 38, to which I return below. Based on the available evidence, however, it is hard to disagree with Frymer-Kensky when she asserts that 'the whole idea of a sex cult – in Israel or in Canaan – is a chimera, the product of ancient and modern sexual fantasies' (Frymer-Kensky 1992: 199).

Where do we find the origins of these 'sexual fantasies'? As important as it is to acknowledge the likelihood that readers have projected their own 'fantasies' onto biblical and other texts, it is also necessary to recognize that the biblical texts are easily appropriated for such fantasies, not because these texts actually speak about 'cultic' or 'sacred prostitution', but because the texts already contain a polemical caricature of the sexual practices of Canaanites. After all, biblical passages such as Leviticus 18 and 20 that proscribe certain sexual practices set up a sharp, rhetorical distinction between the Israelites and the population that is said to have dwelt in Canaan before the Israelites. While the prohibitions against particular sexual acts are assumed by the text to be relevant to both Israelites and the other nations, these other nations are mentioned primarily because they have already been cast out of the land. They suffered this fate, according to the discourse of Leviticus, because they practiced those 'abominations' – and in particular, in context, sexual abominations – that God is now forbidding to the Israelites. Only a small step was necessary for scholars to move from reading such passages as, e.g., Leviticus 18.24–30 or 20.22–6, to attempting to describe or reconstruct the supposed sexual abominations of the Canaanites. Even if scholars went further in their descriptions than the evidence should have allowed, they were surely encouraged in their reconstructions by the link already forged, by the biblical authors, between sexual abomination and the ethnic/religious Other.

As this project of defining the Canaanites negatively on the basis of their supposed sexual misconduct is increasingly critiqued and abandoned, scholars have begun asking whether it might be possible to use archaeological remains to distinguish Canaanites and Israelites in other ways. Given the recurring biblical

---

11. For useful discussion see Hooks 1985; Oden 1987; Westenholz 1989; Frymer-Kensky 1992: 199–202; Henshaw 1994; Bird 1997a, 1997b; Binger 1997: 118–20; Keefe 2001: 36–103.

tendency to slide rhetorically between sex and food, it is hardly surprising that food practices seem to be supplanting sexual abomination. Thus, scholars now debate whether ethnic distinctions between 'Israelites' and their non-Israelite neighbors can be correlated with particular archaeological sites and layers of material remains on the basis of the relative presence or absence in those remains of pig bones.[12] The absence of pig bones in the archaeological remains of certain sites is interpreted by some scholars as evidence for abstinence from the eating of pork, and hence as evidence that the remains in question belong to Israelites, while the presence of pig bones in the archaeological remains of other sites is understood as evidence for the eating of pork, and hence as evidence that the remains in question belong to non-Israelites.

Such an argument depends on the recognition that food is indeed often used to construct ethnic boundaries. It depends also on recognition that pigs are one of those animals proscribed as food sources in the Bible, and the animal that later became, among all proscribed animals, particularly associated with Jewish food avoidance.[13] It is not clear, however, whether, or how far, this argument from ancient pig bones can be sustained. As attempts by previous generations of scholars to establish firm distinctions between 'Israelites' and 'Canaanites' in the archaeological record have often failed, and the distinction still becomes increasingly blurred the closer one tries to define it, there may be good reason to wonder whether the distribution of pig bones in the archaeological record will be sufficient to confirm a distinction that has so far proven elusive. Already, scholars involved in the analysis of the question have adopted conflicting positions.[14]

My own view is that the archaeological-historical questions at stake are rather less important – especially for queer readers – than the ideological-theological questions associated with such debates. For the tendency to define an 'inside' and an 'outside' of identity by defining the Other on the basis of the Other's supposed negative practices – and, in the process, defining oneself by way of contrast – has extremely troubling consequences. These consequences are usefully understood in relation to Iris Marion Young's discussion of 'border anxiety'. Building in part upon Julia Kristeva's theory of the 'Abject' (Kristeva 1982),[15] Young points out that much demonizing of the Other takes place because of basic insecurity occasioned by the presence of that Other. This insecurity arises in part because the

---

12. Cf. Hesse 1990; Edelman 1996: 47–9; Finkelstein 1997; Hesse and Wapnish 1997, 1998; Finkelstein and Silberman 2001: 118–20; Dever 2001: 113; Bloch-Smith 2003.

13. This emphasis upon the pig is underway already by the late second century B.C.E., when 1 and 2 Maccabees are written. Antiochus IV is described there as ordering the people 'to sacrifice swine and other unclean animals' (1 Macc. 1.47, NRSV). The martyrdom of Eleazar takes place when, having been 'forced to open his mouth to eat swine's flesh', he chooses death for 'spitting out the flesh' (2 Macc. 6.18–19); and the martyrdom of seven brothers and their mother follows a refusal 'to partake of unlawful swine's flesh' (7.1). As Douglas notes (1982: 38–41), while these stories emphasize the whole of the Law and not the proscription of pork only, the way in which pork avoidance in particular results in martyrdom probably encouraged the tendency to single out the pig as that animal most detested by (and hence, paradoxically, often associated by others with (cf. Fabre-Vassas 1997)) the Jews.

14. See, especially, the cautious analyses of Hesse and Wapnish 1997, 1998.

15. Kristeva's discussion, in turn, is indebted to Douglas.

Other is not quite so different from oneself as one might wish to believe. Hence, the Other challenges the security of the boundaries of one's self, in much the same way that one's bodily boundaries appear to be threatened by, e.g., eating and sex. Thus, 'border anxiety' arises as part of an attempt to establish those boundaries more firmly and to avoid the 'fear, nervousness and aversion' (Young 1990: 146) that result from any fluidity in those boundaries.

It is certainly not difficult to imagine a scenario in which this sort of 'border anxiety' overdetermined the writing of biblical literature, resulting in biblical rhetoric about the supposed sexual and dietary misconduct of Israel's 'Canaanite' predecessors. In thinking about the historical and social circumstances that produced these passages, we do well to focus on the context in which much biblical literature probably reached its present form: the post-exilic, Persian period of Israel's history. The most significant development in this context, so far as the biblical literature is concerned, was the attempt by those who 'returned' to Judah from Mesopotamia to forge a distinct religious and ethnic identity in a small province on the western end of the Persian Empire, and to do so in opposition to other groups of people who were already living there. This attempt arguably gave us the final form of the major narrative books (Genesis through 2 Kings (cf. Mullen 1993, 1997)). And, if we keep this context in mind, we can see that the rhetoric of passages in Leviticus 18 and 20 that construe sexual misconduct – and in 20.22–6, food misconduct – as the cause for a people's being 'vomited' out of the land serves several different functions. Such rhetoric differentiates the Israelites from other nations, asserts the unwillingness of those other nations to follow the path that God wishes Israel to follow, and justifies the removal of those nations from the land that God has promised to the Israelites. But it also serves as a warning about possible consequences of future transgressions, and, implicitly, as an after-the-fact explanation of the Babylonian exile. By stating, in a post-exilic context, that God had long ago told the Israelites that they would be 'vomited' out of the land if they participated in behaviors that motivated the 'vomiting' out of earlier nations, the passages hint that insufficient attention had been paid to proper observance of these precepts by the pre-exilic Israelites whose actions led to that 'vomiting out' which was the exile. A post-exilic Judahite audience for these texts could therefore conceivably identify with various positions simultaneously – for example, that of the ancient Canaanite who was supposed to have been destroyed but still, paradoxically, continued to exist in the land with the Israelites (cf. Judg. 1); that of the pre-exilic Israelite who is supposed to have known the law but was vomited out of the land anyway for transgressing it; and the post-exilic Judahite who wishes to avoid the fate of previous inhabitants of the land. The existence of these multiple subject positions undoubtedly contributed to the formation of a certain sort of anxiety on the part of the Judahites. To borrow the words of Robert Cohn, the biblical authors 'shaped the Canaanites as the Other whose sin justified their dispossession, but who also threatened to take Israel down the same path. As outsiders who became insiders, the Israelites … seem never quite secure in the land. The Canaanites as the insiders who became outsiders serve as the symbol of that insecurity' (Cohn 1994: 77). The ambiguity of the boundary between 'inside' and 'outside', to which Cohn's language points, correlates with the 'border anxiety' that both produced and was perpetuated by biblical rhetoric about supposed sexual and eating abominations of the Canaanites.

The fact that biblical scholars have often replicated, and even elaborated or exaggerated, rhetoric produced by ancient Judahite 'border anxiety' is in need of explanation. Such an explanation might start with recognition that most biblical scholars have themselves been affiliated with Judaism or Christianity, and so on the basis of their own religious commitments have identified with Israelites or Judahites rather than Canaanites. The boundaries of modern religious and ethnic identities are as unstable as the boundaries of ancient ones and, just as border anxiety among the Israelites or Judahites produced a phantom picture of wicked and sexually deviant Canaanites in the first place, so also border anxiety among modern scholars who identify with the biblical Israelites has contributed to a sensationalized picture of a depraved Canaanite culture and religion, over against which Israel's narrated extermination of its predecessors receives legitimization.

Examples of this process at work can be found in the writings of William Albright, one of the most influential biblical scholars of the twentieth century and a pioneer in the study of the Canaanites. As Burke Long shows in a fascinating book (Long 1997), Albright's impressive scholarly endeavors were tied up with his own involvement in the construction of particular sorts of identities, including that of the modernist Christian who takes full account of 'scientific' archaeological and historical research. In arguing for the importance of understanding the biblical tradition thoroughly, Albright was forthright about his belief that modern Christians must maintain the boundaries of the religious identity that resulted from this tradition. Not only in ancient times, but also today, those boundaries were, in Albright's opinion, under attack: 'Now again we see the religious world confronted by the imperious necessity of choosing between biblical theism and Eastern pantheism, which threatens to sweep away theistic faith as it is reinterpreted by neo-Gnostic religious thinkers of the contemporary West' (Albright 1957: 23). Reading such passages in the context of Albright's work as a whole, it is difficult to avoid the conclusion that Albright's own 'border anxieties' had an impact on his understanding of Israelite identity and the threats that it once faced from the Canaanites. In the discourse of Albright as in the discourse of the biblical texts with which he identified, border anxiety resulted in the production of rhetoric about the sexual abominations of the Canaanites, especially when Albright attempted to justify extermination of those Canaanites (Albright 1957: 280–1):

> From the impartial standpoint of a philosopher of history, it often seems necessary that a people of markedly inferior type should vanish before a people of superior potentialities, since there is a point beyond which racial mixing cannot go without disaster. When such a process takes place – as at present in Australia – there is generally little that can be done by the humanitarian – though every deed of brutality and injustice is infallibly visited upon the aggressor. It was fortunate for the future of monotheism that the Israelites of the Conquest were a wild folk, endowed with primitive energy and ruthless will to exist, since the resulting decimation of the Canaanites prevented the complete fusion of the two kindred folk which would almost inevitably have depressed Yahwistic standards to a point where recovery was impossible. Thus the Canaanites, with their orgiastic nature-worship, their cult of fertility in the form of serpent symbols and

> sensuous nudity, and their gross mythology, were replaced by Israel, with its
> pastoral simplicity and purity of life, its lofty monotheism, and its severe code
> of ethics.

In the wake of postcolonial critique, it is impossible to encounter rhetoric such
as Albright's without being struck by the extent to which its representation of
'sensuous' Canaanites participates in a recurring sexualization of the 'Orient' (cf.
Said 1978; Whitelam 1996: 82–4, *passim*). Such representations underscore the
potentially pernicious effects of using sex to construct symbolic boundaries differ-
entiating one people from another (cf. Bleys 1995; McClintock 1995; Stoler 1997).
It is little wonder that Native American, Palestinian and Asian readers of the Bible,
among others, have suggested that it is time to reconsider biblical religion from the
point of view of the Canaanites rather than adopting the Israelite subject position
uncritically (cf. Said 1988; Warrior 1991; Ateek 1991; Kwok 1995: 90–1, 98–9;
García-Treto 1996; Schwartz 1997).

To reconsider religious tradition from the position of the Canaanites is not,
however, to assume any 'real' identity. The Canaanite, far from being a stable ethnic
or religious entity, is something more like the 'constitutive outside' (Butler 1993:
8) of Israelite identity. Ironically, as a 'constitutive outside', the Canaanite is to
some extent a kind of necessary support for Israelite identity, helping to define the
Israelite by means of differential relation and contrast. We know what the Israelite
is by knowing what it is not, and, in that respect, Israelite identity is dependent
for its existence as a coherent object upon the demarcation and exclusion of the
Canaanite. Thus the Canaanite is not outside Israelite identity at all, but rather
is always already inside Israelite identity as a kind of necessary support for the
illusion that such an identity is coherent and secure. As I suggest in more detail
elsewhere (Stone, in press), those of us who are today defined largely in terms of
deviance from normative heterosexuality have especially good reasons to identify
with, rather than over against, the Canaanites. For the 'Canaanite' is arguably
positioned with respect to the 'Israelite' in something like the same way that the
'homosexual' is positioned with respect to the 'heterosexual'.

Queer theorists argue that the binary opposition between 'homosexual' and 'heterosexual' functions not only to stigmatize individuals classified as 'homosexual'
but also to cover over ambiguities in the notion of 'heterosexuality' (see, e.g.,
Halperin 1995: 43–8, *passim*; Katz 1995; Jagose 1996: 16–19, *passim*; cf. Sedgwick
1990). 'Homosexuality' is, in fact, a kind of necessary support for 'heterosexuality',
serving as its 'constituent outside' and helping to define it by means of differential relation and contrast. As with the 'Israelite', so also with the 'heterosexual',
we know what it is by knowing what it is not; in that respect, 'heterosexuality' is
dependent for its existence as a coherent object upon the demarcation and exclusion
of 'homosexuality'. Thus, 'the homosexual' is not outside heterosexual identity at
all, but rather is always already inside heterosexual identity as a kind of necessary
support for the illusion that such an identity is coherent and secure. The homosexual
is therefore positioned with respect to the heterosexual in something like the same
way that the Canaanite is positioned with respect to the Israelite.

It is thus ironic to recall that advocates for lesbian and gay Christians and Jews
sometimes try to *distance* lesbians and gay men from the Canaanites by arguing

that supposed biblical references to homosexuality in Leviticus are actually references instead to Canaanite cultic practices (e.g., Edwards 1984: 58). As theories about Canaanite 'cultic prostitution', upon which such arguments depend, have been challenged, a curious thing has started to take place. At the very time that scholars studying ancient Israel have turned their attention from Canaanite sex ('cultic prostitution') to Canaanite food ('pig bones'), so Christian theological interpreters of the Bible have attempted to shift their arguments about boundaries, homosexuality, and biblical interpretation away from an exclusive focus upon sex, to a reflection upon Christianity and food.

Thus, gay-friendly New Testament scholars (e.g., Countryman 1988; Siker 1996; Johnson 1996; Fowl 1998) now suggest that struggles in the early church, which led to the eventual rejection of Pentateuchal food guidelines as markers for Christian identity, might serve as a paradigm for approaching disputes over homosexuality. According to this argument, the tendency of Christians today to insist that rejection of homosexuality is required of Christians is no more defensible, finally, than the tendency of some in the early church to insist that rejection of particular food practices (e.g., eating with the uncircumcised, or eating foods considered 'unclean') was a necessary component of Christian identity.

The potential effects of this sort of argument, for at least some Christian lesbians and gay men, are clearly preferable to traditional condemnations of homosexual behavior. It is striking to note, however, that discussions which argue in this fashion against the identification of homosexuality as constitutive of the boundaries of Christianity frequently attempt to draw such boundaries clearly elsewhere. Thus, Luke Johnson cautions that 'inclusivity must follow from evidence of holiness'; and distinguishes 'homosexual covenantal love' that may provide evidence for such 'holiness', from 'promiscuity' and other forms of gay sex to which 'the church must emphatically and always say no' (Johnson 1996: 146–8). So, too, Jeffrey Siker draws a distinction between gays and lesbians in whose lives one discerns the 'good fruit' of 'the Spirit' (in much the same way that Peter and his companions discerned the Spirit among the Gentiles in Acts 10–11), and those whose lives are deemed by 'a broad consensus in the church' to be 'bad fruit' (Siker 1996: 149). It appears, from such rhetoric, that modification of what we might call the heterosexual boundary marker for Christianity only provokes still more 'border anxiety' even on the part of those arguing for modification, resulting in a nervous redrawing of boundaries elsewhere.

Yet those of us who have been in the past, or are in the present, stigmatized or persecuted on the basis of boundaries drawn by others have good reason to think carefully about the ways in which these newer distinctions are likely to be employed within Christian contexts. For who shall have responsibility for determining which lesbian and gay lives manifest 'the Spirit' and which do not? What shall prevent the distinction between 'good fruit' and 'bad fruit' from turning into a distinction between 'good homosexuals' (who, in practice, are likely to be lesbians and gay men whose styles of life most closely conform to heteronormativity) and 'bad homosexuals' (who, in contrast, are likely to be lesbians, gay men or others whose styles of life most directly challenge heteronormative assumptions)? When such boundaries are drawn, those of us whose sexual and gender practices fail to conform to dominant conventions have little reason to be optimistic that 'a broad consensus in the church' will produce anything other than new rituals of exclusion.

And so perhaps the biblical texts that queer readers need to emphasize are not texts that construe religious identity in polarized terms or draw clear borders between insiders and outsiders. Perhaps we might cast our glance instead on such tales as that of Tamar, the daughter-in-law of Judah whose story appears in Genesis 38. Like the daughters of Lot, Tamar secures sexual relations from a patriarch by playing a trick on that patriarch involving a type of food. Whereas the daughters of Lot use wine to get their father drunk and make of him a sexual object, however, Tamar disguises herself as a prostitute and asks for her father-in-law's seal, cord and staff as pledge for the promised food animal that is, apparently, one form of payment for prostitutes in Israel (Gen. 38.17).

It is striking to note that Tamar's ethnic and religious affiliations are quite ambiguous. She is arguably a Canaanite like her mother-in-law, the wife of Judah (Gen. 38.2), and is frequently accepted as such by commentators (e.g., Speiser 1964: 300; Fuchs 2000: 72), yet her Canaanite origins are never explicitly stated in the text. Her identity is further obscured when she disguises herself to achieve what she wants, and when she does so she is referred to by others first as a prostitute and then as a *qedeshah*, that is, the very functionary from Canaanite religion which has motivated so much speculation about 'cultic prostitution'. Frymer-Kensky suggests, convincingly, that we can best explain the fact that Tamar is referred to first by one of these terms and then by the other, not by importing into the religious term dubious notions about 'cultic prostitution', but rather by recognizing that women filling these two roles were among the few women in Israel who were 'at least in male eyes … outside the family system and therefore approachable for sexual encounter or arrangement' (Frymer-Kensky 2002: 271). The fact that both women serve public functions allows Judah's servant to obscure the fact that Judah has been trafficking with a presumed prostitute.

By acting as one of these public women, however, Tamar positions herself at the margins of the gender, sexual and kinship systems of ancient Israel. The chain of events that leads her to do so, moreover, begins when two of her sexual partners die. As a result of these deaths, her father-in-law comes to believe that sex with Tamar will mean death for his youngest son as well. Consequently, he attempts to prevent a sexual union of which he is afraid. Thus, in the age of AIDS, gay men in particular might find it valuable to reflect upon the story of Tamar, in spite of – or, perhaps, partly because of – the complexities of cross-gender identification that result from such a reading. Here we have a tale of a figure at the margins who provokes in others – and, who knows? perhaps in herself as well – a fear that sexual intercourse might lead to death.

Tamar, of course, tricks her father-in-law into having sexual relations with her in order to receive the son that she believes she rightfully should bear. Her story might be criticized for placing women yet again in the position of sexual seductress, or for underscoring yet again the biblical valorization of patriarchal descent (cf. Fuchs 2000: 65–82). Indeed, we have to acknowledge that it was produced (as were all biblical texts) in a patriarchal society that heavily influenced its structuring. Rather than attributing to Tamar's story a single, stable meaning which places Tamar always in the position of victim, I prefer to emphasize the fact that, within a society organized to her disadvantage, Tamar is willing to use whatever tools are at her disposal to achieve her goals, including not only a trick involving food but also the female sexual subjectivity that is often stigmatized in biblical discourse. She acts at first in secret, and only subsequently reveals more about her sexual experience, yet her 'coming out' exposes the hypocrisy of those most eager to defend the system of sex, gender and kinship within which Tamar was expected to live. Her sexual actions, like those of many of us, stand outside accepted conventions of her society, and at one point bring her quite close to being killed (Gen. 38.24). As a woman, a 'Canaanite', and a participant in forbidden sexual activities, Tamar would seem to be the ultimate biblical outsider. Yet, in the end, her sexual relations with Judah produce a son who turns out to be the ancestor of David; her story is referred to positively by the book of Ruth (4.12), and the reference to Tamar in Matthew's genealogy of Jesus (Matt. 1.3) implies that her transgressive actions ultimately make possible the birth of the Christian messiah. Thus, Tamar is neither inside Israel in any conventional sense, nor completely outside Israel in the position usually allotted to Canaanites. Existing upon, and ultimately destabilizing, the border between inside and outside, she both ensures the survival of the line of Judah from which we derive the word 'Judaism', and contributes to the birth of Christianity. In that respect she offers a biblical, 'Canaanite' position from which a 'queering' of theology, biblical interpretation, and the conceptualization of religious 'identity' might usefully commence.

Demands to be allowed *inside* such institutions as the religious community, the ordained clergy, the socially sanctioned marriage contract, the heteronormative academy and so forth may be necessary interim political goals for those of us who are currently excluded from, or marginalized within, those institutions. Nevertheless, we should not ignore the extent to which such demands actually reinforce boundaries between 'inside' and 'outside', boundaries that often rely upon food and sex but frequently become, themselves, justification for stigmatization and oppression. Ultimately, a 'safer' biblical interpretation, and a 'safer' religious practice, may need to work instead at dissolving those very boundaries between 'inside' and 'outside'; or, like Tamar, using sexual transgression and social marginality to turn those boundaries 'inside out' (cf. Fuss 1991).

CHAPTER 3

'BEFORE THE EYES OF ALL ISRAEL':

PUBLIC SEX, MARRIAGE AND FOOD IN THE BIBLE

I

The last chapter suggested that boundaries between the 'inside' and the 'outside' of identities – boundaries often established by appeals to food and sex – ought to be interrogated and destabilized rather than accepted uncritically. Should such an argument be at all persuasive, it might mean that issues and debates which are normally considered beyond the borders of religious or theological reflection need to be given greater attention by scholars and practitioners of religion. In the present chapter I would like to consider a particular case in which, I believe, such attention may prove fruitful.

The last decade has seen a resurgence of disagreement about the parameters of acceptable sexual expression within lesbian, gay, bisexual and transgendered communities in general, and among gay men in particular. Citing as justification the ongoing problem of sexually transmitted HIV, a number of gay writers have critiqued 'the strong traditions of sexual freedom and libertarianism in gay culture' and have called for redirecting gay energies toward monogamous relationships and 'increased sexual restraint' (Rotello 1997: 202, 209, *passim*). Such calls have not been accepted uncritically, however, but have produced in response reaffirmations of the sexual freedom and experimentation often associated with gay men as well as arguments for, in Michael Warner's words, 'a *publicly accessible culture* of safer sex' (Warner 1999: 218, emphasis mine).

As Warner's language indicates, one of the points of contention in these debates is so-called 'public sex'. The phrase 'public sex' is, however, rather imprecise. It can be used to refer to sexual contact that takes place in public parks, 'tearooms', and so forth;[1] but in current debates it is used even more often to refer to sexual contact taking place in commercial establishments which permit or facilitate sexual activity, including bathhouses, sex clubs, backroom bars and adult bookstores. Significantly, though, recent discussions of 'public sex' ask not only about these sexual contacts but also about specific ways in which such notions as 'public',

---

1. The term 'tearoom' is a slang reference, common especially among men who have sex with men, for public restrooms that become known 'as locales for sexual encounters' (Humphreys 1999: 29).

'private', 'sexuality', 'intimacy' and so forth are conceptualized and understood in relation to one another in the modern world.[2]

Now these conflicts over 'public sex' appear to be far-removed from debates about homosexuality that take place within religious communities. Such debates focus more often on the morality of same-sex sexual contact as such, on equal access to ordination, or, most recently, on possibilities for gay marriage. Whether on principle or for strategic purposes, lesbians and gay men in religious communities, as well as their advocates, appear to have accepted the widespread valorization of marriage, or at least of long-term partnerships, as the optimal context for sexual activity. With the adoption of this starting point, serious reflection on public sex seems to be largely ruled out. It is not impossible to find discussions of religion, gay men and public sex (e.g., Boisvert 2000: 82–3; Rudy 1997: 75–84), but such discussions are certainly rare.

In the present chapter I want to reverse the usual way of thinking about such matters. Rather than starting with a focus upon marriage or domestic partnerships and allowing the assumed meaning of such institutions to determine the significance that we give – or more often do not give – to questions about public sex, I wish to reconsider certain biblical texts in light of the debates over public sex and allow the analysis that results to influence the ways in which we think about religion, sex and marriage. For portions of the Hebrew Bible, when read in this admittedly 'queer' fashion, can be used to underscore at least some of the points made by those who today resist the stigmatization of public sex. Just as queer theory emphasizes the instability of such binary categories as 'heterosexual' versus 'homosexual', or 'male' versus 'female', which structure modern discourses of sexuality, so also queer theorists involved in the analysis of 'public sex' emphasize the instability of the binary distinction between 'public' and 'private' and question the assumption that all legitimate sexual activity has been, is now, or should be confined to a 'private' realm of intimacy. Building in part on feminist interrogation of the 'public/private' split, queer analyses of public sex ask about the history, ideological motivations, and effects of claiming to restrict sexual matters to a 'private' sphere. They point out that the circulation of sexual meanings is too complex to allow such restriction ever to be entirely successful.

Whereas some queer theorists challenge the conventional placement of sexual matters in relation to the public/private divide by stressing the instability of that divide in its actual functioning *in modernity* (see, e.g., Harper 1999), it is also possible to question modern ways of construing interrelations among sexual activity, public and private by underscoring the *historical variability* of those interrelations. As Warner puts it (Warner 2002: 8):

> Behind the common sense of our everyday life among publics is an astonishingly complex history. The idea of a public is a cultural form, a kind of practical fiction, present in the modern world in a way that is very different from any analogues in other or earlier societies. Like the idea of rights, or nations, or

2.   My own thoughts about 'public sex' have been stimulated immensely by the analyses in Seidman 1991, 1992; Dangerous Bedfellows 1996; Berlant and Warner 1998; Delany 1999; Harper 1999; Leap 1999; Warner 1999, 2002; Califia 2000; Schifter 2000; and Crimp 2002.

markets, it can now seem universal. But it has not always been so. Its conditions have been long in the making, and its precise meaning varies from case to case.... Its meaning can be seen to change in ways that we have scarcely begun to appreciate.

Inspired in part by Warner's acknowledgment of differences between 'the modern world' and 'earlier societies', I want to point out in this chapter that modernity's particular ways of drawing a distinction between public and private, and relating that distinction to sex, can make little sense of the approaches taken to sexual contact in the Bible. Certain biblical representations of sexual contact are simply incompatible with modern attempts to consign sexual matters to a private realm of affect and intimacy. In a number of cases, biblical sex takes forms that are not only 'non-monogamous', but might even be referred to, plausibly, as 'public'. While recognition of this fact will not, and should not, by itself resolve contemporary disputes about public sex, nevertheless such recognition may at least encourage those of us who are interested in biblical traditions to engage the contemporary disputes in a more direct and constructive fashion.

Before turning to the texts in question it is important to be clear about what I am *not* attempting to argue. I do not wish to imply that the *specific forms* taken by 'public sex' in the Bible ought to be understood as models for emulation. This is not the sort of statement that one would normally have to make when reading an ancient text, but the continued practice of appealing to biblical literature in order to justify or critique contemporary positions – including positions on sexual practice – forces those of us who read and write about that literature to demarcate our assumptions as carefully as possible. This clarification is especially important in the present chapter, as the texts with which I am concerned here rest upon presuppositions about the sexual use of women that are especially disturbing. Some of the implications of this fact for my larger argument about food, sex and biblical interpretation are considered in more detail in the next chapter. Here, the point I wish to underscore is that I am not at all interested in holding up biblical representations of public sex as examples to follow, but rather in using biblical representations of public sex to complicate and unsettle the ways in which modern notions about sex (such as the notion that sex is properly the private expression of intimacy between partners in a long-term, and usually married, couple) are assumed to stand in continuity with the Bible.

This way of putting the matter indicates that the analysis of public sex may have implications for the ways in which we think about 'marriage'. I shall have more to say about this below. For the moment, though, I want to turn my attention to some rather spectacular, if infrequently discussed, instances of biblical public sex. Significantly for the overall purposes of this volume, several biblical texts considered in this chapter, like texts considered in the last two chapters, also associate sex with food.

II

2 Samuel 15–18 narrates events that take place during a struggle for the throne of Israel between King David and his son, Absalom. Toward the beginning of this

section of 2 Samuel, Absalom goes to the city of Hebron, ostensibly for purposes of worship but actually to initiate a revolt against his father (2 Sam. 15.7–12). The choice of city recalls an earlier time in David's life when David, after a lengthy conflict with the house of Saul, was himself proclaimed king at Hebron (2 Sam. 5.1–5). It was apparently from Hebron that David first marched against, and then seized, Jerusalem (5.6–10). So, too, Absalom now leaves Hebron and marches against Jerusalem. There are other ways in which events narrated in 2 Samuel 15–18 recapitulate circumstances from David's own rise to power. Indeed, throughout the books of Samuel, earlier and later episodes allude to one another, a fact we shall have to keep in mind as we proceed. Thus, just as Saul's attempts to hold off David in 1 Samuel were complicated by the fact that people close to Saul (including Saul's daughter, Michal, and son, Jonathan) gave aid to David, so now Absalom's conspiracy against David is joined by David's former counselor, Ahithophel. David is, therefore, on the defensive in 2 Samuel 15. According to one character, 'The hearts of the Israelites have gone after Absalom' (15.13). Consequently, David, his officials, and members of his household flee Jerusalem, leaving behind ten of David's concubines to look after David's house (15.16).

When Absalom and his followers enter Jerusalem, Absalom asks for and receives advice from Ahithophel:

> And Absalom said to Ahithophel, 'Give us your advice. What should we do?' Ahithophel said to Absalom, 'Go in to your father's concubines, the ones he left to watch over the house, and all Israel will hear that you have made yourself a stench to your father, and the hands of all who are with you will be strengthened.' So they put a tent for Absalom on the roof, and Absalom went in to the concubines of his father before the eyes of all Israel. For the advice of Ahithophel was in those days as if one asked for a word of God. Thus was all the advice of Ahithophel to David and to Absalom. (2 Sam. 16.20–23)

The language about Absalom's 'going in to' his father's concubines is, in biblical Hebrew, a way of referring to sexual intercourse. Absalom has sexual relations with the concubines of his father on the roof of the palace and, as the narrator puts it, 'before the eyes of all Israel'.

This passage narrates one of a number of biblical incidents in which male characters use their sexual relations with women to jockey for prestige and power vis-à-vis other male characters.[3] Absalom's sexual relations with David's concubines are clearly not motivated by desires for affection, intimacy, or mutual pleasure (as sexual relations frequently are understood today); neither are they linked to reproduction and the desire for progeny (as sexual relations are in many other biblical texts). Rather, a kind of 'public sex' here serves a semiotic function, transmitting messages primarily among men who share certain assumptions about the interrelations among sexual practice, prestige structures and gender. Following the advice of Ahithophel, Absalom attempts to increase his own prestige in the eyes of 'all Israel' by decreasing the prestige of his father and rival David, shaming David through a public demonstration of David's inability to control sexual access

---

3.   For more detailed discussion of this point and others made in the following paragraphs, see Stone 1996.

to the women of his household. Such a demonstration is, in the cultural world of ancient Israel, tantamount to symbolic castration. Absalom is calling into question David's ability to fulfill the protocols of manhood, hoping that his Israelite audience will begin to doubt that David is, in the words of anthropologist Michael Herzfeld, 'good at being a man' (Herzfeld 1985: 16), that is, capable of acting according to culturally prescribed dictates of gendered – in this case, 'masculine' – behavior. Moreover, Absalom seems to believe, if 'all Israel' no longer perceives David as 'good at being a man', perhaps Israel will no longer perceive him as 'good at being a king' either. Sexual relations with his father's concubines are simply a means by which Absalom hopes to accomplish his communicative goals vis-à-vis David and Israel. The story therefore illustrates well the statement of Jacobo Schifter, in his study of public sex in Costa Rica, that 'public sex prioritizes what we term nonverbal messages ... In public sex places, the body is the paper on which words are written' (Schifter 2000: 63).

However, it is difficult to state with certainty just what we mean here by referring to this instance of sexual contact as 'public'. Absalom's sexual encounters take place on the roof of the palace, 'before the eyes of all Israel', in the words of the narrator, and in that sense are clearly quite public. Absalom's message is only communicated successfully if 'all Israel' understands exactly what has taken place, but the text also causes us to doubt that anyone actually sees the physical contact between Absalom and his father's concubines. After all, the sexual encounters take place inside a tent. The tent is pitched on the roof for everyone to see, but that tent hides from 'all Israel' the actual details of that very thing which is said to take place before their eyes. There is thus a sense in which Absalom's sexual relations with his father's concubines are 'public' and 'private' at the same time. Right away, then, we can see that this text offers an interesting biblical case with which to consider, in Phillip Brian Harper's words, 'how extremely indistinct is the boundary between public and private space' (Harper 1999: 64).

Eventually it is David, rather than Absalom, who prevails in this conflict. Absalom comes to a brutal end in 2 Samuel 18 when, having been caught by the head in the branches of a tree, he is thrust through with spears by David's general. Within the larger narrative complex in which these incidents are recounted, moreover, David is elsewhere represented (in, e.g., 1 Sam. 16.1–13; 28.17; 2 Sam. 7.8; 12.7, *passim*) as the chosen king of Israel's god, a status that is never attributed to Absalom. Thus, the fact that it is Absalom rather than David who is represented in chapter 16 as a practitioner of public sex might be taken as evidence that the narrative understands such public sex to be inherently a bad thing. A reader of the Bible who looks to it for contemporary guidance (as many readers of the Bible do), but who opposes public sex on other grounds (as many readers of the Bible no doubt also do), might be tempted to construe this association of public sex with Absalom as evidence that public sex ought to be viewed with suspicion.

Yet, it is not clear that such a simple conclusion adequately grasps the position assumed by the narrative itself. In the first place, the passage I quoted above indicates that Ahithophel's counsel was received 'as if one asked for a word of God'. The implication of this statement may well be that Absalom assumed that Ahithophel's advice had, or could have had, divine sanction. It is true that David, who knows Ahithophel to be a wise counselor, has earlier prayed for God to turn Ahithophel's counsel to foolishness (2 Sam. 15.31). However, this prayer has little to do with Absalom's actions with David's concubines. Rather, David's prayer is answered when Absalom subsequently chooses to follow the military advice of David's friend Hushai instead of the better advice of Ahithophel. It is at that point, according to the narrator, that Yhwh frustrates Ahithophel's counsel (2 Sam. 17.14).

In any case, a closer reading of David's story reveals that Israel's god, far from being an opponent of public sex, is in fact a cause of public sex in certain circumstances and actually brings about these public sexual acts of Absalom. In order to see this, we need to recognize the link between this incident in 2 Samuel 16 and an earlier incident in 2 Samuel 11–12.

In 2 Samuel 11, David has sexual relations with Bathsheba, the wife of a soldier named Uriah. When Bathsheba becomes pregnant, David first tries to cover up the pregnancy by bringing Uriah back from the battlefield and telling Uriah to 'go down to your house, and wash your feet' (11.8). The fact that 'feet' are, in the Hebrew Bible, sometimes associated euphemistically with the genitals hints at David's intention here (cf. McCarter 1984: 286; Hertzberg 1964: 310): David hopes that Uriah will have sexual intercourse with Bathsheba so that the child of David will be credited to Uriah.

But how does Uriah respond? Unfortunately for David, Uriah declines 'to eat and to drink and to lie with my woman' (11.11) while his fellow soldiers remain in the field. Notice the appearance, in Uriah's reply, of both food and sex. Although Uriah's initial refusal 'to eat and to drink' has not received much attention from commentators, his refusal to have sexual relations with Bathsheba is sometimes associated with the abstention from sexual contact that was apparently required of soldiers during military expeditions (McCarter 1984: 286). The reader who encounters this text while working sequentially through the books of Samuel, and who is cognizant of the fact that various parts of the story of David hearken back to earlier parts of that story, may recall that such abstention from sexual contact has been referred to by David himself in 1 Samuel 21.4–5. Looking back at that earlier passage, one discovers that David is actually attempting there to secure *food* for himself and his men from a priest named Ahimelech. The only food available is holy, presumably consecrated, bread, and Ahimelech agrees to give the bread to David and his soldiers only after he learns that they have refrained from sexual relations with women. Due in part to assumptions about purity,[4] exceptional circumstances with respect to food (the eating of holy bread) require, in 1 Samuel 21, exceptional circumstances with respect to sex (avoidance of intercourse). Uriah's simultaneous reference to food and sex in 2 Samuel 11.11 therefore recalls, ironically, an incident from an earlier period of David's career when David was himself a soldier in the field rather than a king of leisure, and moreover a soldier whose life was, like that of Uriah, being sought by a king – specifically, David's predecessor Saul. Intertextual references to food and sex thus contribute to characterization in 2 Samuel 11, casting Uriah in a positive light by comparing him with an earlier

---

4.   For a helpful discussion of such assumptions see Harrington 2001.

David, and casting David in a negative light by contrasting his present actions with earlier ones and comparing him now, implicitly, to Saul.

David is finally able to persuade Uriah to eat and to drink, and even succeeds in getting Uriah drunk. However, although conventions of biblical narrative pointed out in the last chapter might lead us to assume that a drunken Uriah should be susceptible to the idea of sexual contact, he nevertheless refrains from going to his house and spending the night with Bathsheba. Once again intertextual references to food and sex contribute to characterization, highlighting Uriah's sexual restraint by showing that for purposes of warfare he refrains from sexual contact even in a situation – that is, after the ingestion of food and much drink – in which, on the basis of the actions of other male characters (Lot, Boaz, possibly Noah), we might expect sexual relations to take place. David therefore has to resort to more drastic means to cover his sexual misdeed. He orders his general to place Uriah in the thick of battle and have the other soldiers pull back, insuring that Uriah is killed. Once this plan is carried out, Bathsheba is brought by David to his house, becomes David's wife, and gives birth to David's son.

For our purposes, the most important part of this story appears after the death of Uriah and the birth of David's son. Yhwh becomes angry with David and so sends the prophet Nathan to deliver a message to David, a message that both forges another rhetorical link between food and sex and looks ahead to Absalom's actions with David's concubines:

> And Yhwh sent Nathan to David. He went in before him and said to him, 'There were two men in one city, one rich and one poor. The rich man had many flocks and cattle, but the poor man had only one small ewe lamb that he had bought. He took care of it and it grew up with him and his children. Together with him it would eat from his morsel of bread and drink from his cup and lie in his embrace.[5] It was to him like a daughter. A traveler came to the rich man, but he did not wish to take anything from his flocks or cattle to prepare something for the man on a journey who came to him. So he took the lamb of the poor man and he prepared it for the man who came to him.' Now David was very angry at the man, and he said to Nathan, 'As Yhwh lives, the man who did this ought to die. The lamb he took he should pay for four times, because he did this thing and did not show any compassion.' But Nathan said to David, 'You are the man! Thus says Yhwh the god of Israel, "I anointed you as king over Israel and I rescued you from the hand of Saul. I gave to you the house of your master and the women of your master into your embrace, and I gave you the house of Israel and Judah. And if that were too little, I would have given you that much more. Why did you treat with contempt the word of Yhwh, to do what is evil in his eyes? Uriah the Hittite you struck down with the sword, and his woman you took for your woman, and killed him with the sword of the Ammonites. And now the sword will never depart from your house, because you treated me with contempt and took the woman of Uriah the Hittite to be your woman." Thus says Yhwh, "Now look, I'm going to raise up for you trouble from your house, and I will take your women before your eyes and give them to your enemy, and he will lie with your

---

5.   On the English rendering 'lie down in one's embrace', see McCarter 1984: 292. The more common translation is 'lie in his bosom' (e.g., NRSV).

women in the sight of this very sun. For you did it in secret, but I will do this
thing before all Israel and before the sun." ' (2 Sam. 12.1–12)

There are a number of things to notice about this extraordinary passage. First,
while there is not exactly a one-to-one correspondence between the structure
of Nathan's parable and the structure of 2 Samuel's plotline, it is clear that the
wives and concubines of David are represented in Nathan's parable as 'flocks and
cattle', that is, as animals suitable for food; and that Bathsheba is represented as
the poor man's lamb, taken from the poor man and turned into food by the rich
man. Whereas Uriah has earlier refused 'to eat and to drink and to lie with my
woman' while a war is taking place, David's sexual activity with that very woman
is now ironically symbolized, in Nathan's parable, by the rich man's activity of
turning another man's lamb (a lamb, moreover, that 'eats', 'drinks', and 'lies with'
its owner (12:3; cf. Polzin 1993: 123)) into something to eat. Once again, food and
sex are impossible to disentangle in the language and imagery deployed by the
biblical text.

The comparison that Nathan's parable makes between a woman and a food
animal might seem disconcerting to modern readers, but such a comparison
coheres well with the ideology of gender, marriage and property that undergirds
certain biblical texts. For example, the version of the Ten Commandments found
in Exodus conceptualizes a man's relation to his wife as a sort of property relation,
parallel to other sorts of property relations including the relation between a man
and his animals:

> You will not covet the house of your neighbor. You will not covet the woman of
> your neighbor, or his male slave, or his female slave, or his ox, or his donkey, or
> anything that belongs to your neighbor. (Exodus 20.17)

In Hebrew, this commandment linguistically addresses a male audience: the
generic English pronoun 'you' obscures a masculine Hebrew form. When this linguistic phenomenon is interpreted together with the commandment's third person
reference to wives but not to husbands, we recognize that the content of the prohibition lists things belonging to one male Israelite that another male Israelite might
be tempted to 'covet', including not only houses and animals, but also women.
Thus, when Nathan's parable compares Bathsheba to a lamb that is taken from her
rightful owner and served as food, it builds upon assumptions about wives as a sort
of property, comparable to food animals, which are found elsewhere in biblical
literature. As Regina Schwartz rightly notes, Nathan's parable 'drives home the
point that the king's adultery is also a violation of property rights' (Schwartz 1997:
137). While the typical Israelite man presumably valued his wife more than he
valued his cattle (though Nathan's parable may make us wonder even about that),
nevertheless, biblical rhetoric sets up a structural parallel between a man's women
and his animals; this parallel lends itself, in 2 Samuel, to the conceptualization of
women (like animals) as possible objects not only of male theft but also of male
consumption.

Given the tendency for modern readers to ignore biblical connections between
food and sex, we should not be surprised to find that most commentators do not
discuss this link between food and sex in Nathan's parable. Interpretations of the

parable focus more often on the difference in status and power between the rich man and the poor man (and, hence, between David the king and Uriah the soldier). Since it was the responsibility of the king, in Israel as in other parts of the ancient Near East, to insure that justice was carried out and the poor were not exploited by the rich, David is eager to take action in a theft that represents what Kyle McCarter calls 'the abuse of the poor and powerless by the rich and powerful' (McCarter 1984: 299) and is unprepared for Nathan's revelation that it is actually the king himself who is guilty here (2 Sam. 12.7).

Such an interpretation of the dynamics of Nathan's parable is no doubt correct as far as it goes, but should we assume that the rich man's use of the stolen lamb *specifically as food* is accidental? Or might it not be the case that the parable in 2 Samuel 12 picks up on an association between food and sex already hinted at (as we have seen) in the dialogue between Uriah and David in 2 Samuel 11 and the earlier dialogue between David and Ahimelech in 1 Samuel 21? As Fewell and Gunn note, Nathan's 'parable makes very clear the analogy between eating/drinking and sex' and represents a wider tradition of biblical symbolism according to which 'the female body is a meal for the man' (Fewell and Gunn 1993: 160).

Nathan's parable does not bring to an end the story's interweaving of food and sex. Inasmuch as David is understood in the parable to have earned Yhwh's displeasure by consuming another man's 'meal', it seems appropriate that he attempts to appease Yhwh by fasting. When Yhwh causes the son produced by David's union with Bathsheba to become ill, David refuses to eat while he prays for the boy's well-being (2 Sam. 12.16–17). Once the boy dies, however, David asks for, receives, and eats food (12.20). Immediately after recounting David's explanation for ending his fast (12.22–23), the narrator notes, as if to bring things full-circle, that David comforts Bathsheba by lying with her so that she becomes pregnant again (12.24). According to the symbolism utilized in the story, we might say that one type of meal – that which brings to an end David's fast – is followed here immediately by another type of 'meal' – that which consists of David's renewed sexual relations with Bathsheba.

Apart from the way in which it brings together images of food and sex that intermingle throughout the story of David, Nathan's parable has other features that we have to note as part of our reflections on 'public sex'. In particular, we must look carefully at the giving and taking of women attributed by Nathan to Yhwh. In 2 Samuel 12.8, Yhwh claims (through Nathan) to have given to David 'the women of your master'. In context this claim seems to refer, again, to the period before David was king, a period in which David's power and prestige gradually increased at the expense of his rivals. One of the ways in which David's accumulated power and prestige is signified in that earlier part of his story is through an increase in the number of his wives and concubines (cf. 2 Sam. 3.1–5; 5.13). This earlier increase in wives and concubines is now shown by Nathan's oracle to have been actually accomplished by Yhwh. The reference in 12.8 to a 'master' or 'lord' from whom Yhwh has taken women to give to David is almost certainly a reference to Saul, mentioned explicitly in the previous verse. At first glance this may not be obvious, for although in 1 Samuel David does marry one of Saul's daughters and comes close to marrying another, there is no clear reference outside of Nathan's oracle to David's having taken wives of Saul for himself. The Talmud, however, already concludes from Nathan's oracle that David had married one of Saul's wives (*b.Sanh.18a*). There are a couple of biblical references to a wife of David named Ahinoam, and these references, together with the fact that Saul also had a wife named Ahinoam (1 Sam. 14.50), lead some biblical scholars (e.g. Levenson 1978; Levenson and Halpern 1980) to suggest that we are dealing in both cases with the same woman, and that this very Ahinoam is the woman (or one of the women) referred to in Nathan's oracle. This suggestion is strengthened by the fact that David's wife Ahinoam is referred to on more than one occasion (1 Sam. 25.42–3; 30.5) together with one of David's other wives, Abigail. Abigail is clearly the wife of yet another one of David's rivals before she marries David, and that rival – Nabal – is explicitly said to be killed by Yhwh (1 Sam. 25.38). Thus, Nathan's reference to Yhwh's having given to David 'the women of your master' is plausibly understood as an indication that Yhwh gave to David Ahinoam and Abigail, the wives of Saul and Nabal, as part of that process whereby David gradually assumed the throne of Israel through divine intervention.

The retrospective acknowledgment in Nathan's oracle of Yhwh's role in David's earlier collecting of women is only the prelude to a divine initiative that is, from the point of view of our inquiry into public sex, more significant. Yhwh, through Nathan, says explicitly in 2 Sam. 12.11 that, 'I will take your women before your eyes and give them to your enemy, and he will lie with your women in the sight of this very sun.' This oracle is surely fulfilled by Absalom's actions with his father's concubines in chapter 16. Just as Yhwh warns David in 12.12 that 'I will do this thing before all Israel and before the sun', so 16.22 notes that Absalom's sexual relations with David's concubines take place 'before the eyes of all Israel'. What Israel's god predicts in chapter 12, Israel's god fulfills in chapter 16. This fulfillment means, however, that it is Yhwh rather than Absalom who actually initiates public sex in 2 Samuel 16: Absalom carries out precisely those actions with the women of David's household that Yhwh has promised to bring about. It is, therefore, not only the case that *Absalom* utilizes his own sexual actions to send a message to David; *Yhwh* uses Absalom's sexual actions to send a message to David as well, a message of judgment and disapproval that has been foretold by Nathan in chapter 12. If the bodies of David's concubines function as paper on which words are written (to recall Schifter's statement about public sex), those words come not only from Absalom but also from Yhwh. So we find that public, non-monogamous sex, far from being divinely prohibited in the Bible, is, at least in 2 Samuel, divinely sanctioned and even involves, in a sense, divine participation.

III

The biblical use of sexual practice to send public messages between male characters is not restricted to 2 Samuel. This semiotic function of sex also occurs, among other places, in the story of Sodom in Genesis 19 and a similar story in Judges 19. Significantly, both of these stories make use of another motif that we have seen in the story of David, the motif of supplying food for a traveler that appears in Nathan's parable. At a certain point in both the Genesis and Judges narratives, a male character who provides food for travelers also offers women as sexual objects to other male characters. The circulation of food and the circulation of women are once again interrelated in complex ways.

The importance of the food motif for the story of Sodom becomes most apparent when we remember that the story actually does not begin in Genesis 19 (where we find the infamous threat of same-sex rape that has led, through strange and circuitous paths, to the English word 'sodomy').[6] Rather, the plot of Genesis 19 builds directly upon events narrated in chapter 18, where Abraham is visited by three strangers, one of whom is Yhwh. The story of this visit is narrated in such a way as to emphasize Abraham's hospitality:

> And Yhwh appeared to [Abraham] by the oaks of Mamre. [Abraham] was sitting at the entrance of his tent in the heat of the day, and he lifted up his eyes and looked, and there were three men standing near him. When he saw them, he ran from the entrance of the tent to meet them, and he bowed down to the ground. He said, 'My lord, if I find favor in your eyes, do not pass by your servant. Let a little water be brought, and wash your feet, and rest under the tree. Let me bring a little food so that you may refresh yourselves. After that you may pass on, since you have come to your servant.' And they said, 'Do as you have said.' So Abraham hurried to the tent to Sarah and said, 'Quickly, three measures of the best flour, knead it and make cakes.' Then Abraham ran to the cattle, and took one of the young cattle, tender and good, and gave it to the servant who quickly began to prepare it. He took curds and milk and the young cattle that he had prepared, and put these before them. And he stood by them under the tree as they ate. (Gen. 18.1–8)

This description of Abraham's efforts at food provision is surprisingly detailed, given the relatively spare use of descriptive detail found in most biblical narrative. The extent of the detail signals the importance, for the story, of the matter being described.[7] Abraham is here characterized in relation to a cultural 'protocol of hospitality' (Matthews 1992; Matthews and Benjamin 1993: 82–95) that has had to be negotiated in the Mediterranean and Near Eastern worlds in both ancient and more contemporary times (cf. Pitt-Rivers 1977; Finley 1978; Herzfeld 1987). While the provision of food and drink to visitors is not the only hospitality convention presupposed by this story (which also refers, for example, to the washing of feet), certainly such provisioning plays a central role in the social code at work here. It is this same social code, of course, that the rich man in Nathan's parable attempts to follow when he supplies food for his own visitor in 2 Samuel 12. Where that parabolic character ultimately fails to follow the 'protocol of hospitality' in an appropriate fashion when he feeds his guest with food stolen from another, less wealthy, man, Abraham by contrast generously feeds his guests with several types of food, all of which are taken from Abraham's own supply with the assistance of members of Abraham's household. The contrast is underscored by an overlap in food vocabulary: the rich man in Nathan's parable steals the poor man's lamb

---

6.　See Jordan 1997 for a study that is crucial for understanding the history of 'sodomy'.

7.　Cf. Westermann 1985: 274: 'The introduction is so detailed and carries such weight in itself as to be determinative of the narrative...'

because 'he did not wish to take anything from his flocks *or cattle*' (2 Sam. 12.4); Abraham goes precisely to 'the *cattle*' and selects 'one of the young *cattle*, tender and good' (Gen. 18.7) for his guests.[8] In a text written in a world that placed much value on generous hospitality, Abraham is characterized as a wealthy and honorable, albeit appropriately deferential, host.

Although Abraham is presumably unaware at first that Yhwh is among his visitors, Yhwh subsequently 'rewards the reception and hospitality with a gift, in this case the birth of a child' (Westermann 1985: 274). At the announcement of this gift, however, Abraham's wife Sarah laughs – and for good reason: 'After I am old and worn out, will I have pleasure, and my lord [Abraham] is old?' (Gen. 18.12b) The narrator has already noted that Sarah has ceased having her period (18.11) and here she refers to herself as 'worn out'. Yet her words may indicate more than simply her postmenopausal condition. She notes explicitly, for example, that Abraham is also old. The obscure word that I have translated as 'pleasure' is used only here in biblical Hebrew. Yet most commentators agree that the word probably refers to 'sexual pleasure' (Westermann 1985: 281) or 'sensuous enjoyment' (Skinner 1910: 302). The issue may not be simply a matter of conception, then, but also one of waning interest in intercourse or even, in Abraham's case, an inability to perform brought on by the old age to which Sarah laughingly points. Nevertheless, Yhwh goes on to affirm that, indeed, Sarah will bear a son. Thus, a gift of generous hospitality, described in terms of the preparation of choice food, produces in response a gift of miraculous childbirth at a time when both sexual pleasure and conception appear unlikely. We might even say that Abraham's gift of food is reciprocated with Yhwh's gift of sex.

The hospitality that Abraham gives to his visitors in Genesis 18 seems at first to be paralleled by the reception of these visitors in chapter 19. When two of these visitors arrive at Sodom, Abraham's nephew, Lot, like his uncle, offers the visitors hospitality in the form of a place to stay, the traditional washing of feet, and food. It is striking to note, however, that Lot's hospitality is described in considerably less detail than were the efforts of Abraham to feed these same guests. In contrast to the cakes made from fine flour, the young cattle, the curds and the milk given to the travelers by Abraham in chapter 18, in 19.3 only unleavened bread is referred to explicitly. Consequently, the reception of the travelers in Sodom seems less extravagant, and this shift may function as a hint to the reader that things will not go as well here as they went at the tent of Abraham.

Such an impression is confirmed almost immediately, for just after the description of Lot's food provision at the end of verse 3 we find, in verses 4 and 5, the infamous threat of same-sex rape made against Lot's guests by the men of Sodom. While discussions of this scene have long been tied up with evaluations of same-sex sexual contact prevalent among later readers, it is important to note that the kind of phallic aggression represented here has little to do with modern conceptions of homosexuality. In the socio-cultural context of the ancient Mediterranean and Near Eastern world, sexual penetration symbolizes unequal power relations.

---

8. Both stories use the Hebrew term *bqr*, which is variously translated as 'cattle', 'oxen', or 'herd [of cattle]', depending upon the context.

Thus, the public rape of one male by another constitutes a powerful semiotic mechanism, humiliating the raped man in the eyes of other men by making of him a sexual object (see Stone 1995, 1996; Yee 1995: 164; Brenner 1997: 136–43; Nissinen 1998: 45–49, *passim*; Carden 1999). The men of Sodom are characterized collectively, in this story, as something like the antitype of hospitality. Rather than honoring the travelers with the gift of food, as did Abraham, the men of Sodom attempt to shame these same travelers publicly through the imposition of forced sex.

Many of the story's assumptions about gender, power, hospitality and sexual penetration are made transparent by Lot's subsequent counter-offer to the men of Sodom to take as sexual objects his own daughters rather than his male guests (Gen. 19.7–8). If, as Fewell and Gunn note, 'Lot is willing to sacrifice his daughters in order to uphold his honor as a provider of male hospitality' (Fewell and Gunn 1993: 58), that willingness can only be understood against the background of a social world premised on gender hierarchy and the male control of female sexuality. It is precisely the assumption, found throughout the Hebrew Bible, that women will naturally be given and taken by men, which allows the biblical narrative to make a distinction between, on the one hand, Lot's offer of his daughters as preferable objects of rape and, on the other hand, the wickedness Lot tries to prevent by shielding male visitors from being made objects of rape (Gen 19.7).

As it turns out, Lot's daughters avoid the fate suggested by their father when the men of Sodom reject his offer. However, the potential consequences for women of assumptions such as those made by Lot are spelled out in graphic detail in the parallel version of this story found in Judges. There, too, a threat of male-male rape follows two scenes in which food and drink are shared with guests. There, too, a male host offers two women (including his own daughter) to men who demand sexual access to his male guest. In Judges, however, one woman is actually thrown out of the house and raped all night. When she subsequently dies (at whose hand, the text does not tell us), the woman's husband cuts her body into twelve pieces and sends those pieces throughout Israel as a way of summoning the Israelites publicly to war.

Due in part to the horrific nature of these events, the story in Judges 19 has received a great deal of attention in contemporary scholarship, especially from feminist interpreters.[9] It is not always noted, however, that the use of this woman's dismembered body to send a message to the Israelites – as 'paper on which words are written' – invites an intertextual comparison between a woman and a food animal that reminds us of the way in which David's women are symbolized in Nathan's parable. An intermediary link between the two stories is found in 1 Samuel 11. There Saul takes a 'pair of cattle' (11.7), cuts them into pieces, and sends the pieces throughout Israel to summon the Israelites to battle. The Levite

9.   Feminist readings of the story include Trible 1984: 65–91; Bal 1988b, 1993; Exum 1993: 176–201; Jones-Warsaw 1993; Keefe 1993; Yee 1995; Frymer-Kensky 2002: 118–38. Among other analyses see Cheng 2002, where the story is interpreted from the point of view of 'a queer Asian Pacific American biblical hermeneutic'. For an interpretation of my own, more detailed than the one I offer here, see Stone 1995; 1996.

in Judges, of course, substitutes the body of his concubine for the bodies of Saul's cattle but aims, as does Saul, at using the dismembered corporeal signifier to call the Israelites publicly to action. While the substitution is meant to horrify those with whom the Levite communicates, still his message, like Saul's, is effective: 'all the Israelites' respond to the summons of the Levite (Judg. 20.1) and engage in war with the tribe of Benjamin, whose territory includes the city of Gibeah in which the concubine was raped. Saul was himself from the tribe of Benjamin, and is associated with Gibeah in several biblical texts. Indeed, it appears that he is at 'Gibeah of Saul' (1 Sam. 11.4) when he hears the message that leads him to take his 'cattle' and cut them into pieces. The two stories are obviously related to one another intertextually. The substitution which the book of Judges makes by placing a woman's body in the role filled in 1 Samuel 11 by cattle, further indicates that, when Nathan's parable symbolizes Bathsheba as a lamb, it is utilizing a symbolic comparison between women and food animals with much cultural resonance, at least among the men who no doubt wrote these narratives. When Nathan's parable notes that the rich man (symbolizing David) who steals the poor man's lamb (symbolizing Uriah's wife Bathsheba) did so because he did not wish 'to take from his own flock or from his own cattle' (symbolizing David's own wives and concubines (2 Sam. 12.4)), the word that Nathan uses to refer to the rich man's 'cattle' is the same term used for the 'cattle' that Saul cuts into pieces in just the way that the Levite cuts his concubine into pieces. It is, moreover, the word used to refer to the 'cattle' from which Abraham selects one of the 'young cattle' to give to his guests in Genesis.

In light of this web of intertextual connections, we may well wonder whether the outrage expressed by the Levite in Judges 20 is grounded in care and compassion for his murdered concubine or whether, in fact, he is not responding angrily to a situation in which he feels dishonored by the brutal treatment of his property. It is important to note how the Levite describes the situation to his fellow Israelites: 'The inhabitants of Gibeah rose up against *me*, and they surrounded *me* in the house at night, intending to kill *me*, and they abused my concubine and she died' (Judg. 20.5). Three times the Levite refers to himself before the woman is mentioned. The Levite's own words, therefore, indicate that, as Frymer-Kensky puts it, 'to the Levite, as to his hearers, the attack on the girl was an attack on him...' (Frymer-Kensky 2002: 129; cf. Trible 1984: 79–80). The Levite is arguably expressing outrage quite similar to the outrage that Absalom wishes his father to feel in 2 Samuel 16; in both stories the sexual assault of a man's concubine or concubines functions as a public attack on the man in question. In the ancient context, these sexual assaults would not have been understood by the assumed male audience primarily as offenses committed against the individual women who are raped. The offense is more likely to have been understood by that audience as an offense committed against a man whose honor and prestige have been challenged by the actions of other men. The challenge is public and sexual, and mediated by women.

IV

We may seem to have traveled some distance, by this point, from the debates about 'public sex' with which I opened this chapter. Nevertheless, I want to suggest that careful analysis of the texts discussed here may have implications for the ways in which readers of biblical texts engage those debates. More surprisingly, such an analysis also has implications for contemporary discussions about the nature of marriage with which readers of the Bible are more eager to involve themselves.

In order to explicate these implications, we must underscore the fact that, when we turn to biblical texts such as those considered in this chapter, we are clearly dealing with presuppositions about sex, gender and marriage that are quite foreign to the views likely to be defended openly by most adherents of Judaism and Christianity. The understanding of marriage at work in these narratives does, however, have similarities to that 'political economy' of sex, gender and kinship glossed by Gayle Rubin as 'the traffic in women', in which women circulate along with other goods and serve as the 'conduit' of relations among men (Rubin 1976: 174). Rubin's famous article on 'the traffic in women' consists in part of a feminist rereading of Lévi-Strauss's theory of kinship as the exchange of women (Lévi-Strauss 1969). Women are understood within that theory to be only one part, albeit an important part, of a much larger system in which, in traditional, kinship-based societies, 'all sorts of things circulate in exchange' – including, explicitly, food (Rubin 1976: 171). Such exchanges take place primarily among men, who create through these exchanges a system of alliances that Lévi-Strauss understood to constitute the foundation of society. Rubin, from a feminist point of view, modifies this argument by noting critically that Lévi-Strauss speaks as if the subordination of women to men is a necessary element of human social relations. She goes on to argue, however, that reflection on the systems of exchange analyzed by Lévi-Strauss exposes the symbolic logic of numerous societies in which women are, or have been, subordinated to men. One element of such societies that comes more clearly into view is marriage, which is shown to function in many cases not so much as the expression of intimacy between a man and a woman, nor simply as a mechanism for generating offspring, but rather as a component of social processes by which men establish and manipulate relations with one another.

Discussions about biblical views on marriage and family too often ignore the fact that there are no specific words in biblical Hebrew corresponding exactly to our words 'marriage', 'husband', or 'wife'.[10] However, several biblical texts that refer to something that we today *call* 'marriage' do so by using language about the giving and taking of one another's daughters by groups of men. This language

---

10. But see Berquist 2002: 60–1, where the lack of correspondence between biblical and contemporary vocabularies is taken seriously as an indication that the 'social institution' of marriage 'is not the same in ancient Israel as it is in the modern Western world...' The Hebrew words often translated 'husband' and 'wife' are simply words for 'man' and 'woman', translated variously according to context. In this chapter I have adopted a literal translation of the words 'woman' and 'women', partly to underscore the points I am making here about gender, power and the socio-cultural overdetermination of relations that we group together under the misleadingly simple label 'marriage'. The lack of correspondence between biblical and modern notions of 'marriage' is also noted by Althaus-Reid (2000: 140).

appears in contexts which indicate that such giving and taking of daughters by groups of men was understood to constitute a form of alliance or relationship between the men in question (e.g., Gen. 34.8–24; Deut. 7.3). Such texts, focusing as they do on relations between men rather than on desires of, or consequences for, the women who are given and taken, underscore the relevance of Rubin's construal of kinship as 'the traffic in women' for biblical interpretation. This relevance is broadened significantly by Rubin's recognition that the relations among men which are mediated by women and other exchange items include not only relations of alliance via marriage, but also relations of hostility such as we find when women are 'taken in battle' (175). The same point is noted by Schwartz when, in the course of a reading of the story of David, she argues that 'when women are stolen, rather than peaceably exchanged, all of the relational directions reverse, toward fear, anxiety, and hostility' (Schwartz 1997: 137).

Schwartz also recognizes that animals as well as women play a role in these relations; and she concludes that in Nathan's parable 'the polluting of [a man's] woman is analogous to the slaughter of his animal' (Schwartz 1997: 137). The specific purpose of that slaughter to which Schwartz refers is, of course, the provision of food. This potential interchangeability of women, animals and food is highlighted by Rubin when she reproduces a proverb attributed to the Arapesh: 'Your own mother, your own sister, your own pigs, your own yams that you have piled up, you may not eat. Other people's mothers, other people's sisters, other people's pigs, other people's yams that they have piled up, you may eat' (Rubin 1976: 172). Note the way in which food, animals and women occupy parallel positions in this proverb. So, too, in the biblical texts discussed in this chapter, women, animals and food together are found at points of relation between male characters.

We see in these stories, then, another one of the ways in which food and sex are linked to one another in biblical literature. Food and sex both play a central role in the social exchanges and symbolic associations by which male characters establish and manipulate their relations with one another.

It is striking that Nathan's oracle represents Israel's god as a participant in, rather than a critic of, the economy of sex, gender, marriage and exchange presupposed by a parable in which food animals symbolize wives and concubines. When Yhwh gives David the women of David's rivals (2 Sam. 12.8), Yhwh is assumed by the text to understand, as do the male writers and readers of these texts, that the ability to collect and support multiple women and to take women from one's male rivals allows men to demonstrate publicly their power and wealth and thereby earn prestige in the eyes of male counterparts. A particular perspective on the significance of 'marriage' – one quite different from contemporary Jewish and Christian views on marriage – is not only presupposed by the text but projected onto Yhwh. When Yhwh punishes David by causing David's enemy Absalom to have 'public sex' with David's concubines, the same set of social presuppositions and the same economy of sex, gender and power are at work in the production of the text and the characterization of Yhwh.

Thus, two phenomena, one of which we now call 'marriage' and the other of which I am calling 'public sex', assume a range of meanings and functions in the biblical narratives by virtue of their place in a structured set of assumptions

– assumptions that I have been trying to explicate – about sex, gender, property, power and prestige. The importance of this point must be underscored, for it has implications for the ways in which readers of the Bible think about possible responses to contemporary debates over such matters as 'marriage' and 'public sex'. Neither 'marriage' nor 'public sex' has any inherent, essential meaning or structure. Rather, both 'marriage' and 'public sex' take on forms and significance that are specifiable only within particular networks of assumptions and relations. In the biblical instances, these assumptions include the view that one man's honor and prestige can be attacked via 'his' women, and that the man who launches such an attack (by raping another man's concubine, or taking another man's wife) thereby demonstrates his own power publicly. Because the assumptions underlying such biblical representations of public sex and marriage are not questioned by the authors of the biblical texts, those assumptions can be projected even onto Yhwh (as they are in 2 Samuel), who is, within the world of the text, one male character among other male characters. Such representations of Israel's god serve as a helpful reminder of the fact, which I consider in more detail in chapter 5, that the male god of the Bible is a projection of the Bible's male writers and is often characterized with features that men expected to find among one another.

Now it seems clear to me that such a representation of God's role vis-à-vis female characters in 2 Samuel makes any simplistic theological or ethical 'application' of these texts to our contemporary context, or to the issues that we debate in this context (such as 'public sex' or 'marriage'), extremely problematic. Indeed, reflection on texts such as these ought to raise serious questions about any traditional or neo-traditional approach to biblical interpretation, which would argue or imply that theological or ethical decisions ought to be made, or can be made, on the basis of appeal to biblical precedent alone. As Tolbert notes, assumptions about 'the direct applicability of the [biblical] text to any contemporary context' require relative inattention to the specific ways in which a text's ancient context has shaped the text, and yet paradoxically result in the importation into modern contexts of presuppositions, especially pertaining to matters of hierarchy and gender, that have 'many destructive effects on the church and on society' (1998: 177). Certainly, the texts with which we are dealing here rely upon, and even posit divine approval of, and participation in, presuppositions about gender that can foster exactly the sort of 'destructive effects' which trouble Tolbert – and should trouble anyone concerned about 'safer text'.

Conversely, recognition of *differences* between the presuppositions of these texts and presuppositions of our own might force us to acknowledge, more openly than practicing Jews and Christians are normally inclined to acknowledge, the extent to which assumptions about sexual matters that are actually quite foreign to the biblical texts have already become embedded in much Jewish and Christian rhetoric. Here I am thinking in particular of the ways in which, with the rise of modernity, sexuality has come to be linked to domestic intimacy and considered inappropriate for the public realm. In our own day, it is frequently taken for granted that, as one historian characterizes the situation, one's 'emotional satisfaction and happiness' depend upon the existence of a ' "personal life," sharply distinguished and disconnected from the public world of work and production'. Such a 'personal life' is still

– indeed, is perhaps more than ever – identified with the institution of the 'family' as the context in which 'satisfying, mutually enhancing relationships' are formed (D'Emilio 1983: 103).[11] Much modern rhetoric on marriage, including a good bit of the rhetoric now deployed by advocates for gay marriage, relies upon just such an identification. Sexual contact and its representations are widely deemed appropriate, and appropriate for protection, when they are associated with that 'personal life', but are more likely to be proscribed when such an association is tenuous or absent. As the Christian ethicist Marvin Ellison argues, just such assumptions of liberalism as this particular way of drawing the line between public and private, and the accompanying tendency to restrict sex and love to the private sphere, hinder 'development of an adequate social ethic of sexuality' within contemporary religious communities (Ellison 1996: 7).

The effects of the modern liberal division between public and private are especially damaging for those of us whose sexual, affective and household practices do not fit easily into the narrow assumptions about sex, gender and kinship that are most often promoted in the contemporary world. In a fascinating article titled 'Sex in Public', Lauren Berlant and Michael Warner underscore the extent to which 'heteronormative forms of intimacy' that go routinely unquestioned today are predicated upon those specific historical developments which led to modern ways of consigning most sexual matters to the realm of the private and the personal. To be sure, as Berlant and Warner note, this supposed relegation of sexuality to a private sphere is not the whole story. In late capitalism, sexuality is actually deployed in complex ways on both sides of the public/private divide, as the use of sexual images in advertising indicates. In this respect, at least, we may even be able to make an admittedly anachronistic connection to the biblical texts analyzed in this chapter. Just as Absalom's sexual acts are simultaneously located on the roof where they take place 'before the eyes of all Israel', *and* hidden from view by the tent in which they occur, so also today the boundary between 'public' and 'private' is frequently blurred even as it continues to be affirmed. More importantly, this boundary is often manipulated in moralizing ways to regulate what can and cannot be seen about sexuality – or what can and cannot be seen and acknowledged openly about the actual functioning of heteronormative familial intimacy itself (as opposed to the various official fictions that are allowed to circulate around it).[12] Notwithstanding such manipulations and contradictions, contemporary debates over sexuality and marriage continue to take place in a manner that assumes, as a starting point, what Berlant and Warner call 'a privatization of sex and the sexualization of private personhood'. In such a context, 'sexuality seems like a property of subjectivity rather than a publicly or counterpublicly accessible culture' (Berlant and Warner 1998: 559). Significantly, one's very existence as a

11. Much light is shed on the development of these modern assumptions by Zaretsky 1986; Seidman 1991.

12. For a provocative discussion that uses the realities of sexual infidelity to raise questions about the assumptions concerning love, marriage and sex that structure contemporary rhetoric on intimate coupling, see Kipnis 2003.

social subject can seem to depend upon one's ability to fit into a standard way of construing interrelations among sex, family, intimacy and community:

> A complex cluster of sexual practices gets confused, in heterosexual culture, with the love plot of intimacy and familialism that signifies belonging to society in a deep and normal way. Community is imagined through scenes of intimacy, coupling, and kinship; a historical relation to futurity is restricted to gen-erational narrative and reproduction. A whole field of social relations becomes intelligible as heterosexuality, and this privatized sexual culture bestows on its sexual practices a tacit sense of rightness and normalcy. This sense of rightness – embedded in things and not just in sex – is what we call heteronormativity. (Berlant and Warner 1998: 554)

The attraction of such a heteronormativity is not only felt by heterosexuals. As Berlant and Warner recognize, lesbians and gay men are also tempted to line up behind political projects that 'certify as properly private the personal lives of gays and lesbians' (562). Resisting such temptation, Berlant and Warner mount a powerful argument for the defense and propagation of 'queer counterpublics' that would continue to make room for, among other things, a 'public sexual culture' (563, *passim*).

The point to emphasize here is that the assumed normalcy and rightness of the 'heteronormative forms of intimacy' analyzed by Berlant and Warner are effects of historical developments that led to particular modern ways of construing inter-relations among sex, publicity, privacy, intimacy, politics, economics and so forth. Berlant and Warner underscore the contingency of such construals by contrasting them with the situation in ancient Greece, where very different understandings of sexual practice and its relevance for public life existed (cf. Halperin 1990; Winkler 1990). The same point could be made, however, by pointing to the political economy of sex and gender that we have seen underlying certain biblical narratives.

One of the reasons for underscoring the difference between biblical represen-tations of sexual practice and marriage, and modern 'heteronormative forms of intimacy', has to do with the fact that supposed biblical views are so frequently appealed to by religious advocates for those modern forms of intimacy. In con-nection with this religious function, it is important to recall that religion as well as sexuality has frequently been understood in modernity in privatized and per-sonalized ways. Yet significant strands of contemporary theology have called into question this widespread tendency of modern Christianity, and particularly that 'bourgeois' Christianity which continues to flourish among the white, Western middle class (cf. Metz 1986: 67–81), to privatize and spiritualize religion and separate it from politics. Today some of us who are affiliated, in however com-plicated a fashion, with Christianity, rightly ask what a public, transformative religious practice, albeit one that takes a non-fundamentalist form, would look like. Thus, theologians argue that theology is best approached as a 'public enter-prise' (Davaney 2000: 160), and biblical scholars challenge the understanding of biblical interpretation as a component of individual, devotional spirituality, calling instead for a 'biblical theology as public deliberative discourse of the *ekklesia*' (Schüssler Fiorenza 1999: 191). Obviously, such proposals need to be evaluated publicly. The point I wish to make, however, is that the temptation *among persons affiliated with religion* to privatize *sexual* relations and restrict them to the sphere of familial intimacy should be viewed with great suspicion as one part of that same movement of modernity which has led to the narrowing, privatizing and spiritualizing of theology and religious discourse.

It is crucial to challenge the tendency among Christians, including some lesbian and gay Christians, to accept uncritically, and even mistake as inherently Christian, particular modern ways of relating sexual practice to such phenomena as intimacy, personal fulfillment, kinship networks, domestic arrangements, friendship, social and professional roles, politics, religion, and the division between public and private. The best way of proceeding with such a challenge is *not* to suggest that we must get back behind modernity to initiate a supposedly 'biblical', and hence 'correct', understanding of the interrelations among those phenomena. Such an attempt would run the risk of reproducing economies of sex and gender with implications for women in particular that are, as we have seen, quite horrifying. The tendency of Christian rhetoric to essentialize and sanctify particular configurations of such phenomena as sexual practice, intimacy, personal fulfillment, kinship networks, domestic arrangements, friendship, social and professional roles, politics, religion, and the division between public and private fails to do justice to the thoroughly historical and contextual character of sexual and kinship matters and, indeed, of Christianity itself. Disagreements among religious persons about such matters as public sex or marriage will never be – and should not be – resolved by simplistic appeals to supposed biblical precedent. However, careful attention to biblical texts such as those in 2 Samuel reveals that the religious traditions in which many of us still stand have in the past been able to incorporate a remarkably wide range of assumptions about sexual matters, including the assumption that there are times and places for public sex. A frank recognition of this fact could perhaps lead us to consider in a more open and adventurous fashion a wide range of alternative ways of conceptualizing and experiencing sexual relationality.

The argument I am making is not exactly a positive, constructive argument about the future shape of Christian sexual practice. In certain respects, it is a negative argument. It aims at unsettling the widespread assumption that public, non-monogamous sex could *never* be worked into the structures of Jewish and Christian traditions by demonstrating that such sex has in fact been worked into the structure of biblical traditions *already*. It aims at unsettling the assumption that contemporary debates over marriage are dealing with a single institution with biblical foundations, by pointing out instead that biblical beliefs about marriage are quite distinct from views on marriage that participants in the modern debates would – or should – adopt.

If I have been at pains to emphasize that I am not calling for a replication of *biblical forms* of public sex, I nevertheless wish to stress that positive steps can be made toward the constructive reinterpretation of particular forms of public sex, forms that could receive religious affirmation, albeit forms quite different from those existing in the past. A promising start in this direction is found in Kathy Rudy's construal of gay male public sex as a 'communal' enterprise (Rudy 1997: 75–84). Rudy's reinterpretation of gay male 'promiscuity' as a positive sign of

hospitality offers an important resource for any queer religious reconceptualiza-
tion of radical sex practices. Whereas gay male 'promiscuity' continues to be cited
with horror even by cautious advocates for the Christian recognition of lesbians
and gay men (e.g., Johnson 1996: 146), Rudy suggests that Christians have much to
learn from radical sex practices; for, at a time when 'Christians have forgotten how
to think about social and sexual life outside the family ... the thing they most critique about gay life – "promiscuity" – is the very practice of caring for one another
and the stranger that [Christians] themselves have forgotten' (Rudy 1997: 78–9).[13]
Though Rudy's own concern with 'distinguish[ing] ourselves as Christians' (124)
threatens to reinscribe a boundary between 'church' and 'world' (123) that I
believe needs to be destabilized, her notion of 'promiscuous' sexual relations as a
religious 'practice of caring for one another and the stranger' provides us with one
possible opening for revaluing not only non-monogamous, but even 'public' (in the
widest sense of that term), and for that matter anonymous ('and the stranger'), sex
as a practice of hospitality with positive religious and theological connotations.
Such 'promiscuous' practices may even testify to the strength of our commitment
to that promiscuous God who, in Laurel Schneider's words, 'wants us to be alive
and to love without ceasing' (2001: 32).

As this positive rethinking of radical sexual practice takes place, I assume that
women as well as men will take an active role in shaping and choosing the sexual
behaviors in which they participate (cf. Delany 1999: 197). On this point a clear
distinction between biblical forms of either public sex *or* marriage, and forms of
sexual relationality that we might wish to support or bring into existence today,
must be made.

The fact that *biblical* approaches to public sex sometimes entailed acceptance
of the subjugation of women does not, by any means, lead necessarily to a rejection of public sex. After all, the fact that biblical approaches to marriage or, for
that matter, to 'covenant' or 'justice' also entailed acceptance of the subjugation
of women, seldom leads us to reject 'marriage', 'covenant' or 'justice' altogether
as concepts with potential theological value. As Kathryn Tanner rightly points out
(Tanner 1997: 165):

> The meanings and associations of terms tend to drift with the changing cir-
> cumstances of their use and the differently situated persons employing them.
> Although such contexts of use may help delimit the meaning of cultural mate-
> rials, no particular context has an absolute hold on them; like all meaningful
> materials, it is part of their very nature to be able to be abstracted from one
> context and inserted into another.

Tanner's point with respect to the meanings of terms can be extended to the shapes
and meanings of practices. Avoiding reified, essentialized or ahistorical views as
to what public sex necessarily means or looks like, but recognizing frankly that
something like 'public sex' does play a role in the biblical tradition, we could
construct new forms of, and meanings for, 'public sex' by allowing it to find a

---

13. Rudy also points out, correctly in my view, that even when lesbians, gay men and bisexuals do organize themselves into 'families', 'what gay people mean by families is very different
than what conservatives mean by the term' (Rudy 1997: 81, original emphasis).

place within alternative sets of practices and assumptions that do not involve, for example, the subordination of women to men.

Although my focus on biblical interpretation precludes more detailed discussion of possibilities for alternative sex practices, it should in any case be clear that the reimagination of our approach to sexual matters to which I look forward would have as one of its central components a willingness to 'think' food, sex and religion together. Such a willingness may even assist us with the point that I have just been making about possibilities for non-patriarchal forms of 'public sex', for recognition that the preparation and consumption of a 'meal' often reinforces male domination seldom leads us to conclude that 'meals' are inherently patriarchal affairs. Nevertheless, certain features of the texts that we have considered in this chapter will, by now, have underscored the fact that any attempt to 'think' food and sex together must grapple with difficult questions having to do with assumptions about gender; assumptions that not only structure biblical literature, but also the ways in which human beings conceptualize food and sex. Gender assumptions are clearly at work, for example, when biblical texts characterize Yhwh, as does 2 Samuel, by attributing to him beliefs shared among Israelite men. Gender assumptions are just as clearly at work when biblical texts presuppose, as do all of the texts considered in this chapter, certain forms of the subjugation of women to men. The next two chapters are devoted to further analysis of these gender-related matters, and to reflection on the possible impact of such matters upon my arguments about food, sex and biblical interpretation.

Chapter 4

Pleasure and Danger in Biblical Interpretation:

Food, Sex and Women in 2 Samuel 13 and the Song of Songs

I

If biblical interpretation is going to be reconceived as the practice of 'safer text', attention must be given to the patriarchal structuring of biblical representations of sex. In the last chapter we saw, for example, how certain texts presuppose that the rape of women by men could be tolerated and even brought about by the deity imagined by, and created partly in the image of, biblical authors. Such texts indicate clearly that both biblical interpretation and sexuality present potential risks to women in the context of male domination.

However, feminist discussions of sexuality highlight the importance of maintaining a complex view of sexuality, one that balances recognition of the dangers that sexuality holds for women with recognition of its pleasures. As Carole Vance puts it (Vance 1984: 1):

> The tension between sexual danger and sexual pleasure is a powerful one in women's lives. Sexuality is simultaneously a domain of restriction, repression, and danger as well as a domain of exploration, pleasure, and agency. To focus only on pleasure and gratification ignores the patriarchal structure in which women act, yet to speak only of sexual violence and oppression ignores women's experiences with sexual agency and choice and unwittingly increases the sexual terror and despair in which women live.

Such an emphasis on *tension* between pleasure and danger needs to be taken seriously by readers of the Bible. For the temptation to adopt a single focus – *only* pleasure, *only* danger – is nearly as real, and the difficulty of maintaining the tension between these two poles nearly as severe, within biblical interpretation as within the feminist sexuality debates that motivated Vance's statement.[1]

It may be the case that frank recognition of this tension will raise questions in the minds of my readers about the comparison between food and sex made in this volume. 'Is it not possible', such readers may ask, 'that this comparison between food and sex could have the effect, even if unintended, of trivializing the dangers

---

1. On these debates see Vance, ed., 1984; Snitow, Stansell and Thompson 1983; Seidman 1992: 97–143; Segal 1994; Rubin and Butler 1994; Duggan and Hunter 1995; Hollibaugh 2000.

that sexuality has often presented in the past to, and still often holds in the present for, women living in male-dominated societies?' To what extent does the comparison between food and sex help, and to what extent does the comparison between food and sex hinder, our attempts to take seriously 'the tension between sexual danger and sexual pleasure' in the context of biblical interpretation?

Similar questions have been raised about Gayle Rubin's essay, 'Thinking Sex', widely cited as one of the founding texts of contemporary lesbian and gay studies and queer theory.[2] In that essay Rubin finds it useful to compare conventional responses to sex with conventional responses to food. In the first place, Rubin makes such a comparison to underscore the social, cultural and historical construction and organization of sexuality. While acknowledging that the body's 'biological capacities' serve as 'prerequisites for human sexuality', Rubin argues against approaches to sexuality that focus primarily upon its biological and physiological dimensions. Toward that end she deploys the rhetoric of food, pointing out as an analogy with sexual matters that 'the belly's hunger gives no clue to the complexities of cuisine' (Rubin 1984: 276). Sexuality is in Rubin's view 'as much a human product' as diet (277). It harnesses the body's 'biological capacities', but those capacities tell us relatively little about the practices and meanings that, in any particular society, constitute what we might call (though Rubin does not) the 'sexual cuisine'.

Rubin also compares food and sex to argue that approaches to sexuality suffer from what she calls a 'fallacy of misplaced scale'. Rubin uses this phrase to suggest that sexuality is frequently given symbolic weight and importance far out of proportion to any inherent qualities or effects, such that even small deviations from sexual norms 'are often experienced as cosmic threats' (279). As she puts it elsewhere, 'Part of the problem is that we use different standards when we talk about sex than we do for almost any other aspect of life' (in Hollibaugh 2000: 129). We need, but do not have, any notion of 'benign sexual variation'. By contrast, Rubin points out, 'Although people can be intolerant, silly, or pushy about what constitutes proper diet, differences in menu rarely provoke the kinds of rage, anxiety, and sheer terror that routinely accompany differences in erotic taste' (Rubin 1984: 279). Returning to this point later in her article, Rubin notes that 'a person is not considered immoral, is not sent to prison, and is not expelled from her or his family, for enjoying spicy cuisine' (310). For Rubin, comparisons between food and sex help us to think about sex in a more reasoned and proportionate manner, so that a pluralism of sexual practices and tastes becomes more acceptable.

To Tania Modleski, however, the rhetorical force of Rubin's comparisons between sex and food relies too heavily upon the assumption that practices associated with food and eating are never themselves potentially dangerous. Arguing that Rubin and other 'libertarian feminists' (Modleski 1991: 161) underestimate

---

2. Thus the *Lesbian and Gay Studies Reader* (Abelove, Barale and Halperin, eds., 1992) opens with both a reprinted version of Rubin's essay and an updated 'Postscript' (Abelove, Barale and Halperin, eds., 1992: 3–44); and Judith Butler notes, in an interview with Rubin, the opinion that 'Thinking Sex' helped to 'set ... the methodology for lesbian and gay studies' (Rubin and Butler 1994: 62). See also Turner 2000: 87–90, 101, 178.

the danger that such practices as pornography and sadomasochism present to women, Modleski asserts that the way in which Rubin compares food and sex 'is extraordinarily naïve – and not just about sex'. In Modleski's view, food is already treated more like sex than Rubin's rhetoric allows, for 'both food and sex are ... fraught with taboo and forbidden desire' (Modleski 1991: 153). The first example that Modleski gives to underscore food's problematic potential is anorexia, for the higher incidence of eating disorders among women than men can be taken as evidence that food practices frequently have a more negative impact upon women than men.[3] Of course, eating disorders among men exist as well, and it is possible that their incidence is underestimated or even increasing with the contemporary spread of media-disseminated standardized male body images (cf. Pope, Phillips and Olivardia 2000; Bordo 1999). Nevertheless, the fact that practices of food preparation and consumption can have quite different meanings for, and effects upon, women than men is widely noted in the modern literature on food, even apart from the specific question of eating disorders.[4] It is certainly the case, as Modleski suggests, that potential dangers associated with food are, in many times and places, greater for women than men.

It is, however, doubtful that acknowledgment of this point undermines Rubin's use of comparisons between food and sex to make an argument for sexual pluralism. In the first place, while it may be true that Rubin does not explicitly acknowledge potential dangers associated with food, the fact remains, as Rubin suggests, that in modern Western contexts food practices rarely carry with them the ethical burden of proof routinely assigned to sex practices. This is quite apparent in contexts influenced by Christianity. Even Christian writers who argue for a closer relationship between food practices, religious reflection and biblical interpretation – by exploring, for example, biblical bases for a Christian vegetarianism – acknowledge that, in today's world, many Christians will respond to religious arguments about food with 'surprise' (Webb 2001: 12). Very few people are 'surprised', however, when such arguments are made about sex. Like a good rhetorician, Rubin starts from an assumption that she knows to be widespread among her audience – the assumption that sex practices are assigned greater moral weight than food practices – so as to persuade that audience to accept the specific argument that she wishes to make for 'benign sexual variation'.

Moreover, while I agree with Modleski that both food and sex need to be analyzed in relation to questions about women's oppression, Rubin has recently clarified that her point in 'Thinking Sex' was not (as some of her critics apparently took it to have been) that analyses of sexuality need not take its relation to gender oppression into account. Rather, analysis of the relationship between sexuality and gender oppression, though necessary, is not sufficient for a grasp of the politics of

---

3. On 'eating disorders' among women see Brumberg 1988; Bordo 1993; Bartky 1988; Malson 1998; Lawrence, ed., 1987; Beardsworth and Keil 1997; Knapp 2003, and, in relation to religion, Bell 1985; Bynum 1987; Lelwica 1999.

4. Sherrie Inness suggests that research on women and eating disorders, while valuable, may have 'drowned out other scholarly work on gender and food that does not focus on eating problems' (Inness 2001: 5). For such work see Coward 1985; DeVault 1991; Counihan 1999; Inness, ed., 2001a, 2001b.

sexuality (Rubin and Butler 1994: 97). In that respect, Rubin's comparison between food and sex seems to have been to the point after all. For while it is true that analysis of food practices ought to take their differential gender effects into account, it clearly does not follow that analysis of food in terms of gender oppression is sufficient, alone, for an understanding of the politics or social significance of food. Furthermore, it is unlikely that anyone would argue that awareness of the dangers which food practices pose for women should justify either a failure to appreciate the pleasures that are often also involved in such practices, or intolerance toward a pluralism of such practices. Rather, the goal with respect to food must be similar to that articulated by Vance with respect to sex: to maintain the *tension* between pleasure and danger that shapes the experiences of many women.

It is that tension which I hope to explore in this chapter, specifically in relation to two biblical texts in which food, sex and gender all play a role. If food as well as sex represents a potential danger for women, it should not be surprising if we discover that food and sex appear together in biblical texts where their danger for women is clear. We have seen in the last chapter that this is true, but I will extend the point here by looking at another story from 2 Samuel in which food is associated clearly with a woman who becomes the object of sexual violence. The example underscores the potential dangers of food as well as sex for women in a patriarchal world.

As Vance, Rubin and others argue, however, danger is only part of the story where sex is concerned. As important as acknowledgment of danger is, pleasure has to be acknowledged as well. Such acknowledgment can be difficult to make in relation to biblical texts, for pleasure is not so frequent a topic of biblical discourse as one might wish. Sexual pleasure, and especially sexual pleasure for women, is discussed in biblical literature less frequently still. Indeed, the relative silence of biblical literature on the topic of sexual pleasure may well have contributed to the fact that, as Christian ethicists and theologians note (e.g., Gudorf 1994; Ellison 1996; Jordan 2002: 155–72), the Christian tradition has often had difficulty valuing sexual pleasure as a good in itself, outside the context of procreation. There is, however, at least one biblical text, the Song of Songs, in which female sexual pleasure and desire play a central, and generally positive (if admittedly complex), role, in spite of the fact that concerns about procreation are absent from the book. As the Song of Songs also conjoins food imagery and sexual imagery – indeed, often uses food imagery *as* sexual imagery – it makes a useful point of comparison here.

Food and sex, pleasure and danger, and biblical representations of women – such will be our concerns in this chapter. I will return, at the end of the chapter, to implications of the analysis for 'safer' practices of biblical interpretation.

II

I am discussing 2 Samuel 13 here primarily because of its usefulness for underscoring one pole of the tension between pleasure and danger – specifically, the presence of danger – that shapes the relation of many women to food and sex. Notwithstanding this strategic choice, it is important to recognize that events

recounted in 2 Samuel 13 are an integral part of the story of David that both pre-
cedes and follows it, portions of which have been considered already in the last
chapter. Thus, in 2 Samuel 12, Yhwh, responding to David's actions with Bathsheba
and Uriah, announces to David his intention to 'raise up trouble against you from
within your own house' (12.11). While this oracle is fulfilled most completely by
Absalom's rape of his father's concubines, the predicted 'trouble' in David's house
actually begins earlier, when David's son and Absalom's half-brother Amnon rapes
Absalom's sister Tamar in 2 Samuel 13 and is subsequently murdered at Absalom's
command. There is, moreover, a rhetorical connection between Nathan's words
to David in 2 Samuel 12 and the story of Tamar's rape in 2 Samuel 13. The lamb
in Nathan's tale is said to be 'like a daughter' to the man who owns her (2 Sam.
12.3). As that man and the lamb represent, respectively, Uriah and his *wife*, why
is it the case that the word 'daughter' is used in the parable instead of the word
normally translated 'wife'? It is often suggested that Nathan's comparison of the
lamb to a 'daughter' – in Hebrew, *bat* – is an allusion to the name of the woman
symbolized by this lamb/daughter, Bathsheba, as the first element of her name is
also the Hebrew word for daughter, *bat* (see, e.g., Ackerman 1990: 44; Fokkelman
1981: 79; Polzin 1993: 123). Although this wordplay is at work in the text, Fewell
and Gunn underscore an equally important motivation for the comparison of the
lamb to a 'daughter' when they note that, in the very next episode of David's story
in 2 Samuel 13, David's own 'daughter' Tamar is taken sexually just as Bathsheba
was taken sexually in 2 Samuel 11.

Once again food plays a role in the story. In chapter 13 the association between
food and women involves not metaphorical substitution (as was the case with
Bathsheba and the poor man's lamb) but rather a narrative association between
Tamar and activities of food preparation. This association is made several times
in the text, in words spoken by three different characters as well as the narrator.
We find such words, for example, in advice that Amnon's friend, Jonadab, gives to
Amnon after learning that Amnon has made himself ill with desire for Tamar:

> And Jonadab said to him, 'Lie down on your bed and act sick. When your father
> comes to see you, say to him, "Please let Tamar my sister come and feed me
> food. Let her prepare the food in my eyes so that I may see, and I will eat from
> her hand."' So Amnon lay down and acted sick. The king came to see him, and
> Amnon said to the king, 'Please let Tamar my sister come and prepare two cakes
> in my eyes, and I will eat from her hand.' And David sent to Tamar at the house,
> saying, 'Please go to the house of Amnon your brother and make for him food.'
> And Tamar went to the house of Amnon her brother, and he was lying down. She
> took the dough and kneaded it and she prepared cakes in his eyes and cooked
> the cakes. Then she took the pan and poured it out before him. But he refused
> to eat. Then Amnon said, 'Send out everyone from me.' So everyone went out
> from him. And Amnon said to Tamar, 'Bring the food into the chamber and I
> will eat from your hand.' Tamar took the cakes she had made, and she went in
> to Amnon her brother, into the chamber. But when she brought them near him
> to eat, he took hold of her and said to her, 'Come, lie with me, my sister.' (2
> Sam. 13.5–11)

Tamar then resists Amnon's advance, but she is overpowered by Amnon and raped (2 Sam. 13.14).

The narrator notes explicitly that Tamar's preparation of food is done, literally, 'in the eyes' of Amnon (2 Sam. 13.8; NRSV reads 'in his sight'). As Trible notes, 'Voyeurism prevails' (Trible 1984: 43). It is perhaps no surprise that a woman who is raped is first represented as the object of her rapist's vision. Feminist critics of narrative and film have long called attention to the fact that interconnections among gender, the gaze, desire and structures of representation position women as objects of vision in ways that often support female sexual subordination (cf. Penley, ed., 1988; De Lauretis 1984, 1987; Bal 1991b: 138–76). So, too, feminist biblical scholars argue that the male gaze tends to structure biblical narrative, and that those few 'female characters who dare to look at men … are covered with narrative and doxic scorn' (Bach 1997: 167; cf. Exum 1993; 1996).

It is important to note that Tamar is involved *specifically in activities of food preparation* while Amnon – and the reader through Amnon's eyes – watches her. Once again, the conjunction between food and sex can be read as a significant rather than an accidental textual detail, particularly in light of the emphasis placed in this text on Tamar's activities of food preparation. We can shed light on the gender dynamics at work here by juxtaposing to the story a comment made by Tom Wolfe, who once opined that 'there is no spectacle on earth more appealing than that of a beautiful woman in the act of cooking dinner for someone she loves' (quoted in DeVault 1991: xiv). It seems that Amnon, too, is characterized in 2 Samuel as finding such a 'spectacle … appealing'. Indeed, attention to the role of food in the story allows us to see that the factors which contribute to Tamar's vulnerability go beyond Amnon's superior physical strength, though that strength is noted in the text (2 Sam. 13.14). Both the fact that Jonadab comes up with this food-related scheme in the first place, and the fact that David readily grants Amnon's request to send Tamar to prepare food, are facilitated by the widespread allocation of food preparation tasks to women (as opposed to the widespread association of food production and provisioning tasks (agriculture, hunting, etc.) with men). The anthropologist Carole Counihan, among others, argues that 'in all kinds of societies … women have always had primary responsibility for preparing food and giving it to others' (Counihan 1999: 15).[5] While food and cooking are sometimes associated with men, still, as Sherrie Inness (2001) shows, such associations tend to be made in fairly well-defined ways even in the modern West, where rigid gender roles are sometimes said to be breaking down. Men may be responsible for grilling or barbecuing, as well as carving, meat, but such responsibility results from the traditional provisioning role of men manifest in such gender-coded activities as hunting and fishing (cf. Fiddes 1991: 144–62, *passim*; Inness 2001: 19); so, too, men cook in public situations such as restaurants, holding food-related positions of prestige such as that of chef. Yet such examples of male cooking result from a tendency, going back to the ancient world, to allocate specifically to men positions that garner public prestige and activities that take place in the

5. Cf. DeVault 1991; Ortner 1996: 34; Beardsworth and Keil 1997: 73–99; Diner 2001; Inness 2001.

public world. As one anthropologist puts it, 'the difference between high and low' cuisines has 'tended to be one between male and female' (Goody 1982: 193; cf. Ortner 1996: 34). In contrast, women most often prepare food for their own family members on a regular basis in the domestic sphere.[6]

How does such a generalization square with the biblical literature and our knowledge about ancient Israel? The evidence is not entirely unambiguous. Both male and female characters provide food to others or cause others to eat elsewhere in biblical narrative. Abigail is an extreme case, as she brings David and his men two hundred loaves of bread, two jars of wine, five prepared sheep, five measures of corn, one hundred raisin cakes and two hundred cakes of figs (1 Sam. 25.18), but she is far from being the only female character to play such a role. Jezebel urges her husband Ahab to eat when he is not inclined to do so (1 Kgs 21.4–7);[7] and the wife of Jeroboam (1 Kgs 14.3–4), the widow of Zarephath (1 Kgs 17.11–16) and the great woman of Shunem (2 Kgs 4.8) all provide food to prophets. Prophets are also given food and drink by other male prophets (1 Kgs 13.15–23), however and we have seen that such male characters as Abraham provide food to guests in their role as host.

Yet there is a difference between providing food and *preparing* food. Abraham relies on others to prepare the food that he offers to his guests. Thus, a servant prepares the calf that Abraham serves. While this servant is male, his activity of food preparation can be interpreted as an example of the ways in which assumptions about appropriate gendered activity are complicated by such factors as rank. Even in the case of Abraham's household some division of labor by gender seems to be presupposed; prior to bringing the calf to his male servant, Abraham tells Sarah to take 'three measures of the best flour, knead it and make cakes' (Gen. 18.6). Perhaps the male servant of Abraham prepares the veal simply because it represents an example of, in Meyers's words, that 'aspect of food preparation men are most likely to take on – the cooking of meat' (Meyers 1988: 147). When male characters are credited with food preparation elsewhere in the Bible, the food prepared is indeed most often meat (see, e.g., Lev. 8.31; 1 Sam. 9.23–4;[8] 1 Kgs 19.21). In any case, the male head of household, Abraham, does not actually prepare food that he serves even though honor accrues to him as host.

Lot, in contrast to his uncle, seems to be credited with 'baking' the unleavened bread that he serves to the same visitors in the next chapter (Gen. 19.3). But how should we understand the significance of this fact? Were men normally involved in baking? While the story of Joseph refers repeatedly to a male baker, the context of the royal court makes it difficult to draw conclusions from that story, given the tendency noted by Goody for courts to 'employ men as cooks' (1982: 193). While

---

6.   A different dynamic is at work, of course, in gay male relationships where, in most instances, no woman is present to prepare food. For one attempt to analyze 'feeding work' in gay male couples see Corrington 1999: 29–65.

7.   On the role of food in the story of Jezebel see Appler 1999.

8.   The narrator in 1 Samuel 9.23–4 does not specify the person who prepares the meat eaten by Samuel and Saul, but the reference to a 'butcher' or 'slaughterer' who gives meat to Saul at Samuel's command can be read as implying that the same male figure prepares the food. NRSV translates this figure as a 'cook'.

baked offerings are mentioned in legal texts, normally the gender of the person who bakes is not specified. Samuel warns the Israelites that the king they ask for 'will take your *daughters* as perfumers, as cooks, and as bakers' (1 Sam. 8.13), and elsewhere it is the woman at Endor who takes flour, kneads it, and 'bakes' unleavened bread (1 Sam. 28.24). These texts associate baking specifically with women, as does the warning in Leviticus 26.26 that, in a time of hunger, 'ten women will bake your bread in a single oven'. Thus, Lot's characterization as one who 'bakes' is probably a means of calling into question his ability to act as host in an appropriate, gender-coded fashion, by associating his attempt to play the host with an activity usually carried out by women. Such characterization builds upon the fact that Lot's food provision is less impressive than that of Abraham, and hints prospectively both at Lot's inability to protect his guests and the fact that he will, through a kind of reversal of cultural assumptions about gender and sex, be made an object of the sexual actions of his daughters. The representation of Lot as a man who 'bakes' is part of a textual strategy that calls into question Lot's manhood.

A similar attempt to cast a particular light on a male character by associating him with cooking activities more frequently linked to women is at work in the stories about Jacob. Genesis 25 makes a sharp contrast between Jacob and his brother Esau that clearly depends on a gender distinction: their father, Isaac, prefers Esau whereas their mother, Rebekah, prefers Jacob (Gen. 25.28). From birth Esau is 'hairy' (25.25) whereas Jacob, even as an adult, is 'a smooth man' (27.11). The distinction between the brothers is further underscored by the fact that, as an adult, Esau is 'a man knowing game, a man of the field' (25.27) with 'game in his mouth' (25.28). He is, in other words, a good hunter. Jacob, on the other hand, 'dwells in tents' (25.27). By the time we read that 'Jacob was stewing a stew' (25.29) when Esau comes in from the field, Jacob has already been linked to the world of his mother and is, in the words of Susan Niditch, 'more like her, the smooth son who lives in tents in contrast to red, hairy Esau who is a man of the fields' (Niditch 1998: 23). When Niditch subsequently refers to Jacob as 'the more womanish' brother, she responds to a character effect that is achieved in part by links made in the text between Jacob and domestic food preparation. The fact that cooking in the domestic sphere is associated with the mother who favors Jacob becomes even more clear in chapter 27, where Rebekah knows how to turn two kids into 'tasty food for your father which he loves' (Gen. 27.9). Esau, too, prepares a 'tasty dish' for his father (27.31), but this dish is made precisely from the 'game' acquired in the traditional male pursuit of hunting and not from regular processes of domestic cooking.

Thus, even when male characters are represented in situations of food preparation, the textual evidence gives us little reason to doubt that domestic cooking and related household tasks were in ancient Israel most often associated with women (cf. Meyers 1988: 145–6). When Tamar is told to prepare food for her brother, then, she is told to act according to culturally prescribed dictates for female behavior. Jonadab and Amnon assume, correctly, that David will hear Amnon's request as a conventional one. The traditional role of women in domestic food preparation sets the stage for Amnon's rape of Tamar. Her story illustrates only too well that food as well as sexuality can constitute for women what Vance calls 'a domain of restriction, repression, and danger' (Vance 1984: 1).

III

As Vance, Rubin and others emphasize, danger is only part of the story that must be told where women and sexuality are concerned. Pleasure has to be acknowledged as well, at least if we wish to take to heart Vance's warning that 'to speak only of sexual violence and oppression ignores women's experiences with sexual agency and choice and unwittingly increases the sexual terror and despair in which women live' (Vance 1984: 1). Such a warning presents a difficult challenge to biblical scholarship, since female sexual pleasure and desire are seldom represented within biblical literature in non-stigmatizing ways. How possible is it, then, to speak positively about female sexual pleasure and agency in the context of biblical interpretation?

Although possibilities for generating such speech do seem limited, there is at least one biblical text – the Song of Songs – in which affirmations of female sexual pleasure and desire appear to play a significant role. The positive attention to female sexuality in the Song of Songs no doubt helps to account for the fact that the book has so often provoked positive responses from its feminist readers.[9] Indeed, the focus on female sexual agency is one of several features of the book that have led even male critics to argue, on occasion, that such a text must surely have been written by a female author (e.g., LaCocque 1998). Moreover, sexual pleasure and desire are explored in the Song of Songs largely outside the conventions of marriage, and quite apart from any interest in procreation or descent. As we shall see, the Song of Songs also utilizes food imagery as one way of talking about sexual matters. Can the Song of Songs offer at least a partial counterbalance to the dangers that both food and sex present, in their biblical occurrences, to female characters and women readers?

In attempting to answer this question, it is important to note first that several commentators have recently cautioned against a failure on the part of many of the Song's readers to recognize more disturbing passages and undercurrents in the book (see, e.g., Clines 1995: 94–121; Polaski 1997; Exum 2000; Black 2000, 2001). These, more suspicious, commentators remind us at the very least that interpretations of the Song of Songs must not overlook, but take into account, dissonant elements such as the brutal treatment of the woman in 5.7 or the fact that barriers are sometimes placed in the way of the woman speaker who seeks to be united with her lover. Unless we are prepared to argue that the Song of Songs escaped the influence of its social and historical context (a claim that I would consider contrary to the most important results of modern biblical criticism), we must guard against the temptation to romanticize the book by anachronistically overstating the extent to which it is or could be free of the effects of its patriarchal context.

Yet we also need to avoid the illegitimate assumption that patriarchal contexts produce uniformly patriarchal texts, even in the Bible. As the Bible does not offer a single perspective but, rather, a collection of diverse and sometimes contradictory

---

9.   See, for example, Trible 1978: 144–65; Falk 1982; Meyers 1988: 177–80; Brenner 1989: 87–93, passim; Pardes 1992: 118–43; Brenner, ed., 1993b; Dijk-Hemmes 1993a: 72–81; Brenner and Dijk-Hemmes 1993: 71–83; Weems 1998; Walsh 2000b; and several of the essays in Brenner and Fontaine, eds., 2000.

traditions, it is important to refrain from projecting onto the various books of the Bible a monolithic point of view, even about such matters as gender and sexuality (cf. Carr 2003: 93–5, *passim*). The best way to proceed, when reading the Song of Songs and other biblical texts that deal with female sexuality, is to do so while keeping in mind both the 'polyphonic' nature of biblical literature (Brueggemann 1997: 88-9, *passim*) and the insight of Vance that, so long as conditions of gender inequality and oppression exist (as they certainly did in ancient Israel, and as they continue to do today), the situation of women with respect to sexuality will always be one in which the *tension* between pleasure and danger must constantly be kept in mind. With respect to the Song of Songs, therefore, the question to be considered is not whether the book's approach to sexual pleasure avoids entirely any evidence of its patriarchal context – it does not; no ancient text could. The question is rather whether, within the constraints of a patriarchal context, the Song of Songs is able to assert the importance for women of sexual pleasure, agency and desire, and to do so in a way that surpasses, or causes the Song of Songs to stand out among, other biblical texts. Should the answer to that question be 'yes' (as I believe it is), then interpretations of the Song of Songs can serve the useful function of encouraging its women readers, and perhaps other readers as well (for example, gay male readers), to struggle for sexual pleasure, agency and freedom even in the face of the most formidable obstacles.

Toward this end a comparison of the Song of Songs with the story of Tamar may be productive, and the use of food and sex to 'think' biblical interpretation offers us a way into such comparison. The presence of food and drink images in conjunction with sexual images – and sometimes food and drink images *as* sexual images – is quite striking in the Song of Songs, as it is in the story of Tamar. As Marcia Falk notes, 'Feasting ... almost always has erotic overtones in the Song, and wine is the most intoxicating temptation to the feast' (Falk 1982: 105). These images of feasting and drinking are so striking that they even lead some scholars to suggest that the Song of Songs may have been written to entertain participants at a banquet (cf. Fox 1985: 244–50; Carr 2003: 110). In the Song of Songs, however, in distinction from 2 Samuel, the language of food and sex serves to emphasize pleasure rather more than – but also, as we shall see, *in the face of* – danger.

Right from the beginning of the Song of Songs, the female speaker proclaims that 'your love is better than wine' (1.2b). In this particular formulation the speaker's comparison clearly works to the advantage of the love of her beloved, though of course the nature of the comparison assumes the goodness of wine. The sentiment is repeated two verses later, when the 'daughters of Jerusalem' also proclaim that 'We will savor your love more than wine' (1.4).[10]

Wine is by no means the only foodstuff taken up by the Song of Songs and used to speak about love and sex. The female speaker elsewhere uses fruit symbolism (both simile and metaphor) to talk positively about sexual interaction, once again

---

10. The final clause of this verse may make an additional comparison between love and wine. Whereas NRSV ends the verse with the words 'rightly do they love you', JPS reads 'like new wine they love you'. The difference between the two translations results from two different ways of handling the Hebrew word *mesharim*. See Pope 1977: 305–6.

presupposing the sensory pleasures of food and making those pleasures a point of reference for evoking the pleasures of sex:

> As an apple tree among the trees of the forest, thus is my beloved among young men.
> With great delight I sit in his shadow, and his fruit is sweet to my mouth.
> He brought me to the house of wine, and his intention toward me was love.
> Sustain me with raisin cakes, refresh me with apples, for I am faint from love.
>
> (2.3–5)

Here as elsewhere in the book, fruit images evoke sexual contact, and in this particular instance symbolize the sensory pleasure that the man's body holds for the woman.

Of course the Song of Songs uses many types of images, and not simply images of food and drink, to talk about love, sex and desire, but the Song's use of food (especially fruit) and drink (especially wine) imagery arguably results in particular ways of thinking about sexuality. So, for example, in the last line of the passage quoted above (2.5), the female speaker uses the comparison of sex with food to evoke the nourishing and sustaining qualities of sexual love, and hence its importance. Moreover, as Carey Ellen Walsh points out, fruit, though not necessary for survival, was an important supplement to the ancient Palestinian grain-based diet, adding as it did sweetness, juice, and distinctive flavors, smells and textures. These pleasurable dimensions of the experience of eating fruit allow the Song to evoke a remarkable range of sexual experiences. Significantly for our purposes, Walsh draws attention to the book's fruit images in part because, in her view, the 'taut, delicate skin, pulpy and yielding flesh, and pungent, fresh scents and tastes' of many kinds of fruit are 'associative rather than literal qualities, which fruit shares with a woman' (Walsh 2000b: 119). Walsh notes, in addition, that the fruit and vineyard symbolism of the Song of Songs builds upon ancient Near Eastern and Mediterranean traditions of using agricultural metaphors for sexual activity while avoiding the ubiquitous 'seed/field' imagery that is so common elsewhere (including elsewhere in the Bible) and that, as we shall see in the next chapter, rests upon patriarchal assumptions. Consequently, in the Song of Songs 'seed and procreation give way to ripening, engorgement, and taste' (85). Such food and drink imagery underscores 'the orality of sexual desire' in Song of Songs (121), an orality that Walsh contrasts with more phallic conceptualizations of sexuality. In all of these ways, the fruit imagery contributes to a conceptualization of sexual pleasure that incorporates female desires and experiences to a far greater extent than do most biblical, or for that matter most ancient, texts.[11]

The emphasis on oral pleasures underscored by Walsh is indicated already by the woman's opening adjuration, 'let him kiss me with the kisses of his mouth'

---

11. I do not wish to imply that the Song of Songs stands alone in the ancient Near East. Egyptian love poetry utilizes many of the same literary conventions as the Song of Songs. For analysis of the Song of Songs in light of this Egyptian tradition see Fox 1985 (with particular attention to similarities and differences in their use of garden imagery at 283–7). Cf. Carr 2003: 91–107, where connections with other ancient Near Eastern traditions are stressed as well. Pope 1977 casts an even wider comparative net.

(1.2a). It is clear, however, that much more than simple kissing is being imagined in the Song. The poet uses images of food and drink to evoke other sorts of oral pleasures as well, including both pleasures that the woman receives ('his fruit is sweet to my mouth' (2.3)) and pleasures that the woman gives to her lover. The fact that the woman as well as the man provides pleasurable fruit for the other's enjoyment is clear in the fourth chapter. There, the male speaker, having already spoken of the woman as a garden (4.12), refers apparently to her genitalia (cf. Pope 1977: 490–91) as 'an orchard of pomegranates, with excellent fruit' (4.13) and numerous spices (including saffron and cinnamon). To his description the woman responds by urging the 'wind' to 'blow upon my garden that its fragrance may spread. Let my love come to his garden, and eat its excellent fruit' (4.16). As if in answer to this demand, the man replies that 'I have come to my garden ... I have eaten my honeycomb with my honey, I have drunk my wine with my milk' (5.1). And, in celebration of this oral exchange, the text goes on to exclaim (in a speaking voice that cannot be clearly identified) 'Eat, friends, drink! Be drunk with love' (5.2). This use of food and drink images by multiple speakers in the Song makes it difficult to differentiate the giver and the receiver of pleasure. The person who receives oral sexual stimulation no doubt finds this a pleasurable experience, but when the oral stimulation of a partner is compared to the experience of eating sweet, succulent fruit, it is difficult to insist that pleasure is going only in one direction. Roland Boer points out that when one is 'eating the mouth is the active receptor' (Boer 2000: 290). In that respect, as Boer (like Walsh) rightly notes, the use of images of eating in the Song of Songs disrupts the phallocentric conceptualization of penile penetration, with its frequent demarcation of subjects and objects, known to us from many ancient representations of sexuality (cf. Halperin 1990; Winkler 1990; Keuls 1985) and from other parts of the Bible. Indeed, the clear desire of the woman for oral sexual stimulation, while not absent from heterosexual male fantasy, is hardly the epitome of phallocentric sexuality and – with some adjustment of gendered pronouns – could easily be taken from the pages of lesbian erotica.

We also note in the Song of Songs that the woman's face is compared to 'halves of a pomegranate' (4.3), that 'honey' or 'nectar' drips from her lips, and that 'honey and milk' are under her tongue (4.11). In chapter 7 her abdomen is 'a round bowl' full of 'mixed wine', 'a heap of wheat' surrounded by flowers (7.3 (English 7.2)). Her breasts are like the clusters of fruit growing on palm trees and vines (7.8–9 (English 7.7–8)), her 'breath'[12] like apples or apricots (7.9 (English 7.8)), and her kisses 'like the best wine' flowing smoothly over lips and teeth (7.10 (English 7.9)). Having been described in such terms, the female speaker quickly confirms that this bountiful feast will be given to her lover:

> I am my beloved's, and for me is his desire.
> Come, my beloved, let us go out to the field.
> Let us lie in the cypress.[13]
> Let us get up and go to the vineyards.

---

12. Here I follow the more common translation. Pope, however, suggests that the 'aroma' in question emanates from 'the vulva or clitoris' (1977: 637).

13. On the translation 'cypress' see Pope 1977: 645.

Let us see if the vines have flowered, if the grape blossoms have opened,
If the pomegranates are in bloom.
There I will give my love to you.
The mandrakes give their fragrance,
And over our doors are all excellent fruits.
New ones, also old ones, my beloved, I have stored up for you.   (7.10–13)

Now it is true that, in this passage and others, the woman is represented as something like food for the man (cf. Brenner 1999: 109). She is a vineyard, she is a garden, she is excellent fruit stored up for her lover. Thus, one might object that the man's comparison of the woman to food and drink is disturbingly reminiscent of such texts as Nathan's parable and the story of Tamar, where, as we have seen, the use of such imagery occurs.

Even if we acknowledge that the Song of Songs shares the comparison of women and food with other biblical texts, our interpretation of the food-sex conjunction needs to take into account the specific ways in which the Song recontextualizes that comparison. In that regard, the texts that we have examined from 2 Samuel 11–13 serve as an especially useful contrast, particularly when we ask about the subject/object positions filled by the female characters in relation to sex and food. Recall that there is no indication in 2 Samuel 11 that Bathsheba chooses or desires sexual relations with David, and that Nathan's parable makes the lamb symbolizing Bathsheba an object, taken by the rich man who symbolizes David and turned into food for his guests. Tamar actively opposes Amnon's demand for sexual access, but to no avail: as she was first the object of David's command to prepare food for Amnon, and then the object of Amnon's vision during her act of food preparation, so also she is finally the object of Amnon's rape. In 2 Samuel 11–13 the female characters are granted relatively little agency by the text.

In the Song of Songs female textual subjectivity – that is, the attribution of speech, vision and action (cf. Bal 1991a; 1997) to female subjects in the text – is much more prominent, especially in relation to sex and even, in certain respects, in relation to food. Commentators have long noted that female voices are not only present but are even, arguably, dominant in the Song;[14] Renita Weems states that 'the protagonist in the Song is the only unmediated female voice in scripture' (Weems 1998: 164). Certainly, this female voice articulates some of those passages in which food and sex are closely intertwined. It is the female speaker who praises her lover's 'fruit' (2.3), who asks for her lover to 'sustain me with raisin cakes, refresh me with apples' (2.5) and who uses the language of food to assert her desire for oral stimulation (4.16). The female speaker in chapter 7 urges her lover to come to the garden that is herself, as we have seen. It is arguably the female speaker as well who, in an enigmatic but provocative passage in the sixth chapter, 'went down to the nut grove ... to see if the vines have flowered, if the pomegranates are in bloom' (6.11).

The woman is not only a subject of speech and sexual exploration. Significantly,

---

14. Brenner (1985: 49) notes that 'the female voice(s) account(s) for approximately 53% of the text, while the male voice(s) account(s) for only 34%'.

she is also a subject of vision who makes of the man an object. In 5.10–16, for example, in a reversal of the more common relationship between vision and textual subjectivity (according to which women are objects but never subjects of desiring vision), the female speaker of Song of Songs, not content simply to allow her own body to be the object of the man's focalization, also places his body under her desiring gaze.[15] Given the role of the male fetishistic gaze in those conventional processes whereby sexual representation contributes to the domination of women, it is crucial to refrain from underestimating the potential importance of this reversal of gendered vision by the Song of Songs.

Moreover, the female speaker actively searches for her male lover when they are apart, sometimes successfully (3.3–4) and sometimes unsuccessfully (5.6–7). Although it is now fashionable to interpret these search passages as dreams, I am not entirely persuaded by this view, as 3.2 seems to assert that the woman rises from her bed before beginning her search. Nevertheless, even if we accept the prevalent opinion that the woman is narrating dreams in these sequences, the woman's determination to be with her lover and her desire for sexual agency are asserted throughout the Song, sometimes in the language of food and drink (8.1b-2):

> I would find you in the street and kiss you, and no one would despise me.
> I would lead you, I would bring you into the house of my mother, and into the
> chamber of the one who bore me.[16]
> I would cause you to drink spiced wine, the juice of my pomegranates.

While the woman may here be food for the man, it is she rather than he who initiates the meal, and there is no hint here (as there is, for example, in the prophetic tradition) that such female sexual initiative has negative connotations. Indeed, as the prophetic tradition stigmatizes female sexuality while attributing food provision (as we shall see) largely to *male* characters, we may wonder whether the Song of Songs, by eliminating the stigmatization while simultaneously utilizing images of *female* provision of food (cf. Brenner 1999: 110), is not thereby *actively contesting* the premises of the prophetic tradition (cf. LaCocque 1998: 33–9, *passim*). Moreover, the reference in this passage to 'the house of my mother' can itself be seen as evidence of female focalization. Meyers argues convincingly that instances of this rare biblical phrase 'mother's house', used twice in the Song of Songs (3.4; 8.2) but only two times outside of it (Gen. 24.28; Ruth 1.8), in every case 'involve a female perspective on issues that elsewhere in the Hebrew Bible are viewed from the male perspective that dominates scripture' (Meyers 1991: 50). In this same eighth chapter the woman is also unafraid of challenging male descriptions of her body that she finds inadequate. If, at the beginning of the book, the female speaker responds to the 'daughters of Jerusalem' who 'gaze' at her dark skin (1.6) by asserting that 'I am black and beautiful' (1.5),[17] now, at the end of the book, she counters her brothers' worried observation that 'we have a little

---

15. The importance of this point is noted by Exum (2000: 28).

16. On the concluding phrase of this difficult line see Pope 1977: 658–9.

17. References to the woman's skin color in 1.5–6 can be read as hints that the woman is considered by some of her contemporaries to be an inappropriate, and perhaps unattractive, partner

sister, and she has no breasts' (8.8a) with the bold and contrary assertion that 'my breasts were like towers' (8.10b).

As the presence of the woman's brothers indicates, forces exist in the Song of Songs which oppose the woman and conspire to keep the lovers apart. While there are no references in the Song of Songs to a father (a fact which is itself quite striking in a biblical text), the brothers appear to serve in the Song of Songs, along with the city guards in chapters 3 and 5, as spokespersons for and enforcers of patriarchal attitudes toward female sexuality. The woman's assertive statements throughout the Song contrast with the position taken by her brothers, who are described early in the book (1.6) as being angry with her for not having kept her own vineyard. That vineyard symbolizes the woman's sexuality (cf. Walsh 2000b: 129–32). This concern on the part of the brothers about control of the woman's 'vineyard' can be interpreted anthropologically as an expression of the well-known 'vigilance' (Schneider 1971) with which brothers in many cultures attempt to guard the sexual purity of their sisters – and, hence, the sexual honor of their families and themselves (cf. Giovannini 1981, 1987; Pitt-Rivers 1977). In assessing the role of this fraternal vigilance in the Song of Songs, the narratives of 2 Samuel once again provide a useful point of comparison. As I argue elsewhere (Stone 1996:117–18), Absalom's killing of Amnon in 2 Samuel 13 is an expression of this honor-driven fraternal vigilance, as is the response of Simeon and Levi to Shechem's sexual relations with their sister Dinah in Genesis 34. By including both a reference to such concern on the part of the woman's brothers, and a narration (in 5.7) of the sort of brutal response that assertive, sexually active women were likely to receive from male Israelites who disapproved of their behavior (cf. Black 2001), the Song of Songs explicitly acknowledges the patriarchal attitudes toward female sexuality that dominated the context in which it was produced. The book therefore makes no claims to having been written in a feminist utopia.

But whereas male struggles for honor and power around female sexuality dominate 2 Samuel, the woman in Song of Songs has little regard for her brothers' opinions or concerns about female chastity. Instead, she proclaims defiantly in 8.12 that the vineyard over which these brothers obsess is hers, not theirs, and that her vineyard and its fruit are superior even to all the vineyards and fruit that belong to King Solomon. The Song of Songs ends not with a denial of patriarchy or of its negative consequences for female sexuality, but with a strong affirmation of female sexual agency *in defiance of* patriarchy. As Christopher King notes, the female speaker in the Song, 'disregard[ing] any extrinsic norm whereby her choice to love as she pleases might be condemned ... fearlessly and joyfully proclaims her erotic autonomy' (King 2000: 134). This proclamation is expressed, in part,

───────────

for her lover, either because she comes from a different ethnic or geographical background (if we assume that her black skin is here an ethnic or geographical signifier) or because she has been forced to work in the sun (whether for reasons of social rank or simply because of the demands of her brothers (cf. 1.6)). See, e.g., Goulder 1986; Weems 1998; King 2000; Carr 2003. Such interpretations rightly note the opening chapter's references to both the woman's skin color and the gaze of the Daughters of Jerusalem, though it is important to recognize with Fontaine (who also underscores the woman's black skin) that, in the rest of the Song, 'the Daughters of Jerusalem do not seem actively hostile or dismissive of the Shulammite' (2000: 179, n. 22).

through the very type of symbolism – food symbolism – that in 2 Samuel communicates female sexual vulnerability.

IV

What should we make of this defiant affirmation of female sexual desire and pleasure in the face of frankly acknowledged patriarchal constraint? Such features of the Song of Songs seem to lead in a rather different direction from that taken by David Clines when he proposes that 'the implied author [of the Song] is male, and I think the balance of historical probability about the actual author is overwhelmingly in the same direction' (Clines 1995: 99). While I am cautious about our ability to know or say very much about 'the actual author', I am inclined to argue that, if the book's literary features and dominant attitudes toward sexuality (including the ways in which it uses food to imagine sex) can be taken at all as 'implying' an author of a particular gender, then an equally strong, if not stronger, case can be made for the position that the 'implied author' of the Song of Songs is female. To support such a case, I would not only appeal to the presence in the text of those female subjects of voice, vision and action noted above. I would also stress the fact that the Song of Songs recognizes, *but at the same time resists*, the male obsession with the chastity of women (e.g., sisters) whose sexual purity potentially reflects upon male honor. If the Song's perspective is going to be characterized as 'male', it is a male perspective that incorporates a rather critical attitude toward, and even openly contests, dominant concerns of circum-Mediterranean manhood and patriarchy. It is hardly surprising that various scholars conclude instead, on the basis of the book's extraordinary features, either that the author of such a text is likely to have been a woman (Goiten 1993; LaCocque 1998: 41, *passim*), that female authorship of some or all of the book's passages is at least a plausible hypothesis (Brenner 1985, 1989; Brenner and Dijk-Hemmes 1993: 71–81; Bekkenkamp and Van Dijk 1993; Arbel 2000; Carr 2003), or that women must have participated in the folk traditions informing the Song's poetry (Meyers 1993).

Such conclusions about authorship may also allow us to reframe, without rejecting entirely, the association that Clines makes between the Song of Songs and 'pornography' (Clines 1995: 119). This association is especially intriguing in the present context, because pornography is one of the issues at stake in that disagreement between Rubin and Modleski with which I opened this chapter. An association between pornography and the Song of Songs may seem intentionally provocative to many readers of the Bible, who would perhaps be more willing to characterize the Song as 'a book of erotica' (Walsh 2000: 2), but the line between 'pornography' and 'erotica' is notoriously difficult to draw. As Laura Kipnis puts it, 'one person's pornography is another person's erotica, and one person's erotica can cause someone else to lose her lunch' (Kipnis 1999: 64). Given the difficulties of definition, it is important not to dismiss too quickly Clines' invocation of 'pornography'.

What is the actual significance of such an invocation? Clines draws this link between the Song of Songs and pornography on the basis of his view that, in the opening chapter of the book, 'the poet invites his readers to share his sight of the woman's humiliation' (Clines 1995: 119). Although it should be clear already that I have serious reservations about the adequacy of this statement as an interpretation of the Song of Songs, I am also concerned about the limited view of pornography that the statement presupposes. The definition of pornography as an objectification of women's sexual humiliation does represent *one* contemporary feminist understanding of pornography, according to which pornography as such is defined as something like the 'abuse' of women 'made into a spectacle for other people's sexual pleasure' (MacKinnon 1992: 131). This way of thinking about 'pornography' has had some impact among biblical scholars, influencing the discussions of troubling passages in such prophetic books as Hosea, Jeremiah and Ezekiel. Scholars increasingly characterize these passages as 'pornographic', not because the passages utilize graphic sexual imagery but, rather, because the graphic sexual imagery in question involves the sexual humiliation of women (see, e.g., Setel 1985; Brenner and Dijk-Hemmes, van, 1993: 167–95; Exum 1996: 101–28; Brenner 1997: 153–74). Clines' characterization of the Song of Songs as 'pornography' works with a similar understanding of the nature of 'pornography', but applies that understanding to an object – the Song of Songs – seldom associated with such damaging images of women.[18]

As important as discussions of 'prophetic pornography' have been for our understanding of the brutal nature of those prophetic texts, I find myself agreeing with those (Carroll 1995: 281–82; Boer 1999: 54–5) who suggest that a rather narrow definition of 'pornography' is being deployed within biblical scholarship. Only a partial selection, even of contemporary *feminist* views on pornography, seems to have been taken into account by most biblical scholars. The situation within biblical studies appears to replicate the situation within the larger fields of religious and theological studies, where 'pornography', if it is spoken about at all, is discussed almost entirely in pejorative terms. Alternative, and in many respects more nuanced, feminist analyses of pornography (e.g., Segal and McIntosh, eds., 1992; Strossen 1995; Duggan and Hunter 1995; Williams 1999; Kipnis 1999; Hollibaugh 2000: 125–37) are not taken into account at all.

Suppose, however, we tentatively grant the association made by Clines (and, from a radically different point of view, Boer [1999: 53–70]) between the Song of Songs and pornography, but use as our point of departure feminist accounts of pornography other than those most often deployed in biblical scholarship. Kipnis (1999), for example, refusing to adopt a uniformly negative stance toward 'pornography', makes a compelling argument that texts classified as 'pornography', responses (positive and negative) to those texts, and even the very gesture of deciding what is and is not 'pornographic', constitute a complex representational field in which issues of significant cultural concern are constantly being negotiated. From this perspective, Clines' assertion that the Song of Songs is, in its approach to gender, 'the very stuff of pornography' (119) actually tells us very little. What

---

18. It is striking to note, in fact, that the title of one Presbyterian study on 'pornography' (Thorson Smith 1988) explicitly contrasts the Song of Songs with 'pornography', which that study, like analyses of 'prophetic pornography', associates largely with the domination of women.

we need to determine is the sort of intervention that this or that particular instance of pornography makes within the field of social forces from which it emerges, and to which it responds. What we need to know, more specifically, is whether the pornographic text affirms uncritically, *or rather contests*, the patriarchal assumptions around gender and sexuality that structure its context.

When it is approached from that point of view, the Song of Songs might be construed as 'pornography', not in the negative sense intended by MacKinnon, Clines, and numerous biblical scholars, but rather in the positive sense intended by the feminist writer Amber Hollibaugh. Hollibaugh argues that 'we need non-sexist sexual images. A lot more of them. In short, maybe what we need even more than Women against Pornography (WAP) are women pornographers, or eroticists, if that sounds better' (Hollibaugh 2000: 130). From this particular feminist perspective (which, like that of Kipnis, acknowledges the impossibility of distinguishing absolutely between 'pornography' and 'erotica'), 'pornography' is not by definition always and everywhere a force for domination but, in some cases at least, a potential tool for women's sexual freedom. If we allowed ourselves to work with a more flexible notion of pornography, would it not be possible to interpret the Song of Songs *positively* as the sort of pornographic text that Hollibaugh desires? The Song of Songs can, after all, be read as a surprisingly graphic representation of physical sexual pleasure. By 'graphic' I do not exactly mean 'literal', for, in spite of the current trend to argue for 'literal' rather than 'allegorical' interpretations of the Song of Songs,[19] it is obvious that most of the book's sexual content is communicated by way of symbolism and metaphor and not by straightforward descriptions of sexual activity. Such symbolism does not lessen the book's sexual impact, as anyone who attempts to translate and interpret it can attest. The nature of the book's language may even enhance the provocative sexual effect, as readers imagine a range of possible referents for the book's imagery and find themselves tempted to extend the sexual interpretation ever deeper and further.[20] It was not for nothing that Origen warned that an encounter with the Song of Songs could become, for the fleshly reader, an invitation to carnal lust.[21] The heavy use of food imagery in the book is no barrier to a positive 'pornographic' interpretation, as there exists a whole sub-genre of what we might call 'food pornography',[22] Most importantly, the Song of Songs can

19. Moore (2001: 21–89) observes that this trend toward more 'literal' interpretations may actually result in a less 'queer' book, since it eliminates the homoerotic dynamics that were often put into play between male worshippers and male deities in the context of allegorical interpretation.

20. This feature of the book's language is exploited in a provocative way by Boer (1999: 53–70).

21. Thus Origen:

But if any man who lives only after the flesh shall approach [the Song of Songs], to such a one the reading of this Scripture will be the occasion of no small hazard and danger. For he, not knowing how to hear love's language in purity and with chaste ears, will twist the whole manner of his hearing of it away from the inner spiritual man and on to the outward and carnal; and he will be turned away from the spirit to the flesh, and will foster carnal desires in himself, and it will seem to be the Divine Scriptures that are thus urging and egging him on to fleshly lust!

The translation is that of R.P. Lawson (quoted in Pope 1977: 117).

be plausibly and safely interpreted, not only as abounding in those 'nonsexist sexual images' that Hollibaugh desires, but also as a provocative, and sometimes quite graphic, affirmation of female sexual desire – arguably written by a woman but in any case featuring a woman's voice and vision – that recognizes the *danger* of patriarchal restrictions on women's sexuality but continues to seek out female sexual *pleasure* nonetheless.

With this invocation of pleasure and danger we return to the issues that I began with. Although I happen to agree with gay scholars (e.g., Boisvert 2000: 53–4; Long 2002) who conclude, partly on the basis of the specific roles that gay porn plays among gay men, that it may be important to consider positive *religious* functions for some pornographic texts, I am not especially interested in arguing at length over the question of whether the Song of Songs 'is' or 'is not' 'pornography'. Like Kipnis and Hollibaugh, I am not convinced that a rigid boundary between 'pornography' and 'erotica' can or should finally be drawn. I have chosen to raise the possibility of such a classification here primarily because the issue of pornography illustrates well some of the stakes raised by efforts at maintaining the tension between pleasure and danger that Vance insists upon. In a context such as our own, where sexual agency and pleasure are themselves too often stigmatized (frequently with the help of biblical interpretation), there are good reasons to remember that both sex and food can function in both positive and negative ways for women who live (as biblical women clearly did, and as too many women still do) under patriarchal social conditions. Attitudes toward, and practices associated with, sexual contact can certainly play a role in male domination, as MacKinnon, Modleski and others note. Other forms of domination – such as racial domination – also take sexual forms, just as they can influence and be influenced by certain ways of preparing, serving and consuming food (cf. Witt 1999). Nevertheless, at a time when sexuality is already frequently stigmatized, it is crucial to be clear about the fact that *it is the use of sexuality to buttress domination, and not sexuality* as such, which must be combated. By recognizing that food as well as sex is now, and has long been, associated with both pleasure *and* danger for women (and no doubt for others as well), we may challenge those essentializing tendencies which attribute to sexual practice that inherent 'cosmic' significance noted critically by Rubin. It is, after all, possible to recognize the contribution of food practices to domination without making that contribution determinative for our attitudes toward food. Just the sort of nuanced approach to food that allows such recognition to take place on a daily basis needs also to be deployed in relation to both sexuality in general and to particular sexual phenomena – including, perhaps, pornography – in particular.

22. I refer, here, not to the 'food pornography' discussed by Coward (1985: 101–6), in which food images are used to manipulate 'oral desires and pleasures for women' (105), but to the proliferation of explicit images of persons performing sexual acts with food. Although many of these images involve women and could be interpreted as 'pornography' in the negative sense (as involving the exploitation of women for the pleasure of men under conditions of gender inequality), a significant portion of this sort of 'food pornography' involves only images of adult men and caters to gay male consumers.

Because appeals to the Bible continue to play a role in debates about gender and sexuality, it is crucial for biblical scholars who wish to contribute to these debates to challenge one-sided or simplistic analyses, not only of sex or food but also of the Bible itself. It should be clear by now that I have no desire to adopt an apologetic stance toward the Bible, and I wish to take with complete seriousness the critique of biblical patriarchy as well as other forms of social domination that are justified by appeals to biblical texts. If we can demonstrate that it was possible, even under the patriarchal conditions that shaped the writing of biblical literature, for both food and sex to be articulated with women's pleasure as well as danger, then we may contribute to the construction of more complex approaches to sexuality, food and the Bible that refuse to attribute acontextual, ahistorical, or monolithic meanings and effects to any of them.

It is precisely the *contrast* between the Song of Songs and many other biblical texts (such as 2 Samuel) that allows such a demonstration to be made. The drawing of such contrasts relies upon recognition of one feature of the Bible that is, in my view, crucial for any attempt to foster practices of safer text. In chapter 1, I emphasized the fact that biblical texts can be read in a wide range of plausible ways. In the next chapter I will suggest that even when a particular text appears to take a position that we find ethically problematic, it frequently fails to do so in a consistent fashion. In this chapter my reading strategy has focused not upon the instability of textual meaning but upon the multivocality of the canon as a whole. 'The Bible' is not, as many of its defenders *and* critics suppose, a unified document that speaks in a single voice. It is not even a collection of voices that always articulate consistent, or compatible, points of view. As Barr puts it, the Bible is not 'the mouthpiece for a standard orthodoxy', but is 'more like a battlefield, in which different traditions strive against one another' (Barr 1981: 28). Barr's military language may be more useful for those of us interested in queer practices of biblical interpretation than are the more tepid terms (e.g., 'diversity') normally used to discuss the Bible's pluriform nature. For if we accept Halperin's proposal that a queer practice 'acquires its meaning from its oppositional relation to the norm' and 'is by definition *whatever* is at odds with the normal, the legitimate, the dominant' (Halperin 1995: 62, original emphasis), then Barr's reference to the Bible as a 'battlefield' allows us to see the existence of conflicting traditions within the Bible as an opportunity to take up tactical positions in the context of specific struggles that involve, or could involve, biblical interpretation. Confronted with the fact that the Bible is so often utilized, not only by those who tolerate or support gender inequality, but also by those who wish to restrict legitimate sexual pleasure to the context of monogamous heterosexual marriage, we should not conclude that our only alternative for taking up an 'oppositional relation to the norm' is to reject the Bible out of hand. Instead, we might seize upon 'this deviant text' (Pardes 1992: 143) which is the Song of Songs, calling attention to the book's defiant affirmation of active, female, and – importantly – non-marital[23] sexual desires and pleasures. Inasmuch as such non-marital female desires and pleasures were normally stigmatized within the context that produced the Song of Songs, we can usefully understand the book as a canonical 'countertext' (Ostriker 2000) with which to authorize a range of sexual desires and pleasures that are stigmatized in our own context.

Among the forms that such sexual stigmatization takes, surely none require more ardent opposition than the religious stigmatization of bodily pleasure itself. I have already pointed out that some Christian ethicists and theologians now insist upon the need for approaches to sex and the body that are built upon the affirmation of pleasure as a good. It is hardly surprising that, when such arguments are made for a positive notion of bodily pleasure, they sometimes affirm the Song of Songs as a useful biblical resource (e.g., Ellison 1996: 71–3; Jordan 2002: 164). The Song of Songs can safely be read as a stirring testimony to the potential counter-patriarchal pleasures, not only of sex, but also of food.

23. Although the Song of Songs is sometimes read as advocating or assuming marriage as the context for sexual relations, the trend in contemporary biblical scholarship is toward the position of Brenner, for whom the Song thematizes 'sexual love' (1989: 67, passim), which 'is unmarried love, and ... marriage is not necessarily envisaged as its ultimate objective, although sexual consummation is'. See also Trible 1978: 162; Falk 1982: 64; Fox 1985: 251; LaCocque 1998: 7–8; Walsh 2000: 137; Carr 2003: 119, 140.

CHAPTER 5

LOVERS AND RAISIN CAKES:

FOOD, SEX AND MANHOOD IN HOSEA

I

The last chapter stressed the importance of taking gender into account when reading biblical passages that deal with food and sex. Although gender analysis plays a central role in this chapter as well, both the biblical texts to be interpreted and the analytical questions asked are rather different.[1] My textual object here is the prophetic book of Hosea, and my emphasis lies on male characters rather than female ones. More specifically, it is the male character Yhwh, the god of Israel, in which I am interested, though lines of demarcation between divine males and human males, and between male characters (e.g., male Israelites) and female characters (e.g., Gomer), are blurred constantly by the book. Leaving aside many difficulties that vex readers of Hosea, I will examine a number of issues that arise from the curious conjunction, in this book, of language about food and drink, and language about sex and gender. My primary focus is upon interrelations among food, sex and *manhood* in the rhetoric of Hosea, for those interrelations constitute key but troubling components of Hosea's 'theology' in the strict sense of that term as 'speech about God'.

Now this emphasis upon 'manhood' is conceivably a controversial one. After more than a decade of feminist and womanist scholarship on Hosea,[2] one might object that my focus on notions of food, sex and *manhood* is a reactionary move that carries with it the risk of extending the marginalization of women long carried out by both the text of Hosea and its readers. This objection is a serious one, and before going further I want to affirm explicitly that analysis of the textual representations of women and female sexuality found in the book of Hosea has been, and remains, an important task for contemporary research on biblical sexual rhetoric. Nevertheless, the gender questions that need to be posed to the Bible are not exhausted by questions about textual representations of women, and my own, rather queer, relation to norms of 'manhood' leads me to agree with those feminist

---

1. This chapter is a revision of material that first appeared in Stone, ed., 2001: 116–39.
2. See, e.g., Setel 1985; Frymer-Kensky 1992: 144–52; Weems 1989, 1995; Brenner 1995a: 40–241; Keefe, 1995, 2001; Sherwood 1996; Exum 1996: 101–28; Bird 1997a: 219–36); Yee, 1998, 2003: 81–109.

scholars (Bach 1993: 192–3; Sherwood 1996: 302) who suggest that one important role for male scholars working in the wake of feminism is to analyze critically the ideologies of masculinity constructed by biblical texts and their readers. Though such analyses have started to appear (e.g., Eilberg-Schwartz 1994; Clines 1995: 212–43; Tarlin 1997), much work remains to be done, and gay male readers of the Bible may have a particular contribution to make here. Such a contribution need not be seen in opposition to either feminist work on masculinity (e.g., Bordo 1999) or other feminist goals. In spite of the important reservations expressed by some queer theorists (e.g., Rubin 1984; Sedgwick 1990) about the tendency to reduce questions of sexuality to questions of gender, any absolute separation of sexuality and gender seems equally flawed (cf. Butler 1994; Spurlin 1998). As Judith Butler points out,

> Although forms of sexuality do not unilaterally determine gender, a non-causal and non-reductive connection between sexuality and gender is nevertheless crucial to maintain. Precisely because homophobia often operates through the attribution of a damaged, failed, or otherwise abject gender to homosexuals, that is, calling gay men 'feminine' or calling lesbians 'masculine', and because the homophobic terror over performing homosexual acts, where it exists, is often also a terror over losing proper gender ('no longer being a real or proper man' or 'no longer being a real and proper woman'), it seems crucial to retain a theoretical apparatus that will account for how sexuality is regulated through the policing and the shaming of gender. (Butler 1993: 238)

Though I shall return at the end of this chapter to Butler's work, I cite it here to underscore my belief that feminist projects and queer projects, while not reducible to one another, are likely to remain intertwined due to the fact that both sets of projects have a stake in exploring, and contesting, hegemonic notions of proper gendered behavior – including notions of manhood found in Hosea.

In order to tease out those notions it is important to resist certain assumptions that could hinder an analysis of food, sex and manhood. In the first place, it is necessary to guard against imagining that men's relations with food and sex, by virtue of being distinct from the relations that many women have with food and sex, are simple and uncomplicated. Links between notions of manhood and notions about food and sex need to be explicated and analyzed critically, instead of being simplistically assumed. Moreover, it is important to resist the assumption that Hosea's – indeed, patriarchy's – notions of manhood are necessarily more coherent or stable than the biblical notions about women which have been so convincingly critiqued by feminist scholarship. I will argue instead, through a somewhat circuitous route, that by using food and sex to 'think' Hosea we can recognize the incoherence and insecurity of the views of manhood and deity which the book presupposes, and that this recognition makes an important contribution to the contemporary 'queering' of the biblical texts.

II

Like many prophetic books, the book of Hosea makes frequent use of language and imagery that involve food and drink.[3] In continuity with biblical themes discussed

---

3.   Carroll (1999) provides a helpful overview of the role of food in prophetic discourse.

already, Hosea refers to food most often in ways that underscore both the agricultural context that gave us the Bible and the particular anxieties (e.g., anxieties about a successful harvest) that were prevalent in such a context. These references have long generated questions about the role of agricultural concerns in the religious practices and beliefs promoted and/or criticized by Hosea. At the same time, Hosea's references to food and drink frequently appear in or near passages in which controversial sexual imagery is also utilized. Consequently, attention to Hosea's references to food and drink can lead quite naturally to questions about Hosea's sexual rhetoric. The combination of language about food and drink, and language about sex, occurs in chapter 2, for example, where Yhwh explains his motivation for punishing his symbolic 'wife', Israel, by stating:

> Because their mother was sexually promiscuous, she who conceived them brought about shame. For she said, 'I will go after my lovers; they give me my bread and my water, my wool and my flax, my oil and my drink'. (2.7 (English 2.5))

One of the ways in which Hosea conjoins language about food and drink and language about sex is through representations such as this one in which, apparently, a sexually profligate woman who represents Israel seeks out lovers who give to her gifts of food, drink and other agricultural products.

The recognition that such passages contain references to both sex and agricultural products plays an important role in one influential theory about the situation in Israel to which Hosea is supposed to have been responding. According to this theory, the Israelites of Hosea's day were falling away from a 'pure' devotion to Yhwh into some sort of Canaanite 'fertility religion', either as a way of worshipping Yhwh or as a way of worshipping other gods instead of, or alongside, Yhwh. Within the framework of this reading of Hosea, the concern of the female speaker in 2.7 (English 2.5) for gifts or payments of food, drink and other agricultural products symbolizes the concern of the Israelites for a successful harvest, and the imagery of sexual infidelity used by Hosea was motivated by the cultic sex rites in which Israelites participated to ensure fertility and agricultural success. Indeed, in some versions of this hypothesis (e.g., Wolff 1974), Gomer, the wife of the prophet Hosea,[4] is herself supposed to have been a participant in such 'ritual sex acts of the Baal cult' (Anderson and Freedman 1980: 166).

This interpretation of the book of Hosea has recently fallen upon hard times, and for good reasons. As I indicated in chapter 2, a growing number of scholars point

---

4. This is a convenient point at which to acknowledge (without solving) a problem of terminology caused by the fact that the name 'Hosea' is conventionally used to refer to several different entities: the prophet Hosea, a character in the book by the same name who is assumed by the language of the book to be the speaker or mediator of the book's oracles; a supposedly 'real' prophet Hosea who may have lived in ancient Israel and whose actual words and deeds, were they available to us, might stand at some greater or lesser distance from the words and deeds of the biblical character; the book that today carries the name of the prophet Hosea; and the actual author (or authors) of the book. Although these variable uses of the term 'Hosea' can be confusing, I have not tried to disentangle the complex issues involved in the confusion. My own interest lies primarily in the literary text that we have before us and the cultural assumptions with which the text can be read as interacting.

out that detailed reconstructions of a Canaanite 'fertility religion' incorporating sexual rites rest upon a rather flimsy set of arguments. There is, for example, little evidence for such practices in Israel as 'cultic prostitution', practices that were long considered central to modern reconstructions of 'Canaanite fertility religion'.[5]

Yet criticism of conventional accounts of 'Canaanite fertility religion', though necessary, should not lead us to discount altogether the possibility that Hosea's rhetoric is motivated in part by issues traditionally associated with the term 'fertility'. Such a discounting seems to be partly at work, for example, in the thesis about Hosea put forward by Alice Keefe (1995, 2001). Keefe, who rightly critiques popular ideas about Canaanite fertility cults, argues that Hosea was not concerned principally with either the worship of other gods or the fertility of the land, as commentators have traditionally assumed, but with unjust practices of land appropriation associated with the commercialization of agriculture in eighth-century Israel. Prior to this time, according to Keefe, it was the patrilineal family, with its inalienable claim to land, which functioned as the foundational unit in Israelite social and political life. In Keefe's opinion, the social chaos that accompanied the appropriation of land for commercial agriculture in the eighth century had as one of its features a breakdown in family structures, a breakdown signified by the chaos in Hosea's family.

Like the older theories of a Canaanite sex cult, this interpretation of Hosea accounts for Hosea's sexual rhetoric (by understanding it to be motivated by widespread family disintegration in the eighth century) as well as the book's references to agriculture (and hence to food). It also takes a prophetic book that is difficult to fit into the popular portrait of the prophets as proponents of social justice and assimilates the book to that portrait by imagining the book to be a protest against unjust land policies – without denying the book's patriarchal orientation. Keefe's positing of a link in Hosea's time between familial breakdown and a wider social crisis will no doubt seem compelling to many readers, especially in the United States (where such links are frequently asserted).

But although Keefe calls our attention to possible socio-political dimensions of Hosea's rhetoric that are often missed,[6] I am not convinced that one can go as far as Keefe does in disposing of Hosea's interest in either the worship of other gods or so-called 'fertility' concerns. With respect to the former, it certainly is the case, as Keefe suggests, that some of the references to Israel's metaphorical 'lovers' refer to political alliances with other nations rather than the worship of other gods (e.g., Hos. 8.9–10), but in spite of the presence of such passages, the traditional conclusion that Hosea is also worried about the worship of other deities – and in particular the worship of Baal – seems inescapable. Keefe downplays this concern by excluding the third chapter of Hosea from serious consideration (Keefe 1995: 75–6; 2001: 17–18). However, the first verse of that chapter tells us explicitly that the people of Israel 'turn to other gods', and it does so by referring to food and sex:

> Yhwh said to me again, 'Go, love a woman who is loved by another and is an adulteress, just as Yhwh loves the Israelites, though they turn to other gods and love raisin cakes.' (3.1)

5. See the discussion in chapter 2 and sources cited there.
6. See also Yee 2003: 81–109, where similar socio-political issues are stressed.

Hosea's concern about the worship of other deities is, in this passage, both explicit and closely tied to the rhetoric of food and sex. A parallel is established between the desire of Hosea's woman for male lovers, and the desire of Yhwh's people for divine lovers; the promiscuous nature of the latter desire is evidenced by the Israelites' love of a specific food – raisin cakes – which apparently played a role in those offerings made to gods that were subsequently eaten by worshippers. Because 'raisin cakes' could also be offered and ingested in the context of the worship of Yhwh (see, e.g., 2 Sam. 6.19), it is sometimes suggested that Hosea's polemical reference to them here must be related to the unsavory use to which they were being put. As these raisin cakes also appear in a sexual context in the Song of Songs (2.5), Anderson and Freedman conclude that 'the cakes seem to be an aphrodisiac' (Anderson and Freedman 1980: 298). This suggestion misconstrues the point of Hosea's symbolism by taking Hosea's sexual references in too literal a fashion. Hosea is attempting to underscore Israel's religious infidelities by characterizing Israel metaphorically as a sexually insatiable woman. The characterization highlights Israel's voracious appetite. In just the same way that a sexually voracious woman will (according to the logic of Hosea's symbolism) seek out multiple lovers, so also Israel in 3.1 seeks out multiple gods, and this active religious pursuit is represented in terms of hunger for the food that is eaten in the context of sacrifice. Religious gluttony, food gluttony and sexual gluttony all combine here in a feast of rhetorical symbolism. Although Keefe, in distinction from Anderson and Freedman, rightly avoids the error of finding references to a literal sex cult in such passages, she does so partly at the expense of eliminating, nearly altogether, the significance of Hosea 3.1 from her interpretation of the book.[7] Should we choose instead to emphasize the importance of this passage, we will have to integrate Hosea's anxiety about the worship of other gods into our overall analysis of the book's approach to food and sex in a more thorough fashion than Keefe's thesis allows.

Moreover, while Keefe correctly criticizes the interpretation of Hosea as a polemic against a sex-centered fertility cult, she paradoxically fails adequately to question a stubborn binary opposition which sustained that interpretation, specifically, the opposition between the worship of Israelite Yhwh and the worship of Canaanite Baal as two radically distinct types of religion. This opposition is simply transposed into a 'sociological distinction between the commercial and mercantile orientation of Canaanite civilization', and 'the communitarian and egalitarian ethos' of 'Hebraic culture' (Keefe 2001: 131).[8] The boundary between wicked

7.   Keefe is disarmingly blunt about the fact that her decision to exclude 3.1 from her interpretation is partly 'strategic' (2001: 17). Though she gives 'stylistic' justifications for the exclusion, she acknowledges explicitly that an interpretation which grants to 3.1 a more significant role, as mine does, will result in a different understanding of the book. Of course, my own decision to highlight 3.1 is also in certain respects 'strategic', and results in part from my decision to exploit the conjunction in that verse of food and sex. As a general rule, however, the decision to include rather than exclude a particular verse from interpretive significance requires less methodological justification.

8.   Keefe is influenced here, in part, by Gottwald 1979. However, Hillers suggests that Gottwald's sociological reading of 'Canaanite' culture perpetuates the tendency to use 'Canaanite' largely as a foil against which 'Israelite' can be defined positively (Hillers 1985: 266–8).

'Canaanite civilization' and good 'Hebraic culture' remains intact and shapes Keefe's interpretation of Hosea. Yet, as Yvonne Sherwood (1996: 207–35) points out, the language of the book of Hosea itself deconstructs the opposition between the worship of Israelite Yhwh and the worship of Canaanite Baal that is so often proclaimed both elsewhere in the text and throughout the commentaries, and it does so, in part, by attributing to Yhwh characteristics frequently associated with the deities of so-called fertility religion, including Baal himself.

Rather than rejecting fertility concerns altogether as concerns of Hosea, or explaining away apparent references to fertility concerns by arguing that they symbolize other social and political issues, it may be preferable to acknowledge instead that, so far as the book of Hosea is concerned, the religion of Yhwh *is* a sort of 'fertility religion', but one in which fertility is properly credited to Yhwh rather than Baal. Such an acknowledgment raises terminological difficulties involving the gender connotations of the word 'fertility', and I will return to these difficulties (rightly stressed by Keefe) below. For the moment I wish to recall that many of the pragmatic concerns which are generally in mind when the *phrase* 'fertility religion' is deployed – concerns about the production of food through agriculture, for example, as well as concerns about conception and childbirth – are more often associated with male than female deities in Northwest Semitic religions. As Jo Ann Hackett points out in her critique of popular representations of 'fertility goddesses', it is actually male gods such as El and Baal who are most often associated with childbirth and agricultural success among Israel's neighbors (Hackett 1989). As biblical representations of Yhwh incorporate features of both El and Baal (cf. Smith 1990; Mettinger 1990), it is not surprising that some of these representations, including passages from Hosea, also attribute success in childbirth and agriculture to Yhwh. In Hosea 9, for example, it is the male god Yhwh who, as part of Israel's punishment, demonstrates control over reproduction and the successful nurturing of children:

> Ephraim, like a bird their honor will fly away – no birth, no pregnancy, no conception! Even if they bring up children, I will bereave them ... Give them, Yhwh – what will you give? Give them a miscarrying womb and dry breasts... Ephraim is stricken, their root is dried up, they will not bear fruit. Even if they give birth, I will kill the precious products of their womb. (9.11–12a, 14, 16)

According to these verses, Yhwh controls the bearing of fruit – which is to say, in this passage, the production of children. This attribution to Yhwh of control over reproduction coheres well with other biblical passages in which Yhwh 'opens' and 'closes' the womb (e.g., Gen 20.18; 29.31; 30.22 ('God' rather than Yhwh); I Sam. 1.6; Isa. 66.9). Like those passages, Hosea construes a womb that cannot bear children as a sign of divine displeasure and punishment (cf. Fuchs 2000: 63, *passim*). Ultimately, successful childbirth is not so much determined by the female body, but rather by the actions of a male deity.

According to Hosea, however, Yhwh does not control only that bearing of fruit which is, within the framework of biblical symbolism, the generation of offspring. Yhwh also controls the more literal bearing of fruit. Yhwh, who gives food and drink to Israel, can also punish Israel by preventing agricultural success and withholding food and drink, as several passages from Hosea testify:

> She did not know that I gave her the grain, and the wine, and the oil, and mul-
> tiplied silver for her, and gold which they made into Baal. Therefore I will turn
> back and take my grain in its time and my wine in its season, and I will take
> away my wool and my flax, that were supposed to cover her nakedness... And
> I will lay waste her vine and her fig tree, about which she said, 'These are my
> pay, which my lovers have given me.' I will make them a forest, and the beasts
> of the field will eat them. (2.10–11, 14a (English 2.8–9, 12a))

> For they sow in a wind, and they reap in a whirlwind. Grain without growth, it
> will not produce flour; if it does produce, foreigners will swallow it. (8.7)

> Threshing floor and wine vat will not feed them, and new wine will fail them.
> (9.2)

Such passages build upon a wider tradition of biblical thought, found especially
in the prophetic literature (cf. Carroll 1999: 116), but also in such books as
Deuteronomy, which understands agricultural success and the production and
acquisition of food and drink to be brought about or prevented by the god who
controls them.

According to Hosea both the fruit of the womb and the fruit of the earth are
given to, or withheld from, Israel by Yhwh. It would appear from such passages
that the issue in Hosea is not a conflict between an ethical religion of Yhwh and
a fertility-centered Baal cult, as some older commentaries would have it; neither
is the issue simply a critique of unjust land policies, as Keefe argues. The issue in
Hosea is rather a contest between two male gods, Baal and Yhwh, both of whom
are considered by adherents to be the source of agricultural and reproductive
success. Hosea, standing clearly on one side of this conflict, wants to insist that
Yhwh is the true provider for Israel, and had been known in this role already at the
time of the wilderness wanderings:

> It was I who fed you in the wilderness, in the land of drought. When I fed them,
> they were satisfied; when they were satisfied, and their heart was proud, there-
> fore they forgot me. (13.5–6, NRSV)[9]

The reference to food in this verse is obviously related to that biblical tradition
which characterizes Yhwh as the god who gave food and drink to Israel in the wilderness (e.g., Exod. 15.22–17.7; Num. 11.1–35; 20.2–13; Ps. 78.15–31). Although
this verse and the tradition behind it may not focus, as other biblical food traditions do, on Yhwh's role in guaranteeing or preventing *agricultural* produce, its
identification of Yhwh as the provider of food for Israel, and the one whose food-
providing abilities are more powerful than drought, is obvious.

From Hosea's point of view, those Israelites who worship Baal and thank him
for the fruit of the land and the rain which nurtures such fruit sin thereby against

---

9.   The text here is widely acknowledged to be problematic. NRSV follows the Greek and
Syriac in reading 'fed' rather than 'knew' in v. 5 and reconstructs the obscure Hebrew beginning
of v. 6. Both of these moves receive support from commentaries (cf. Mays 1969: 173; Wolff 1974:
220; Anderson and Freedman 1980: 634–5). The NRSV rendering coheres well with my interpretation, and I have chosen to follow it. However, I do not believe that the substance of my larger
argument would be affected seriously by a more literal rendering of the Masoretic Text here.

the true provider, Yhwh. In this transgression they are encouraged, apparently, by priests, who thus 'eat the sin of my people' (4.8). This latter verse is sometimes taken as a reference to the greediness of priests who make haste to devour sin offerings (Anderson and Freedman 1980: 358) or as a reference to priests who exchange true devotion to Yhwh for a religion of profit and prosperity (Mays 1969: 70). In context, however, it is likely that these priests are described as eating 'sin' precisely because they are eating offerings made to some other god (probably Baal) or gods, rather than offerings made to Yhwh. Thus, several verses later, eating is placed in parallel with the 'whoring' that clearly symbolizes, for Hosea, the worship of other gods:

> They will eat, but not be satisfied;
> They will be sexually promiscuous, but not increase [i.e., by giving birth];
> Because they abandoned Yhwh to devote themselves to promiscuity.
>
>   (4.10–11a)

We see in this passage that eating and its desired result (satisfaction) are placed in parallel to sexual activity and its desired result (production of children). The illicit sexual activity, which here as elsewhere is a symbol for the worship of other gods, is unfruitful – that is, does not result in the agricultural produce and the birth of children and animals that one expects a god to bring about – because Yhwh, the one who actually provides fruitfulness and fertility, has been forsaken. The hunger of the Israelites will not be satisfied because Yhwh, the one who truly provides food for Israel, has been abandoned for his rivals.

One of the issues underlying the rhetoric of Hosea, then, is a controversy over which god or gods can really provide for Israel food that will satisfy. Given the book's use of the symbolism of female promiscuity as a way of speaking about the Israelites' worship of other gods, and the book's references and allusions to Baal (e.g., 2.8, 16–17; 13.1), the controversy over provision of food seems to be primarily a conflict between the male gods Yhwh and Baal, characterized respectively as a husband and a male lover between which Israel (characterized as a woman) must choose.

If the Israelites (or at least those whose views are represented most often in the Bible) associated agricultural success and the provision of food with male rather than female deities, this association may be due not only to the continuity between Israelite religion and other Northwest Semitic religions but also to the fact that, among humans, agricultural success was more closely associated with men than with women. This association is clear in Genesis 3.17–19, for example, where, as we have seen, it is the man rather than the woman who is condemned to spend his life extracting food from the earth through agricultural labor. What we have in such passages is, of course, evidence for a *conventional notion* about the division of labor in ancient Israel rather than empirical evidence about the *actual* division of labor. Women in Israel may well have played a more important role in subsistence activities (including agricultural production) than the biblical texts acknowledge (cf. Meyers 1988: 47–63); and, in addition, there may also have been Israelites – perhaps especially women – who associated food provision primarily with female rather than male deities (cf. Jer. 44: 15–19). Nevertheless, based on the picture we get from Genesis 3, we might conclude that Hosea and other biblical texts, by attributing agricultural success ultimately to the male deity Yhwh, simply project onto that male deity an association between manhood and agricultural labor that was already made at the human level.

III

How and why does the association between manhood and food provision come to be linked with the notorious sexual imagery that we find in the book of Hosea? Exploration of this question benefits from the use of an anthropological lens to examine Hosea's sex and gender imagery. Gale Yee, in a brief but insightful discussion (Yee 1998), suggests that Hosea's sexual rhetoric can plausibly be interpreted in relation to that network of conceptions about gender and prestige known to us from the anthropology of the Mediterranean basin and the Middle East, and referred to in chapter 3. Recall that such conceptions, often associated (though somewhat simplistically (cf. Herzfeld 1980; Wikan 1987; Lindisfarne 1994)) with the phrase 'honor and shame', emphasize, among other things, the cultural importance to men of the control of female sexuality (see Gilmore, ed., 1987; Blok 1981; Pitt-Rivers 1977; cf. Stone 1996: 37–49). As a way of insuring their own reputation and status, the paternity of their children, and above all their ability to be (in Herzfeld's telling phrase) 'good at being a man' (Herzfeld 1985: 16), these men must demonstrate their ability to father children and to be absolutely vigilant with respect to both the sexual purity of the women of their household and the sexual intentions of other men. The failure to perform these tasks adequately puts one's manhood at risk, and leaves one open to a sort of symbolic castration in the eyes of others. Thus, as Yee points out, the scenario utilized by Hosea, in which one's wife and the mother of one's children is characterized as sexually promiscuous, represents a horrifying possibility that haunts the men who share these cultural values. Such values are used by Hosea to characterize Yhwh, for Yhwh reacts to the religious infidelity of Israel in much the same way that an Israelite man is expected to react to the sexual infidelity of his wife (Yee 1998: 210, *passim*; cf. Weems 1995).

As productive as it is to read Hosea in the light of these notions about masculine honor and the control of female sexuality, it has been insufficiently noted by biblical scholars[10] that, in the anthropological literature used to explicate such notions, the domain of sexuality is only one of several domains in which a man must embody norms of masculine behavior. Among the other components of a man's skill 'at being a man', we also find references to the provision of food for one's dependents. Thus John Davis, to cite one example, suggests that displays of economic success, including 'feeding a family', may actually be more important for a man's honor than the widely discussed displays of sexual vigilance (Davis 1977: 77–8; cf. Davis 1969: 70). A review of the relevant anthropological literature seems to indicate that these two components of male honor – sexual vigilance and the ability to provide – often go together (cf. Gilmore 1987: 6–7; 1990: 43).

---

10. Including myself in previous publications (e.g., Stone 1995, 1996).

Let us suppose that a man's ability to control sexual access to the women of his household, and a man's ability to provide food for his dependents, are interrelated, as Davis and others suggest, in the 'honor and shame' cultures to which Yee directs our attention in her reading of Hosea. What might this tell us about the symbolic significance of attributing the results of one man's provisioning efforts to another man? Would not such misattribution be in some ways parallel to the claim that one's children are really those of another man, and that one has therefore been a cuckold? In both cases, within a certain cluster of assumptions about masculine performance and male honor, a man's skill and success at manhood are at stake. Within the protocols of Mediterranean and Middle Eastern masculinity, both types of questioning demand a 'riposte', to borrow Bourdieu's term (Bourdieu 1979), which is to say, an assertive response to the challenge that has been brought against one's socially acknowledged 'manliness'.

With these considerations in mind we can return to Hosea's rhetoric. As we have seen, Hosea can be read as indicating that the Israelites (or some portion of them) were thanking Baal rather than Yhwh for agricultural success. I would argue that Hosea, in response to this perceived misattribution of Yhwh's produce to Baal, ascribes to Yhwh emotions and reactions that were expected from any Israelite male whose produce, whose fruit in the literal sense, was credited to another man. Assuming that a human male would feel compelled, as a point of honor, to respond angrily and assertively to this sort of misattribution of provisioning ability, Hosea attributes just such a response to Yhwh, who is characterized in Hosea through the projection onto the divine of certain norms and expectations about manhood. The misattribution of agricultural and economic success to other gods such as Baal triggers in Hosea's Yhwh the angry retort, 'She [Israel] did not know that I gave her the grain, the wine, and the oil' (2.10 (English 2.8a)). Such a retort serves a function not altogether dissimilar to the function of that retort made by Bourdieu's Algerian male subjects who, playing upon the cultural link between facial hair and virility, insist that 'I've got a moustache too' when they want to assert the equivalence of their manliness alongside that of other men (Bourdieu 1979: 100). Both Bourdieu's subjects and Hosea's Yhwh are asserting their adequacy within the framework of particular protocols of manhood. Yhwh's male honor has been challenged by misattribution to Baal of Yhwh's provisions, which specifically take the form, here, of the ubiquitous 'Mediterranean triad' (Garnsey 1999: 12–21, *passim*; Longo 1999: 155) of grain, wine and olive oil. The book of Hosea represents Yhwh's 'manly' riposte.

If it is the case, however, that food provisioning plays a role in the notions of manhood presupposed by Hosea, we might wonder whether Hosea's interpretation of divine judgment as, at least in part, Yhwh's response to Israelite misattribution of food and other provisions to Yhwh's rival, Baal, *generated* the biblical symbolization of Yhwh's relationship with Israel in terms of sexual infidelity and sexual vigilance. It is sometimes suggested that, within Israel, Hosea was 'the originator of the (in)famous depiction of God as faithful husband to Israel, his faithless wife' (Yee 2003: 81). If there is any truth to this suggestion (and chronologically, at least, it seems to make sense of the biblical literature), then we must ask about the motivation behind this shift from a religious to a sexual register. Older theories about Canaanite sex cults active in Hosea's day provided such a motivation, and Keefe's link between socio-economic chaos and family disintegration attempts to do so as well. My own view is that connections between food and sex provide us with a more plausible explanation of the appearance of this symbolism in Hosea.

In order to recognize this possibility, it is important to underscore the fact that rhetorical strategies deployed by the book of Hosea rely to a significant degree on mobilizing male fears of emasculation, of being feminized. To borrow Butler's language, Hosea capitalizes on male 'terror over ... no longer being a real and proper man' (Butler 1993: 238). One relatively subtle way in which this mobilization of gender terror works is through the comparison of God's relationship with the Israelites to the relationship between a man and his wife. As some commentators note (e.g., Eilberg-Schwartz 1994), this symbolic structure must itself have produced discomfort among Hosea's largely male audience as it represents that audience as a woman. Hosea further mobilizes male fears of emasculation by utilizing the image of a sexually promiscuous woman, an image that is threatening in part because, within a particular framework of cultural assumptions, control of female sexuality is partially constitutive of manhood.

In choosing this image, is Hosea simply making use of powerful and shocking rhetoric to communicate the message of covenant unfaithfulness? I believe the link between Hosea's chosen imagery, and the situation to which Hosea is trying to respond, is somewhat closer than this and can be understood better precisely when we 'think' food and sex together. Yhwh's 'manhood' is first called into question (Hosea imagines) when Yhwh's Israelite 'wife' attributes agricultural fertility to Yhwh's rival, Baal. In order to communicate, to a male audience, the scandal of this threat to Yhwh's manhood as well as the assumed need for a harsh divine response, Hosea compares such misattribution to the sexual infidelity of a wife. Hosea's vivid sexual language is largely a rhetorical tool for underscoring symbolically, and in a provocative fashion, the offense that Hosea assumes Yhwh must have felt when Yhwh's gifts of produce were attributed to Baal. Such a rhetorical tool was chosen by Hosea, not because of any actual sexual misconduct on the part of the Israelites, but rather because of the parallel importance of both food provisioning and sexual vigilance to demonstrations that one is 'good at being a man' – or, in this case, good at being a male god.

IV

The possibility that Yhwh's manhood is at stake in Hosea's language about food and sex brings us back to the vexing question of 'fertility religion'. The term 'fertility' tends not to be used primarily in connection with men and manhood, but in connection with women, female deities and feminized entities such as the earth. It is difficult even to use the phrase 'fertility religion' without calling to mind popular but dubious ideas about such phenomena as, e.g., 'fertility goddesses' (cf. Hackett 1989). Given the conceptions and misconceptions that circulate in connection with the phrase 'fertility religion', perhaps it is better to avoid such terminology altogether as a way of speaking about the worship of Yhwh.

If we abandon the phrase 'fertility religion', how are we to talk about the real concern of biblical texts like Hosea with such issues as food production and childbirth, and link this concern with assumptions about gender and sexuality presupposed by Hosea's sexual rhetoric? How are we to make clear that the major issue with which Hosea is concerned is not a contest between two different types of religion – one centered on agricultural fertility, the other on ethics – but a contest between two male deities, both of whom were understood by worshippers to play an active role in the generation of life and the products that sustain it? The problem here is not simply a problem of terminology, but also of the various conceptual frameworks within which relations are established among gender, sexual reproduction, agricultural production and deity.

The anthropologist Carol Delaney offers us a way to begin to unravel this conceptual tangle when she suggests that 'honor and shame are functions of a specific construction of procreation', by which she means not simply sexual reproduction but a broader set of 'beliefs related to the question of *how life comes into being*' (Delaney 1987: 36, emphasis mine). As Delaney points out, folk models of procreation dominated by Judaism, Christianity and Islam tend actually to valorize, not so much the fertility of women and the earth (emphasized in so many accounts of 'fertility religion'), but rather what she calls 'the primary, creative, engendering role' of males, whether human or divine (Delaney 1991: 11). While the importance of women to the process of child*birth* is empirically obvious, the relative contributions of men and women to the processes of *conception* are not. Thus, these contributions are said in many cultures to be analogous to the perceived relations between seed and soil. According to the terms of this analogy men plant the seed, in which one already finds the basic substance of life, in women, who as soil are more or less inert vessels in which the seed develops and from which it receives nutrition. This analogy brings together agricultural production and sexual reproduction in a way that emphasizes male potency rather than (as reconstructions of 'fertility religion' sometimes imply) female fertility. The network of assumptions undergirding the analogy, known to us from elsewhere in the ancient world (cf. duBois 1988) and of great importance for understanding such figures as Clement of Alexandria (see Buell 1999), is referred to by Delaney by the term 'monogenesis'; for the analogy seems to presuppose that one human parent, the father, is primarily responsible for the 'genesis' or 'generation' of new life. The mother, on the other hand, serves as something like an incubator.

Delaney argues that the attribution to men of the primary role in contributing the substance of life is both justified by, and justifies in turn, the belief in a male creator god responsible for the generation and cultivation of life not only among humans but also in the wider cosmos. Just as human males must water the soil (both literally and figuratively) for which they are responsible, so also the male creator god waters the soil with rain to produce the fruit of the field (Delaney 1991: 45). The symbolic associations at work in such language are complex, as one can see from the fact that it speaks about male contributions to intercourse as *both* seed *and* rain (in distinction from the female contribution of soil). Nevertheless, the effect of such imagery, in relation to both sexual reproduction and agriculture, is to conceptualize the contributions of human males and divine males in terms of one another in such a fashion that patriarchal beliefs and practices are reinforced.

Delaney goes on to argue for a close association between, on the one hand, the beliefs about gender and procreation that she explicates and, on the other hand, monotheism. Her analysis is developed in dialogue with monotheistic cultures, among which she includes ancient Israel, and Delaney has recently argued more explicitly that a monogenetic view of procreation is presupposed in the Bible (Delaney 1998). Indeed, while Delaney's terminology is not always used, biblical scholars also sometimes note the existence of a sort of 'monogenetic' view of procreation in the Bible (e.g., Rashkow 2000: 75–8). It is well known that the Hebrew word for 'seed' is not only used to refer to 'seed' in the agricultural sense, but also to a man's semen and progeny. Eilberg-Schwartz argues (1990: 141–76) that the assumption of a kind of analogy between agricultural fruitfulness and the fertility of the male organ can best account for numerous biblical texts, including those pertaining to male circumcision. The assumption that something like a monogenetic conceptualization of human sexual reproduction is at work in the Bible surely helps us understand the fact that biblical genealogies, which trace descent almost exclusively through male lines, also (in the words of Esther Fuchs) 'validate the idea that though mothers are admittedly important participants in giving birth, "the fruit of the womb" belongs to the fathers' (Fuchs 2000: 81). Certainly, Delaney is correct to link monogenesis to biblical literature.

As the application of the term 'monotheism' to ancient Israel and the Hebrew Bible may be more complex than Delaney's discussion of monogenesis and monotheism seems to allow (cf., e.g., Halpern 1987; Smith 1990; Gnuse 1997), it is important to note that there may not be a necessary relationship between monogenesis and monotheism. Marcia Inhorn points out that versions of monogenesis can already be detected in writings from pharaonic Egypt, which clearly do not presuppose a monotheistic framework (Inhorn 1994: 53–5). The crucial dimension of monogenesis is not its link with monotheism, but rather the fact that it attributes to male gods (and male humans) the principal role in the generation of life. As Inhorn notes (55), one of the most striking expressions of this attribution is found in those Egyptian myths that refer to masturbation on the part of a male god to account for the generation of other beings (cf. Schumann Antelme and Rossini 2001: 8, 11; Matthews and Benjamin 1997: 8).

In any case, one could imagine from Delaney's own discussion of the ways in which these views play out on the human plane that such views are compatible with versions of henotheism or monolatry involving, not a single male god, but rather an agonistic contest for precedence between two male gods. As Delaney points out, the symbolic understanding of human women as soil, waiting for the sowing of male seed, tends to be accompanied by language about an individual woman as a sort of field. This field has to be protected by its male owner from other males. In order to be certain, as a point of male honor, that his wife bears children who are the product of his own seed, a husband has to put a fence around his field. This language about fencing a field, in Delaney's view, both symbolizes and justifies the segregation of the sexes, the 'vigilance' (Schneider 1971) with which sexual access to a woman is guarded, and the vehemence with which female sexual misconduct is punished. Such vigilance and vehemence result from male anxiety about the possibility that children born to a man's wife are actually the result of another man's sowing. In order to ensure that the fruit produced in one's field is one's own, one has to assert and guard anxiously one's rights as owner – and sower – of the field in question.

Is it not the case that such images circulate throughout the discourse of Hosea, as Hosea continually reflects upon the contest between Yhwh and Baal? Although the language of 'sowing' and 'reaping', which is used in more than one context in the book, can take a human subject (see, e.g., 10:11–14), it also refers to activities carried out by Yhwh. Yhwh tells the prophet to name his firstborn son 'Jezreel', 'God sows', a name which, though not itself incorporating the name Yhwh, contributes in context to Hosea's argument that Yhwh rather than Baal sows in Israel. Israel's god produces the food that Israel eats, a fact that is driven home at the end of the second chapter:

> And the earth will answer the grain, the wine, and the oil, and they will answer 'Jezreel' ['God sows'], and I will sow her myself in the land. (2.24–25a (English 2.22–23a))

Once again Hosea refers explicitly to those specific food staples – grain, wine, and oil – that form a conventional set in the ancient world, appearing together in other texts both biblical and non-biblical, and even elsewhere in the book of Hosea, as we have seen (2.10 (English 2.8)). Significantly, this same series of foodstuffs is associated with Yhwh's rival, Baal, in the Ugaritic Keret text; in that text it is precisely the scarcity of these staples that will be brought to an end by the arrival of the 'rain of Baal' (Gibson 1977: 98; cf. Mays 1969: 41; Wolff 1974: 39). In distinction from such texts, Hosea wants to insist that it is Yhwh who generates these food staples, that it is Yhwh who should be associated with the rain (cf. 6.3; 10.12), and, here in the second chapter, that it is Yhwh who 'sows'. Here as elsewhere, Hosea's rhetoric, insisting that Yhwh rather than Baal owns, sows, waters and generates life in the field of Israel, tends to slide from an agricultural to a sexual register. For while translations frequently substitute the personal pronoun 'him' in place of 'her' in 2.25 (English 2.23) – thus NRSV, 'I will sow him' – there is no textual warrant for this substitution. In fact Yhwh 'will sow her', that is, Israel, who thus serves as Yhwh's field in both senses of the term: Israel is Yhwh's land, and Israel is Yhwh's wife.

Jezreel, however, is the only one of Gomer's three children who is explicitly said (in 1.3) to be born *to Hosea*. When we read about the next two children, by contrast, we are told that Gomer conceives and bears them, but not *to whom* they are born. Although commentators often understand these children to be born to Hosea (e.g., Anderson and Freedman 1980: 172), one could argue instead that textual ambiguity around the paternity of these last two children communicates what it means, from Hosea's point of view, for a man to take as wife a 'promiscuous woman' or 'woman of whoredom'. Such women are dreaded by men in part because their perceived trafficking with other men makes it impossible for any one man to know with certainty that particular children are the result of his sowing rather than another's. The anxiety experienced by Hosea's readers, condemned by the ambiguity of the text to wonder about the paternity of Gomer's second and third children, therefore reproduces exactly the anxiety of the man – or the god – whose field has no fence.

V

With this experience of anxiety we confront one of the more paradoxical aspects of Hosea's use of cultural norms of manhood to characterize Yhwh. For anxiety is not a characteristic that readers of the Bible generally attribute to God. Yet the notions about manhood that are utilized in Hosea's characterization of Yhwh are grounded in a profound sense of anxiety about masculinity. The anger with which a man responds to the implication that he has failed to embody adequately the 'poetics of manhood' (Herzfeld 1985) results from a certain fragility and instability of masculinity as a construct. As David Gilmore points out, one has to 'prove' publicly one's manhood 'because it is undermined perpetually by incredulity and suspicion from within and without' (Gilmore 1987: 15). The fervor with which manhood's protocols are publicly demonstrated has its roots in 'shared male anxieties about feminization' (11), anxieties characteristic of male subjects who fear the symbolic castration that results from being exposed as something less than 'real' men. Thus, by characterizing Yhwh in terms of such recurring demonstrations of manliness as the vehement insistence that one is an adequate food provider, or the harsh punishment of women suspected of sexual infidelity, Hosea ironically leaves the Yhwh that he constructs open to the charge of revealing through anxious assertion a sort of divine insecurity about Yhwh's ability to be (playing here again on Herzfeld's phrase) 'good at being a male god'. That is, Hosea's rhetoric of food and sex exposes, on the part of Hosea's god, an anxiety about the possibility of symbolic divine castration.

Now Gilmore suggests at one point that extreme forms of such anxiety are especially characteristic of males raised in families from those areas of the Mediterranean and Middle East that have so often served as objects of interpretation for the anthropologists of honor and shame. The predominant household structure within these areas is, according to Gilmore, based on a sharp division of female and male spheres that young boys must negotiate in their riteless passage from boyhood to manhood. As Gilmore sees it, the uncertainties of this passage generate a lasting anxiety about its successful completion, which is to say, a lasting anxiety about the successful demonstration of one's manhood (Gilmore 1987: 8–16).

A reader familiar with accounts of sex and gender emerging at the intersection of feminism and queer theory, however, might well wish to place Gilmore's psycho-social suggestion in a larger frame. If one finds compelling the argument of Butler, for example, that gender is *always* a contingent effect of the 'stylized repetition of acts', and hence *always* subject to destabilization as a result of discontinuities from one repetition to another (Butler 1990: 139–41), then one might well imagine that the anxious assertions of manhood described ethnographically by anthropologists of honor and shame are simply context-specific cases of an insecurity that is inherent (at least as potential) within a great deal of what passes for 'manhood' elsewhere as well – including, perhaps, in the biblical texts. As Butler points out, gender norms may be demanded by culture but 'the compulsory character of these norms does not always make them efficacious'. For Butler, the supposed coherence of the 'male/female' binary opposition that undergirds the 'heterosexual contract' (Wittig 1992) is maintained by the compulsory reiteration, citation, and consequent materialization of social norms of sex and gender. Just as speech acts rely upon and reaffirm prior sets of socio-linguistic conventions and norms, so also the 'citation' of gender norms (whether linguistically or through the embodied enactment of such norms) both presupposes and reaffirms the norms in question. Yet careful analysis reveals that the coherence of these norms of sex and gender is not total. Just as speech acts can 'misfire' (when, for example, the required context and conditions for a certain type of speech act are not met), so also the reiteration of gender norms frequently produces citations in which sex, gender and sexual practice are not, according to the dominant ideologies, aligned consistently.[11] That is, 'male' and 'female' actors or speakers often act or speak in ways that stand in some tension with the norms of 'manhood' and 'womanhood' to which, supposedly, 'males' and 'females' must respectively conform. According to Butler, then, gender norms 'are continually haunted by their own inefficacy', and so they are accompanied by an 'anxiously repeated effort to install and augment their jurisdiction' (Butler 1993: 237). The repetition of gender norms seems to be closely related to the inherent instability of these norms, and this instability produces anxiety at the site of repetition.

It is therefore important to note that, while the book of Hosea can be seen as an instance (or perhaps a series of instances) of the representation of the stylized citation or iteration of gender norms (and I take this to be one way of recasting in Butler's terms the argument of Yee, Weems and others that Hosea plays upon audience expectations about appropriate gendered behavior when characterizing Israel and Yhwh), nevertheless, the book is finally unable to sustain a coherent and consistent picture of that 'manhood' which it presupposes and attempts to reproduce or 'cite'. This inability, which is exactly what Butler's view of gender might lead us to expect, manifests itself in several ways in Hosea's text, most of which have been pointed out by others: the hints of maternal imagery for a previously male Yhwh toward the end of the book (cf. Schüngel-Straumann 1995; Yee 1998: 213); the striking gender reversal accomplished by the representation of an intended Israelite audience that was composed largely of males as Yhwh's wife (cf. Leith 1989; Eilberg-Schwartz 1994); and the implication that this wife finds her husband, despite his vehement protestations to the contrary, to be inadequate as provider and/or lover.

Among these slips in gender intelligibility, the one I would like to return to in conclusion is the one with which the book opens: the command by Yhwh that Hosea marry a 'woman of whoredom' or 'promiscuous woman' in the first place (1.2). Although this image, no doubt chosen in order to shock, is key to the symbolic communication of Hosea's overall message (that Yhwh has chosen a people, Israel, which has continually proven itself incapable of fidelity, as evidenced for example by Israel's tendency to expect Baal rather than Yhwh to supply food), the command to marry such a woman also tends to undermine the book's arguments. As Sherwood has shown, the symbolism of a husband deliberately choosing to

11. While the term 'misfire' is taken from Austin's influential account of speech acts (Austin 1975: 16, *passim*), Butler's use of Austin depends crucially on Derrida's reading of Austin's speech act theory (Derrida 1988).

marry a whoring woman runs counter to the claim, made elsewhere in the book, that Israel's relationship with Yhwh, though now adulterated, was once pure (Sherwood 1996: 207–14). Moreover, the fact that Hosea, standing in for Yhwh, marries a woman whose character is already known undermines the force of Yhwh's/Hosea's recurring complaint about Israel's/Gomer's infidelity. As Carole Fontaine puts it, such a complaint ends up 'castigating the woman for the very behavior that caused her to be chosen in the first place' (Fontaine 1995: 63).

For my purposes, however, the intriguing fact about Hosea's/Yhwh's decision to marry a woman/nation whose infidelity is already known in advance is that such a decision may also undermine the divine manhood which, I have argued here, Hosea's rhetoric of food and sex elsewhere presupposes. For if, as Gilmore and others argue, a man is symbolically emasculated in his own eyes and in the eyes of his peers when his wife has sexual relations with other men (Gilmore 1987: 10–1; cf. Blok 1981: 431), then Hosea's culturally ascribed manhood – and, to the extent that Hosea symbolizes Yhwh, Yhwh's culturally ascribed manhood – may paradoxically be *surrendered* from the start by virtue of Hosea's informed decision to marry a woman whose (supposed) 'promiscuous' or 'whoring' character is already known. With that decision, Hosea/Yhwh actually transgresses in advance, or at least opens the door knowingly for a transgression of, the cultural protocols of masculinity according to which a man should ensure the sexual purity before marriage (cf. Deut. 22.13–21) and the sexual fidelity within marriage of the women of his household.

I hasten to add that I would not want my language about the 'surrender' or 'transgression' of manhood to be misunderstood as apologetic for Hosea's rhetoric of sex and gender. The devastating consequences of the gender notions that Hosea presupposes have been well-documented by the feminist research on Hosea cited earlier, and I have no intention of minimizing the book's phallocentric norms or suggesting that Hosea is in any sense a model for contemporary manhood. However, as we have seen, Butler alerts us to the fact that the embodiment or materialization of gender norms (even, or especially, phallocentric gender norms) frequently fails to live up to the ideals on which it is based. It may be precisely this failure that offers opportunities for a certain sort of 'queering' of the biblical texts, a queering that works by destabilizing – or, better perhaps, by calling attention to the inevitable instability of – cultural imperatives surrounding gender and sexuality. The identification and proliferation of misalignments among sex, gender and sexual practice has become, in the wake of Butler's work, a goal for many queer theorists, for such misalignments represent both weak spots in the heterosexual matrix and openings for a reconfiguration of that matrix. As Butler argues, the 'institution of a compulsory and naturalized heterosexuality requires and regulates gender as a binary relation in which the masculine term is differentiated from a feminine term' (Butler 1990: 22–3). If such a 'compulsory and naturalized heterosexuality' is to find a secure grounding in the biblical texts (as many contemporary readers already assume it does), it should ideally be able to rely upon a clear and consistent demarcation of masculine characters, divine and human, from their feminine or ambiguously masculine counterparts. To the extent, however, that Hosea's characterization of Yhwh not only relies upon, but also transgresses, particular norms of manhood (such as those surrounding food and sex), the book helps to expose the inability of masculinities – including divine masculinities – to establish themselves over against what Butler calls the 'feminine term' in a consistent and nonproblematic fashion.

In the previous chapter I emphasized the strategic importance, for the development of queer practices of 'safer text', of attention to the Song of Songs as one text that contests patriarchal attitudes toward sexuality and gender so characteristic of other biblical texts. When biblical scholars decide to point to a text that embodies the patriarchal attitudes which the Song of Songs contests, they frequently and rightly refer to Hosea. The recognition that even so relentlessly patriarchal a text as Hosea is, in the end, not entirely successful at constructing a consistent and secure representation of patriarchal manhood (whether human or divine) is thus a crucial component of queer practices of 'safer text'. It serves as a check on our tendency to essentialize, or overestimate the stability of, such phenomena as 'patriarchy' or, for that matter, 'manhood'. Recognizing that such phenomena are, in fact, already characterized by contradiction and instability, we may find ourselves better prepared to imagine alternative, and even queer, religious and theological scenarios of masculinity that also involve the surrender, rather than the embrace, of the structures of agonistic manhood.

CHAPTER 6

WISDOM AND PLEASURE

I

In my Introduction, I suggested that chapters of this book might be characterized as something like 'courses' in a meal. From that point of view, this chapter could logically be understood as 'dessert'. Dessert, however, occupies an ambiguous position in the symbolic sequence of a meal. Coming as it does at the end of a meal, dessert can be seen as that meal's 'climax', insuring, in Margaret Visser's words, that the meal 'ends on a high note' (1986: 19). Visser herself, however, makes a contrast between 'the seriousness of the entrée and the frivolity of dessert' (216). Is dessert, then, the satisfying culmination toward which everything else moves? Or is it, rather, a kind of luxurious afterthought, which might be skipped if one has had enough already?

Given the ambiguous connotations of dessert, it may be appropriate that this closing chapter has as its textual focus the biblical Wisdom literature. For Wisdom literature, too, occupies an ambiguous position within the various Jewish and Christian canons, seldom playing a significant role in attempts by biblical scholars and theologians to work out a contemporary way of thinking about our use of the Bible. Thus, such influential practitioners of 'Old Testament Theology' as von Rad (1962: 418–59) and Wright (1952: 102–5) seem to have had difficulty deciding how, or whether, the Wisdom literature could be made to fit into their theological scheme (cf. Barr 1999: 46, 380–1). Yet many of the same features of the Wisdom literature that provoke uneasiness on the part of such readers may cause us to wonder whether the Wisdom approach does not have something important to contribute to our attempts at reconceptualizing biblical interpretation as 'safer text'. Wright notes, for example, that Wisdom teachings are often 'chiefly practical, prudential, and utilitarian' and result in a 'commonsense ethic' (ibid). This 'practical' approach tends, as Walter Brueggemann puts it, to 'ask about "what works", what risks may be run, what realities can be trusted, and where the practice of human choice, human freedom, and human responsibility can be exercised' (Brueggemann 2002: 232). Exactly a 'practical' and 'utilitarian' approach to sex (as opposed to a moralizing one) is often invoked by safer sex educators, who speak less about what is inherently right or wrong, sexually, and more about pragmatic ways in which risk can be reduced without eliminating pleasure. Like the Wisdom literature, advocates for safer sex focus upon '"what works", what risks may be run, what realities can be trusted, and where the practice of human choice, human freedom, and human responsibility can be exercised'.

A dialogue with elements of the Wisdom tradition may therefore provide a fitting form for our closing course. We shall not assume a unified Wisdom perspective, however, but a multiplex tradition within which diverse points of view are articulated. The Wisdom literature is, like all biblical literature, a product of its agrarian and patriarchal world. Nevertheless, attention to its approach to that world may provide us with hints about the ways in which we can approach our own very different world and our practices of biblical interpretation. As one way of exploring that possibility, we can ask about the manner in which the Wisdom literature reflects upon food and sex.

II

There is near unanimous agreement that, if the term 'Wisdom literature' is going to be used in relation to the Bible, the book of Proverbs belongs under that rubric.[1] Though the opening nine chapters form a single, relatively unified discourse, much of the rest of the book consists of brief sayings that appear to be collected in a somewhat haphazard manner. These sayings are grounded in practical observations about human behavior and experience, the natural and agricultural world, and the whole of creation. It is therefore no surprise that the sayings which begin in chapter 10 include numerous references to food and drink, as do the sayings found in other ancient Near Eastern texts sometimes associated with the biblical Wisdom literature.[2] Food and drink played an important role in those day to day realities which served, for the Wisdom tradition, as ingredients for critical reflection.

Proverbial references to food in Proverbs 10–31 may appear at first to provide few connections between food and sex. It is, however, the case that connections can sometimes be made on the basis of juxtaposition. Chapters 23 and 31, for example, appear to draw a parallel between the dangers of strong drink and the dangers of certain women (Prov. 23.27–35; 31.3–6); and in chapter 27 it is possible that the juxtaposition of a proverb about food (v. 7) and a proverb about men wandering from home (v. 8) is grounded in a perception of structural similarities between appetites for food and appetites for sex.

Such structural similarities are explicit, however, in a striking proverb in chapter 30:

> This is the way of the adulterous woman:
> She eats, and wipes her mouth,
> And says, 'I have not done anything wrong.' (Prov. 30.29)

In distinction from texts that represent sexual relations by speaking about a man who eats and a woman who is his meal, this proverb places the female sexual subject clearly in the position of the one who dines. However, the context for this representation of female sexual agency has a negative impact on the connotations of the

---

1.   For overviews of academic discussions of biblical Wisdom literature, see the introductions of Crenshaw (1981) and Murphy (1990).
2.   Thus one finds recurring references to food and drink scattered throughout the Egyptian *Instruction of Any* and *Instruction of Amenemope* (the latter of which is closely associated with Proverbs). See Lichtheim 1976: 135–63.

symbolism. The woman who in 30.29 eats and participates in sexual activity is focalized by a male speaker (30.1), who identifies her as an adulterous woman (understood, within Proverbs, to be a dangerous thing), and her speech is embedded in, subordinate to, and reported only by his. Thus, while Proverbs 30 shares with Song of Songs this image of a woman whose sexual agency is symbolized by eating, the ideological connotations of Proverbs 30.29 are obviously quite different from those found in the Song of Songs, where female voices dominate and the book is structured so as to highlight the woman's points of view. The male fear of a voracious female sexuality, and the use of language about eating to signify this female appetite, remind us instead of a scene from the Epic of Gilgamesh. When Ishtar asks Gilgamesh to 'be my lover, bestow on me the gift of your fruit' (Dalley 1989: 77), Gilgamesh in his refusal recalls Ishtar's earlier attempt to seduce her father's gardener Ishullanu, during which attempt her use of the language of eating functioned as, in the words of Walls, 'a veiled threat to utterly consume, not just taste, Ishullanu's virility' (Walls 2001: 39).[3] Both Gilgamesh and the speaker in Proverbs 30.29 use female appetites for food to communicate, to men, perceived dangers in the sexual activity of particular female subjects.[4]

The connection in Proverbs between food and sex is even more apparent in the lengthy discourse found in chapters 1 through 9. These chapters include several references to the figure of personified Wisdom, who prepares and offers food and drink. In Proverbs 9, we find Woman Wisdom represented as follows:

Wisdom has built her house, she has hewn her seven pillars.
She has slaughtered her food, she has mixed her wine, also she has set her
    table.
She has sent out her servant girls, she has called from the heights of the town,
... 'Come, eat my bread, and drink the wine that I have mixed.'

(Prov. 9.1–3, 5)

This particular picture of Wisdom does not have explicit sexual connotations. Woman Wisdom is contrasted in this same chapter, however, with another female figure, the woman of 'folly' or 'stupidity'. While this figure, like Wisdom, invites others to eat and drink, her meal not only has negative consequences (9.18) but contains sexual overtones as well; she states at one point:

Water that is stolen is sweet,
And bread eaten secretly is delightful.   (Prov. 9.17)

As commentators recognize (e.g., McKane 1970: 366; Scott 1965: 77; Fox 2000: 302), the stolen water and secret bread represent, here, furtive sexual pleasures. Elsewhere Proverbs makes use of drinking water as a symbol for intercourse. Chapter 5 includes a warning against the 'strange woman', whose lips 'drip honey' and whose mouth is 'smoother than oil' (5.3). The imagery of honey and oil is probably used in Proverbs 5 to signify the woman's seductive speech (cf. 2:16)

3. Foster captures the reference to eating in Ishtar's request with his translation 'let us have a taste of your manliness' (1987: 35).
4. Rivkah Harris points out that the myth of Nergal and Ereshkigal also uses the language of food and sex to express the 'view that women have voracious appetites for sex' (Harris 2000: 136). For an English translation, see Dalley 1989: 163–81.

rather than actual sexual contact, though given the role of 'honey' in the Song of Songs we should not rule out sexual connotations altogether. The specific type of contact that Proverbs 5 is warning against is clearly adultery, as is also the case in chapter 2 (where the strange woman is, in addition to being 'strange', explicitly an adulteress (2.16)). When the narrator turns to the preferred alternative of sexual relations with one's own wife, that speaker uses the symbolism of drinking water and intoxicating beverages to signify sexual intercourse:

> Drink water from your own cistern, and streams from your own well,
> Lest your springs flow outward,[5] in the plazas, channels of water.
> Let them be yours alone, and not for strangers with you.
> Let your fountain be blessed, and be joyful in the wife of your youth,
> A doe of love, a graceful gazelle, may her breasts satisfy you at all times,
>   In her love may you always be intoxicated.
> Why should you be intoxicated, my son, with a strange woman?
>   And why embrace the bosom of a foreign woman?   (Prov. 5.15–20)

The language of this passage is at several points reminiscent of the Song of Songs, which also uses the symbolism of fountains and springs of water to speak about the female lover (see, e.g., Song 4.12–15). If the Song of Songs urges lovers to 'be drunk with love' (Song 5.1), so here the speaker tries to make clear that the 'intoxication' his listener ought to seek is provided by a wife and not the 'strange woman'. Both texts find it useful to conceptualize sexual activity as drinking and eating.

Proverbs 5, however, betrays an anxiety about adultery that is largely missing from the Song of Songs. This obsession with adultery appears at several other points in Proverbs 1–9, including a passage in chapter 6 where sex is referred to in conjunction with food. Trying to dissuade the assumed male reader from having sexual relations with another man's wife (6.24), the speaker observes:

> For the cost of a prostitute is only a loaf of bread,
> But a married woman hunts a man's very life. (6.26)

This frank acknowledgement of prostitution argues that prostitution is preferable to, because less risky than, adultery, and it indicates (like Genesis 38) that food served as payment for prostitutes. It is not, however, the only point of conjunction between food and sex in this passage. The argument that prostitution is better than adultery is followed by further reflections on the dangers of adultery for the man who might be caught by his partner's husband. There we find an assertion that, while thieves are seldom despised for stealing bread when they are hungry, even they will be punished (6.30–31). As in 9.17, so also here, stolen food is a symbol for sexual relations with the wife of another man.

Similar concerns are developed in chapter 7, where we find the tale of a young man falling into the clutches of a woman who is the adulterous wife of another man. Though dressed like a prostitute (7.10), she is married to a man who is away on a journey (19–20). Her seduction begins in a way that seems at first odd, for her first statement to the young man is a report that she has just offered sacrifices

---

5.   The best translation and interpretation of this clause is disputed. For discussion see Fox 2000: 200–1, whose general translation I am adopting here.

and paid her vows (14). The type of sacrifice referred to, however, is an offering of well-being, or so-called 'peace offering', which is simply 'an accepted manner for slaughtering any animal that was to be used for human consumption' (Anderson 1992: 879 (cf. Lev. 7.11–18; 17.1–7)). The point behind the woman's opening statement, then, is that she has freshly prepared food waiting to be eaten. The adulterous wife in Proverbs 7 is seducing her victim by offering him a meal, which, conveniently, she has on hand as a result of the fact that she has just returned from making her offering. As Fox puts it, she 'baits her trap with food' (2000: 246).

If food and sex both contribute to the negative representation of the adulterous woman in Proverbs 7, we may wonder whether they are also linked in the case of her counterpart, Woman Wisdom. We have already seen that, in chapter 9, Wisdom offers food and drink. In that chapter, Wisdom's portrait has no sexual connotations. Chapter 7, on the other hand, speaks about Wisdom in language that can carry sexual connotations, though it is not always interpreted in such a fashion. At 7.4–5 we:

> Say to Wisdom, 'You are my sister',
> And call Understanding an intimate friend,
> To keep you from a strange woman,
> From a foreign woman whose speech is smooth.

This passage introduces the discourse (7.6–27) on the adulteress with food, and clearly a distinction is being drawn here between the 'strange' or 'foreign' woman, and Woman Wisdom. In that light, it is significant that the word chosen to refer to Wisdom in 7.4 is 'my sister'. For the term 'my sister' is used several times in the Song of Songs (as well as certain Egyptian poems) to refer to a female lover (e.g., Song 4.9–10, 12; 5.1–2). It would seem that Wisdom, who has her own food to offer (as we have seen), is represented here with language that has, at the very least, erotic overtones, as commentators recognize (cf. Ringgren 1947: 106; Camp 1985: 94, 100; McKinlay 1996: 88, 130). The use of erotic language for Woman Wisdom is not restricted to this passage. In chapter 4, the listener is urged not only to 'love' Wisdom (4.6), but also to 'embrace' (4.8), and possibly even 'caress', her.[6] Just as chapter 5 presents sexual pleasures with a wife as alternative to sexual pleasures with 'strange' women, chapter 4 counters the sexual pleasures of 'strange', 'foreign', and 'adulterous' women by presenting an alternative picture of Woman Wisdom as object of erotic affection. Woman Wisdom is, in Ringgren's words, 'described as the bride whom the young man should cleave to and love' (Ringgren 1947: 134; cf. Frymer-Kensky 1992: 181; Yee 2003: 156). This is a bride who not only offers sex but, particularly in chapter 9, food as well. The connection is picked up later, in the Jewish Wisdom tradition, by Ben Sira:

> Whoever fears the Lord will do this,
> And whoever holds to the law will obtain Wisdom.

---

6. 'Caress' is the least certain of these three admonitions and depends on the translation of the hapax legomenon *salsleha*. In verse 8, however, this hapax does not stand alone as evidence for the point I am making; the verse ends with a word (which I have translated 'embrace') that, as Camp points out, in its piel stem (which is the stem used here) 'always refers to an erotic embrace' (1985: 94). The use, at the end of this verse, of the verb 'embrace' in its erotic form strengthens the possibility that the hapax at the beginning ought to be translated as 'caress'.

> She will come to meet him like a mother,
> And like a young bride she will welcome him.
> She will feed him with the bread of learning,
> And give him the water of wisdom to drink.

(Ben Sira 15.1–3, NRSV)

By representing Woman Wisdom as both bride and provider of food and drink, Ben Sira simply picks up a motif already present in Proverbs.

When Proverbs 1–9 utilizes images of food, sex and gender, it relies upon a sharp, binary contrast between female figures perceived negatively by the speaker of Proverbs (e.g., 'strange woman', 'foreign woman', 'woman of adultery', etc.) and female figures perceived positively, such as one's mother, one's wife, and Woman Wisdom. Feminist scholars of the Wisdom literature have long noted, and debated the implications of, this binary opposition, which grants a great deal of power to certain female characters, but only by contrasting them dualistically with other, heavily stigmatized, female characters.[7] Carol Newsom notes that the gender ideology of Proverbs 1–9 rests upon a contrast between positive and negative female characters, who together 'define and secure the boundaries of the symbolic order of patriarchal wisdom' (1989: 157). Newsom also underscores the continuing significance of such contrasts by making a comparison between the discourse of Proverbs and the film *Fatal Attraction*.[8] As Newsom acknowledges, when the film draws a binary distinction between Alex (the 'strange woman' of *Fatal Attraction*, with whom the male protagonist, Dan, has a brief but dangerous sexual affair) and Beth (the good wife who ultimately saves her foolish husband), it associates Beth not only with sex but also with kitchen:

> It is 'the wife of his youth' who must rescue him. The wife has been presented, as is the wife of Proverbs 5, as herself a deeply erotic, desirable woman. Equally, she is the center of the domesticity of the patriarchal family. Her symbol is the house, where, more than once, we see the brightly burning kitchen hearth.

(Newsom 1989: 158)

What Newsom does not note, however, is that eating and drinking play a significant role in the characterization of Alex as well. Alex and Dan initially speak while getting drinks at a party, and their first sexual encounter is preceded by a second drink and a meal. A crucial moment in their affair, moreover, is a second meal, with wine, that takes place secretly at Alex's apartment. Like the 'strange woman' of Proverbs, then, Alex is characterized in stark opposition to her female counterpart even while her own associations with food and drink are underscored. The polarization of female 'types' is accomplished in both film and biblical text not only through images of sex (good and sexually attractive wife versus dangerous female sexual subject) but also through images of food (good food associated with

---

7.   For feminist discussions of Proverbs, see Camp 1985, 1991, 1997, 2000; Newsom 1989; Frymer-Kensky 1992: 179–83; Brenner and van Dijk-Hemmes 1993; Brenner, ed., 1995b; McKinlay 1996; Fontaine 1998a; Brenner and Fontaine, eds., 1998; Yee 2003: 135–58.

8.   *Fatal Attraction.* Directed by Adrian Lyne. 121 min. Paramount Home Entertainment, 1987. Videocassette.

the kitchen of a good woman versus dangerous food and drink offered in public or consumed in secret).

This ideological continuity between Proverbs and *Fatal Attraction* underscores the need for a careful and critical reception of the biblical Wisdom literature. The way in which Proverbs and *Fatal Attraction* attempt to distinguish safety and danger by projecting danger, in a dualistic way, onto despised classes of women raises questions about possible risks involved in my notion of 'safer text', which I shall return to below. The 'strange' or 'foreign woman' functions in Proverbs as a 'multivalent symbol' (Camp 1991: 18), which not only expresses male anxieties about adultery but also condenses Israelite anxieties about intermarriage across ethnic boundaries in postexilic Judah (cf. Camp 1997, 2000; Washington 1995; Berquist 2002: 135–61; Yee 2003: 135–58).

When I suggest, then, that attention to the biblical Wisdom literature is useful for reflection on queer 'practices of safer text', I am not suggesting that this literature ought to be viewed uncritically. Quite the contrary: one of the contributions of biblical Wisdom literature is the way in which, taken as a group of texts rather than a single text, it demonstrates the fact that one can stand in conscious relationship with, and learn from, a particular tradition while also, at the same time, analyzing it critically and pragmatically. In order to make this point it is necessary to turn from Proverbs to another biblical Wisdom book that also links food and sex: the book of Ecclesiastes, or Qohelet.

III

Like Proverbs, Qohelet is traditionally grouped under the rubric of 'Wisdom literature'. Yet the book is frequently characterized in such a way as to draw a contrast, or highlight a tension, between the two books. While scholars debate how close or distant Qohelet stands in relation to a more traditional Wisdom approach to the world, nearly all scholars agree that Qohelet can be read as both standing within the same Wisdom tradition, broadly construed, as Proverbs while simultaneously voicing alternative positions that stand in some tension or even contradiction with conclusions reached, not only by Proverbs, but also by most other biblical books.

That Qohelet understands himself[9] to be involved in a Wisdom enterprise is clear enough from the opening chapter of the book. Qohelet asserts, 'I set my mind to study and to seek out *by wisdom* all that is done under the heavens' (1.13). Like other adherents of the Wisdom tradition, Qohelet wishes to understand life and human existence; he wishes to understand everything 'under the heavens' and 'under the sun', and he chooses a Wisdom method – reflection on human experience and on the natural world – in order to do so.

Many of the conclusions that Qohelet reaches are quite unexpected for a biblical text. His discoveries are summarized by an opening refrain often referred to (by, e.g., Crenshaw 1987: 57–9; Fox 1999: 161–3) as the book's 'motto': '"Utterly

---

9.   I am adopting the scholarly convention of using the word 'Qohelet' to refer not simply to the book as a whole but also to the personage implied by its dominant speaking voice. It is clear that this voice is a male one.

absurd," says Qohelet, "Utterly absurd. Everything is absurd"' (1.2). The sense of this motto is not altogether easy to capture in translation. The phrase *hebel hebelim*, which I have just translated as 'utterly absurd', is variously translated as 'vanity of vanities' (KJV, NRSV), or 'utter futility' (JPS); but the literal meaning of *hebel* as something like 'breath' or 'vapor' has connotations of something that is ephemeral or fleeting. However one translates this motto, much of the book goes on to elaborate upon it by recounting the processes of observation and reflection that led Qohelet to it. Along the way, numerous ideas associated with biblical religion are called into question, either explicitly or implicitly. Qohelet questions the assumption, quite common in Proverbs, that things generally work out better for the wise person than for the fool (2.12–16; 6.8). He recognizes the terrible reality of oppression and suffering, while also raising the disturbing possibility that power arrangements prevent justice from ever actually existing for the oppressed (4.1–3; 5.7). He gives us good reason to wonder whether the good person is really rewarded and the evil person really punished (7.15; 8.9–14; 9.2–3), suggesting instead that our fates are determined largely by time and chance (9.11–12). He notes the opinion of others that some form of existence continues for humans after death, only to call such an opinion into question (3.18–21), and he seems to doubt that anything new ever really occurs (1.9–10). Though Qohelet does not question the existence of God, one carries away from the book a picture of God as rather distant and uninvolved. And how many Christians or Jews open the Bible expecting to learn that being too good or too wise is just as dangerous as being too wicked or too foolish, so that perhaps one should be a bit moderate in one's virtues (7.15–18)? With good reason Brueggemann refers to Qohelet as 'a lively dissenter from what is generally the consensus of Old Testament faith' (2003: 331; cf. 1997: 393–8).

James Crenshaw, more willing than most readers to face the apparently pessimistic dimensions of Qohelet's message, notes that, faced with the realities of chance and death, Qohelet finally 'opts for life' (Crenshaw 1987: 27). Such a statement can hardly fail to catch our attention in the context of reflection on 'practices of safer text', for the rhetoric of AIDS activists has, from the beginning of the HIV/AIDS crisis, been full of such life-opting slogans as, 'Silence = Death' and 'Choose Life'.[10] Significantly, it is precisely when we turn to passages in Qohelet used to support Crenshaw's statement that we find a connection between food and sex.

In 2.1–11, Qohelet, having already determined that the quest for wisdom in which he has been engaged is a futile 'chasing after wind' (1.14, 17), sets out on a quest for 'pleasure' or 'joy' (2.1). The first specific pleasure mentioned by Qohelet is wine (2.3); and, in a subsequent description of pleasurable things acquired, Qohelet refers to vineyards (2.4) and fruit trees (2.5), as well as cattle, herds and flocks (2.7). Clearly, then, the pleasures of food and drink are included among those things with which Qohelet attempted to satisfy himself.

---

10. Although the phrase, 'Choose Life', is used by opponents of abortion in the United States, the United Fellowship of Metropolitan Community Churches (UFMCC) has published a brochure on HIV/AIDS under the title 'Choose Life'. The inspiration for this title is, of course, Deuteronomy 30.19.

It seems, however, that sexual pleasures were also pursued by Qohelet. At the end of a list, in 2.8, of pleasures acquired, Qohelet states that he got 'human delights, many mistresses'. The English phrase 'many mistresses' translates a very difficult phrase, which some modern translations (e.g., JPS) and commentators (e.g., Seow 1997: 131) render otherwise. At least as far back as the twelfth-century Jewish writer Abraham Ibn Ezra, however, other commentators have concluded that these words probably refer to 'mistresses' or 'concubines' (see, e.g., Gordis 1955: 140, 208–9; Ginsburg 1970: 285–6; Crenshaw 1987: 81; Longman 1998: 92–3). This way of understanding the conclusion of 2.8 seems especially likely in light of the fact that the very word for 'delights' in this same verse is used specifically for the sexual delights that the male speaker finds in his female lover in Song of Songs 7.7. As we shall see, the appearance of sex in Qohelet 2.8 together with food and drink in the preceding verses parallels an important recurrence of food, drink and sex later in the book.

In chapter 2 Qohelet decides that the process of testing pleasure is finally fleeting, another 'chasing after wind' that does not ultimately 'profit' (2.11). The implications of this judgment for Qohelet's overall attitude toward the pleasures of food and sex have to be assessed in the light of the remainder of the chapter. At the end of the same chapter, Qohelet, having reflected further on wisdom, toil and worry, finally concludes that 'there is nothing better for a person than to eat and drink and allow himself to see enjoyment from his work' (2.24). While this conclusion is hardly unqualified praise, an affirmation that 'there is nothing better' than the enjoyment of life's physical pleasures is rather unexpected in biblical literature, and constitutes a message that many readers of the Bible choose to ignore.

This affirmation does not stand alone in the book. 'I knew', says Qohelet in the next chapter, 'that there is nothing better for them than to be joyful, and to do what is good with their lives, and also that whenever one eats and drinks and sees good from all one's work, it is a gift from God' (3.12–13). 'To do what is good', here, is not a moral activity, but rather a pleasant one; thus, one can translate 'experience good' (e.g., Crenshaw 1987: 92) or even 'enjoy themselves' (e.g., Longman 1998: 122). A similar refrain is found in 5.17–19, where the goodness of such pleasures is less qualified. Here, Qohelet does not say that 'there is nothing better', but rather, 'Look, this is what I found to be good: that it is beautiful to eat, and to drink, and to see good from all the work at which one works under the sun, during the numbered days of the life which God has given one, for that is one's portion' (5.17). Again, in chapter 8, Qohelet, having observed correctly that individuals do not always receive the reward or retribution appropriate to their conduct, concludes that the enjoyment of one's pleasures in life is the appropriate response: 'And so I praised pleasure, for there is nothing better for anyone under the sun than to eat and to drink and to enjoy oneself, and that can accompany one in return for one's work during the days of the life which God has given to one under the sun' (8.15). Such passages, taken together, lead to the conclusion that the book of Qohelet, for all of its supposed cynicism or pessimism, has as one of its 'basic themes' what Gordis calls 'the duty to enjoy life and taste its pleasures to the full' (Gordis 1955: 240).

These sorts of passages are placed in the book and phrased in such a way as to steadily increase the emphasis placed by Qohelet upon this theme of the enjoyment

of life (cf. Whybray 1982). For our purposes, the most important among such passages, and the climax of Qohelet's stress upon the enjoyment of life, is found in
chapter 9. There Qohelet arrives at last at the following verdict:

> Go, eat your bread with joy and drink your wine with a glad heart, for God has
> already approved your actions. At all times let your clothes be white, and may
> oil on your head never be lacking. Enjoy life with a woman whom you love all
> the days of your fleeting life that God has given you under the sun – all your
> fleeting days. For that is your portion in life and in the work at which you work
> under the sun.   (Eccl. 9.7–9)

It is clear that not only the speaker, Qohelet, but also his implied audience, is
male (cf. Crenshaw 1987: 163). For our immediate purposes, though, the point to
underscore is that we have, once again, a conjunction of food and – in the form
of a female partner – sex. If, in chapter 2, Qohelet's quest for goods and pleasure
led him to pursue (among other things) wine, food and sexual partners before discovering that the quest for pleasure is, like the quest for wisdom, ephemeral, here
Qohelet concludes that the enjoyment of food, drink and sexual companionship,
while indeed fleeting, is nevertheless the primary goal that one can realistically
pursue during the brief span of human life. Food, drink and sexual companionship
come to represent the pleasures that, in the opinion of Qohelet, God has approved
for human existence. As Gordis (1955: 119) puts the matter:

> For Koheleth, joy is God's categorical imperative for man [*sic*], not in any
> anemic or spiritualized sense, but rather as a full-blooded and tangible experi-
> ence, expressing itself in the play of the body and the activity of the mind, the
> contemplation of nature and the pleasures of love.

The inclusion here of 'the activity of the mind' and 'the contemplation of nature'
within Qohelet's approved course of action, though appropriate within the context
of the book as a whole, is inferred by Gordis from Qohelet's narrated practice elsewhere. Qohelet's explicit recommendation in 9.7–9 places the emphasis squarely
upon those physical experiences captured by Gordis's phrases 'the play of the
body' and 'the pleasures of love'. Gordis's use of the word 'imperative' rightly
underscores the fact that the language of 9.7–9 changes from mere observation and
reflection to command: the verbs appear mostly in the imperative form ('go', 'eat',
'drink', 'enjoy',[11] etc.). Qohelet is not simply allowing for physical pleasure as com-
pensation for a generally gloomy human existence. Qohelet is 'opting for life' by
urging his audience to enjoy the God-given pleasures of food, drink and sex while
they can, understanding that enjoyment of such pleasures is not merely something
to be tolerated but is the form of life that God has approved for us.

Readers of this passage are frequently tempted to see in it praise for marriage. In
this temptation they are assisted by translators, who render verse 9 as, for example,
'enjoy life with the wife whom you love' (NRSV) or 'enjoy life with your wife,

---

11. The imperative 'enjoy life' at the beginning of v. 9 is a rendering of a phrase that could
be translated, more literally, as 'see life', but the sense of the verb 'see', here as in chapter 2, is,
as commentators recognize (e.g., Ginsburg 1970: 416; Seow 1997: 126, 301; Fox 1999: 294), one
of enjoyment and pleasure.

whom you love' (NIV). As there is no Hebrew word referring specifically and exclusively to 'wife', the meaning 'wife' must be inferred from contexts in which the Hebrew word 'woman' is used. Should one simply assume, then, that 'wife' is to be understood here?

Certain features of the passage may cause us to think otherwise. The word 'woman' has, in this instance, neither a definite article (as NRSV misleadingly implies with its translation, '*the* wife') nor a possessive pronoun (as NIV misleadingly implies with its translation, '*your* wife'). Literally we have, simply, 'a woman whom you love'. The fact that translators so often render a general recommendation in a more determined and definite sense ('the' or 'your' instead of simply 'a') already raises suspicions that normalizing sexual assumptions are being imposed upon a verse for which alternative interpretations are possible. In fact, numerous commentators (e.g., Ginsburg 1970: 416; Barton 1959: 162; Gordis 1955: 296; Tamez 2000: 168) note, though occasionally with discomfort, that when this verse is read together with the probable reference in 2.8 to physical sexual pleasures with women, and in light of the fact that there is here no definite article on 'woman', one can more plausibly conclude that Qohelet does not have marriage, in particular, in mind in 9.9. As Gordis puts it, Qohelet 'was certainly no apologist for the marriage institution' (1955: 296).

Such conclusions do not sit well with all readers of the Bible. Against the argument that marriage is not here specified, Seow (1997: 301), for example, argues that a similar passage in the Old Babylonian version of the Gilgamesh Epic, often cited as a parallel to this section of Qohelet, uses an Akkadian word most often understood as 'wife' rather than an alternative word that simply means 'woman'. The section of Gilgamesh to which Seow appeals comes at that point in the story where the female tavernkeeper Siduri recommends to Gilgamesh a course of action rather close to the life advocated by Qohelet in chapter 9. Dalley (1989: 150) translates Siduri's recommendation as follows:

> Gilgamesh, where do you roam?
> You will not find the eternal life you seek.
> When the gods created mankind
> They appointed death for mankind,
> Kept eternal life in their own hands.
> So, Gilgamesh, let your stomach be full,
> Day and night enjoy yourself in every way,
> Every day arrange for pleasures.
> Day and night, dance and play,
> Wear fresh clothes.
> Keep your head washed, bathe in water,
> Appreciate the child who holds your hand,
> Let your wife enjoy herself in your lap.

This passage is frequently cited as a parallel to Qohelet 9.7–9; and it does show that Qohelet's emphasis upon enjoyment of life has continuities with other ancient Near Eastern texts.[12] Not only does Siduri recommend to Gilgamesh several of the

12. Also frequently cited, in this regard, is an Egyptian 'Harper's Song', translated in Lichtheim 1973: 194–7.

specific pleasures mentioned by Qohelet (including the pleasures of food and sex), but the context for such recommendation is, in the Epic of Gilgamesh as in Qohelet, an attempt to come to terms with mortality. Other Mesopotamian texts also indicate that death was dreaded in the ancient world in part because after death one could no longer enjoy such pleasures as food, drink, and sex (cf. Leick 1994: 222–3).

Whether this parallel from Gilgamesh actually confirms that Qohelet is talking about a 'wife' in 9.9, however, as Seow suggests, is less clear. The Akkadian word to which Seow appeals (and which Dalley translates as 'wife') is a rare one;[13] and Tzvi Abusch suggests, in his detailed study of Siduri's dialogue with Gilgamesh, that here the word was originally understood 'not as "wife", but as "prostitute/harlot" or the like' (Abusch 1993: 9). Thus Seow's confident appeal to Siduri's speech to justify the translation 'wife' in Qohelet 9.9 gives an impression of scholarly certainty that may be unwarranted.

Whether Qohelet refers in 9.9 to 'women' or 'wives', it is sex, rather than companionship, that seems to be in his sights. Qohelet is clearly an advocate for the importance of human companionship, or 'solidarity' (Tamez 2000: 72, *passim*), in the face of life's difficulties, and it might be possible to derive from that advocacy biblical support for the theme of 'friendship', which is probably more helpful than 'marriage' for rethinking relationality in a queer context.[14] However, Qohelet's specific discussion of the importance of companionship (in 4.7–12) does not single out the spouse as the person who provides such companionship. Indeed, it only refers explicitly to male categories when it provides specific examples (e.g., 4.8). When he refers to the pleasures of women alongside the pleasures of food and drink in chapter 9, Qohelet is more likely to be referring specifically to physical, sexual pleasures with those women (as he is in 2.8) than to the pleasures of companionship between lovers or spouses so often associated with 'marriage' today. His emphasis is, as Ginsburg noted, on 'sensual gratification' (Ginsburg 1970: 417).

When Qohelet comes to his central argument in chapter 9 that enjoyment of pleasure is the appropriate and divinely approved manner of living one's life, the specific pleasures referred to include the bodily pleasures of food, drink and sex. Food, drink and sex are apparently more important for Qohelet, or at least more worthy of recommendation, than any number of other things that we might expect a biblical author to emphasize. No attempt is made here to recommend the observance of covenant stipulations, worship, communion with God, holiness, virtue, the bearing and raising of children, political activity, or even justice. The importance of any one of these things may or may not be presupposed by Qohelet. We might be able to argue from what Qohelet does say here in such a way as to elaborate implications that would logically entail some of these other things. Perhaps the importance placed here on food and drink could be used to argue, for

13. Abusch (1993: 9) points out that, outside of the Gilgamesh Epic, it is found in extant texts only twice.

14. Cf. Stuart 1995; Vasey 1995; Hunt 1991. Given the role of food and eating in the solidification of friendship, it seems to me that an approach to sex which thinks about it in relation to food would have much to contribute to efforts at developing a theology or ethics of sexual friendship.

example, that, as God wants all of us to enjoy food and drink, political work for justice that ensures food and drink for everyone ought logically to be implied by Qohelet's recommendation (cf. Gordis 1955: 119–20). By extension, perhaps the importance placed here on sex could be used to argue that, as God wants all of us to enjoy sex, political work to ensure sexual pleasures for everyone ought logically to be implied by Qohelet's recommendation as well. I would make both of those arguments myself. The fact remains, however, that, having sought wisdom, and having observed his world carefully, and having reflected upon the realities of life and death, Qohelet ultimately urges us simply to enjoy the bodily pleasures of food, drink and sex as the best thing which we can do, and the thing which God has approved for us, during the few days that we have in this ephemeral life under the sun, the only existence (Qohelet explicitly reminds us (3.18–21; cf. 9.5–6, 10)) of which we can be certain.

IV

We have, then, in Proverbs and Ecclesiastes, two biblical books that both make some use of the recurring biblical conjunction of food and sex. However, although Proverbs and Qohelet stand in the 'same' Wisdom tradition, they are in several respects quite different from one another. Allowing for some over-simplification, we could say, for example, that Proverbs is characterized by relative confidence in the sage's ability to detect orderly structures underlying the world, to discern how best to conform one's life to those structures, and to reap the benefits of security and contentment that follow from such conformity. Qohelet, on the other hand, raises critical questions about all of these assumptions. Qohelet seems uncertain that moral order underlies the world. Even if such order exists Qohelet doubts whether human beings can find it out. Moreover, Qohelet boldly questions whether the person who searches for this order and attempts to live by it will be any better off than the person who does neither of these things: the same fate awaits us all. Thus, Proverbs and Qohelet stake out rather different positions in the Wisdom tradition. And, of course, Job, Ben Sira and the Wisdom of Solomon represent still other perspectives within that tradition. The fact that differences between these texts and perspectives exist, not only within the canon as a whole but even within that more narrow part of the canon known as 'Wisdom literature', reminds us of the need to attend, always and carefully, to heterogeneity, contradiction and particularity within those phenomena and persons in our own world that we are otherwise tempted to interpret in totalizing or homogenizing ways. I would even go so far as to argue that the activity of discerning differences of detail in texts and perspectives that we normally imagine as unified, 'canonical' wholes ('The Bible'), or lump together in essentializing categories, serves as good exercise for the practice of resisting attempts at repressing differences among one another, attempts that, as we know too well, often take violent forms.

Let us think further about the implications of the fact that Qohelet stands in identifiable ways *within* the Wisdom tradition, but simultaneously critiques that tradition from a position that is recognizable as a radical alternative, not only to more conventional Wisdom texts, but even to the main streams of biblical thought. Could one not argue that, exactly for these reasons, Qohelet may have far more to offer to attempts at queer theologizing than do many of the tame arguments for 'inclusion' and 'equality' that are more frequently deployed? There may be a sense in which Qohelet can usefully be imagined as a 'queer' biblical text.

Such a statement may surprise many readers. Qohelet contains no real hint of homoeroticism, unless one interprets liberally the reference to those fellows who lie together to keep warm (4.11). Although Gordis remarks that 'Koheleth was almost surely a bachelor' (1955: 296), the references to sex that I have pointed out are clearly references to women placed in a male voice.

Nevertheless, I believe it may be useful to think of Qohelet as a 'queer' text for at least two reasons. The first of these reasons is more formal or structural in nature, while the second concerns portions of Qohelet's content that I have underscored here. With respect to the structural argument, Qohelet can be read as standing in relation to the primary streams of biblical tradition in something like the same way that, Halperin argues, a 'queer' position stands relative to heteronormative society. Halperin, writing under the influence of Foucault, suggests that a 'queer' position is perhaps *not* most usefully understood as a position 'rooted in the positive fact of homosexual object-choice'. Rather, 'queer', for Halperin,

> acquires its meaning from its oppositional relation to the norm. Queer is by defi-
> nition *whatever* is at odds with the normal, the legitimate, the dominant. *There
> is nothing in particular to which it necessarily refers.* It is an identity without an
> essence. 'Queer', then, demarcates not a positivity but a positionality vis-à-vis
> the normative. (Halperin 1995:62, original emphasis)

How might we explicate implications of this positional and oppositional notion of 'queer' for our attempts to think through possibilities for queer readings of the Bible? While Halperin himself may not have anticipated such a question, it seems consistent with the spirit of Halperin's suggestion that '"Queer" … describes a horizon of possibility whose precise extent and heterogeneous scope cannot in principle be delimited in advance' (ibid). If we attempt to relate Halperin's discussion to the 'horizon' of possibilities for a 'queer' biblical interpretation, it seems to me that one of several arguments which could be sustained[15] is the argument that, within the context of the canon as a whole and the Wisdom tradition in particular, Qohelet is a book that occupies something like an 'oppositional relation to the norm'. It was not for nothing that early Jewish authorities questioned whether the book should be excluded from the holy scriptures, or even suppressed, containing as it does not only internal contradictions but also potentially heretical views.[16] Most early Christian lists of canonical books include Qohelet, but the book's difficulties were largely handled by Christians through the use of allegorical exegesis, by which method, as Ginsburg notes, 'all difficulties [in Qohelet] disappear, and the most heterodox sentiments are easily converted into thoroughly orthodox admonitions' (Ginsburg 1970: 102). A Christian reader, Theodore of Mopsuestia,

---

15. For an attempt on my part to relate Halperin's discussion to a different part of the Hebrew canon – specifically, the biblical laments – see Stone 1999.

16. See Seow 1997: 3–4; Ginsburg 1970: 9–16; and sources cited there.

widely remembered for his more literal approach to biblical interpretation, seems to have raised questions about the inspiration of Qohelet, and the influence of Theodore is sometimes credited with the apparent exclusion of the book from the Nestorian canon (Seow 1997: 4). Still today a reader of the book can reach the conclusion that Qohelet 'is undeniably the most heterodox' book in the Bible (Merkin 1987: 396), and it is quite common to find among commentators the opinion that the book only achieved canonical status either because it was associated, erroneously, with Solomon (see, e.g., Gordis 1955: 39–42) or because it was given a more orthodox epilogue (12.9–14) by its secondary editor (see, e.g., Crenshaw 1987: 52). At a purely formal level, Qohelet's radical departure from many of the accepted truths of both biblical thought and the religions that claim biblical provenance allow us to characterize it as a book that is, in Halperin's words, 'at odds with the normal, the legitimate, the dominant' – and hence as 'queer'.

There is a less formal sense in which Qohelet might be characterized as 'queer', and this has more to do with the book's appreciation of the bodily pleasures of food and sex. Here again, reflection on Halperin's discussion may help us to make a connection. For although Halperin's presentation of possible connotations of 'queer' allows us to imagine the term to have a wide potential scope, still there remains a sense in which Halperin's discussion of the term seems to presuppose that sexual matters will remain a central focus of most 'queer' activism. This is implied, for example, by the particular way in which Halperin, arguing against a narrow understanding of 'queer', insists instead that it represents 'a positionality that is not restricted to lesbians and gay men but is in fact available to anyone who is or who feels marginalized *because of her or his sexual practices*' (62, emphasis mine). Continued attention to matters of sex is assumed by even this expanded definition of 'queer positionality'.

But what about matters of food? Halperin, building upon Foucault's late work on the 'practices of the self',[17] advocates for the development of 'queer practices of self-fashioning' (82), or even 'spiritual exercises',[18] through which 'one can transform oneself; one can become queer' (79). It is notable that, when Halperin turns to consider several specific practices which, in his view, might or already do fulfill such a function for gay men, most of his examples involve, in one way or another, the body.[19] To be sure, Halperin also gives attention to the creation of unforeseen relational forms (81–5) and 'other expressions of subcultural development', including social and political expressions (99). Yet even these possibilities

17. Although Foucault's late writings on the 'practices of the self' are not among his most influential works, Halperin is not the only person to recognize their importance. See, e.g., McWhorter 1999; O'Leary 2002; and McLaren 2002. For an earlier attempt of my own to think about Foucault's later writings in relation to biblical interpretation, see Stone 1997a. Julianne Buenting suggests, in a paper delivered to the American Academy of Religion (2003), that Foucault's work on practices of the self are potentially valuable for rethinking the interrelations among food, sex, gender and religion.

18. The term 'spiritual exercises' makes its way into Halperin's discussion by way of his attempt to take seriously the influence on Foucault of the work of Pierre Hadot (e.g., Hadot 1995).

are never entirely separated from bodily pleasure, as they derive in part from Foucault's injunction 'to use one's sexuality henceforth to arrive at a multiplicity of relationships' (Foucault 1997: 135). Halperin's major emphasis, in any case, is on possible techniques for, and effects of, that queer 'asceticism' to which Foucault looked forward when he recommended the development of

> a homosexual ascesis that would make us work on ourselves and invent – I do not say discover – a manner of being that is still improbable ... What we must work on, it seems to me, is ... *to make ourselves infinitely more susceptible to pleasure.* (Foucault 1997: 137, emphasis mine)

Foucault's own interest in 'asceticism' or *askesis*, which inspires Halperin's meditation on queer 'spiritual exercises', makes what is perhaps its most prominent appearance in *The Use of Pleasure* (1985). There, *askesis* is discussed in the context of reflection on those relationships to self by which certain Greek writers attempted to learn how to make use of one's pleasures. As I indicated in my Introduction, that volume emphasizes throughout that, for these writers, the pleasures of food, drink and sex played not only central but also structurally parallel roles in the ethical reflection and bodily regimen by which one worked on one's self. There is a real sense in which Halperin is attempting to develop a model of queer 'spiritual exercises' that could be said to be grounded in – or at the very least partly derived from – a Foucauldian highlighting of those same bodily pleasures of food, drink and sex with which Qohelet urges his readers to happily occupy themselves. What Halperin, Foucault and Qohelet all share is a recognition of the importance of what Gordis calls, in his discussion of Qohelet, 'the play of the body ... and the pleasures of love' (Gordis 1955: 119).

Could one not argue that exactly this positive emphasis upon bodily pleasure has also been one of the most important contributions made by queer interventions in theological discourse? After all, Christian theology has only on rare occasions been able to grant to bodily pleasure, not simply a begrudging tolerance, but rather a position of central importance. In principle, at least, the positive valuation of bodily pleasure that often seems to be fostered among gay men, lesbians, bisexuals and transgendered persons, even in the face of much opposition, has the potential to effect a radical transformation in both the nature of religious communities and the shape of theological discourse. It is quite striking that many of those theologians and ethicists who today call, in one way or another, for a positive theological account of bodily pleasure issue this call from non-heterosexual speaking positions (e.g., Ellison 1996; Boisvert 2000; Jordan 2002: 155–72; Goss 2003). While much energy in gay and lesbian religious life is devoted to organization around the fight for inclusion within religious communities, or for equal access to the roles (e.g., the clergy) and functions (e.g., the blessing of unions) associated with those communities, some of the most creative queer theological work being done today aims instead at transforming religion and theology by bringing to bear on them

---

19. Thus, Halperin discusses 'sadomasochistic eroticism' (85–91), or S/M, while mentioning as well 'bathhouse sex' (94), 'fist-fucking' (90–3, 98–9), and 'gay male bodybuilding' (115–18).

precisely those 'indecent' realities of body, pleasure and sex that Christianity has preferred to stigmatize (cf. Althaus-Reid 2000).

I do not myself believe that such projects require biblical legitimization. To the extent, however, that one does wish to find biblical precedents for this affirmation of bodily pleasure, Qohelet's admonition to enjoy food, drink and sex may serve as a resource. Qohelet does not find it necessary to justify such pleasures by making them vehicles for some other, presumably higher, religious goal. Food, drink and sex are not justified by Qohelet on the grounds, for example, that through the very real communion with others that takes place through them we may better experience or understand our communion with God. Such pleasures are, according to Qohelet, good in themselves. Indeed, 'there is nothing better for anyone under the sun than to eat and to drink and to enjoy oneself' (Eccl. 8.15). This affirmation – let us never stop reminding ourselves – is a *biblical* affirmation. It may be an unusual one. It may stand in opposition to a great deal that passes for traditional Judaism and, especially, Christianity. Yet, in exactly that respect, its 'heterodox' (Merkin 1987: 396) affirmation, from within the 'orthodox' canons of Judaism and Christianity, of the enjoyment of food, drink and sex as the course approved by God, undermines the supposed boundary between 'orthodoxy' and 'heterodoxy' and contests the normative and normalizing tendencies either to view bodily pleasure with suspicion or, at best, to relegate it to secondary status. Here we surely have a 'queer' biblical text.

Qohelet is not the only biblical book about which some of these statements could be made. The Song of Songs has much more to say about sexual pleasure than does Qohelet, and also uses imagery that presupposes the pleasures of food and drink, as I have pointed out. Perhaps more significantly, it also contests patriarchal assumptions, prevalent within the context that gave us the Bible, in a way that Qohelet does not. In light of the latter difference between the two books one could make a strong argument that the Song of Songs is even more appropriately characterized as a 'queer' biblical text than is Qohelet.

I have nevertheless chosen to end my discussion with a reflection on Qohelet for several specific reasons. I find it intriguing, in the first place, that Qohelet's affirmation of bodily pleasure is, in distinction from that affirmation made by the Song of Songs, articulated explicitly in relation to language about God – that is, to 'theology'. The particular representation of God that we find in Qohelet may or may not be attractive to all of Qohelet's readers, or even to all of Qohelet's queer readers. To the extent, however, that Qohelet does make an explicitly 'theological' statement – by insisting that it is *God* who has approved our enjoyment of the bodily pleasures of food, drink and sex – Qohelet stands as a reminder that the affirmation of bodily pleasure can have specifically *theological* consequences. With this reminder, we may be led to the conclusion that matters of food, sex, body and pleasure need not be understood only as matters for a secondary 'application' of theological ethics, but rather can have a direct impact on the kind of God that we confess.

Attention to Qohelet and its history of interpretation also reminds us that attempts to link God to the affirmation of bodily pleasure are likely to be opposed by those who understand themselves to be guardians of tradition. It has sometimes been suggested that the Wisdom of Solomon – a 'biblical' book for many Christians – is responding, in part, to Qohelet when it describes conclusions reached by the 'ungodly' in Wisdom 1.16–2.11. That passage from Wisdom attributes to the 'ungodly' a position that is in several respects similar to the views promoted by Qohelet. The position that Wisdom is opposing recognizes the fleeting nature of life, the fact that life has no certain remedy after death, and the likelihood that those who die are quickly forgotten; all of these themes appear in Qohelet. More significantly, the 'ungodly' position described by Wisdom promotes the enjoyment of life on the basis that 'this is our portion, and this is our lot' (Wisdom 2.9, NRSV). Such language sounds remarkably similar to the argument for the enjoyment of bodily pleasure made by Qohelet in 9.7–9; and commentators on the Wisdom of Solomon (e.g., Winston 1979: 119) rightly note the parallel. Whether or not the author of Wisdom is referring specifically to Qohelet (as some commentators believe (e.g., Gordis 1955: 295)), it is obvious that Wisdom is opposing a perspective that is close to the one espoused by Qohelet. In this instance, it is the Wisdom of Solomon, rather than Qohelet, that promotes the more orthodox view, and, in light of this fact, it is somewhat ironic – and queerly appropriate – that Qohelet is now included in all of the official canons of Judaism and Christianity (even if it is more often than not ignored) whereas the Wisdom of Solomon is excluded from 'the Bible' by all of the various branches of Judaism and by most Protestant forms of Christianity. The primary point I wish to make, however, with my reference to the Wisdom of Solomon, is that the very sort of affirmation of the enjoyment of bodily pleasure that Qohelet promotes was opposed as 'ungodly' by the guardians of orthodoxy no later than the first century of the Common Era.[20] We should not be surprised, then, but should assume as a matter of course, that queer affirmations of bodily pleasure are, and will continue to be, fiercely denounced today. We should not be surprised, but should assume as a matter of course, that religious opponents of lesbians, gay men and bisexuals will attack our unapologetic appreciation of the pleasures of life as 'high-risk, aggressive, and dehumanizing behavior ... behavior that God finds detestable' (Gagnon 2001: 475, 489). Such orthodox chatter should not in any way cause us to doubt that the enjoyment of the bodily pleasures of food, drink and sex are, as Qohelet insists, approved by God.

Is my appeal to Qohelet consistent with my call for 'practicing safer text'? The occasional inclusion in Qohelet of obviously patriarchal statements (e.g., 7.26–28) rightly gives us pause. A crucial goal of education around 'safer sex', it needs to be recalled, is to foster awareness that one can respond to the dangers of sexually transmitted disease without abandoning the desire and determination to enjoy the pleasures of sex. Working toward this goal, safer sex educators increasingly recognize the need to avoid discussing sexual activity in simplistic, 'either-or' categories. Safer sex is not about the rejection of particular types of sexual partners (e.g., gay men, or persons infected with HIV) or particular types of sexual practices (e.g., anal intercourse), but rather about careful and responsible reflection on the possibility that HIV or other pathogens will be transmitted between particular

20. Although the Wisdom of Solomon is difficult to date, most scholars place its composition during the first century B.C.E. or the first century C.E. See Winston 1979: 20–5.

people participating in particular activities in particular contexts. Attention to the difference that is made by particularities of context and situation is crucial if one wants to promote both responsible awareness of relative risk and a non-moralizing affirmation of sexual pleasure. So, too, the relative risks of the ingestion of particular foodstuffs depend a great deal on factors that vary from situation to situation – including the way in which the food in question has been prepared, the health condition of the person who is eating, the type and amount of food and drink (and hence, the amount of calories, nutrients, fat grams and so forth) that have been or will be consumed in temporal proximity, and so forth. What one needs in such situations, in order to distinguish relative risk from relative safety, is not a firm list of universalized sex or food rules, or a firm list of acceptable and prohibited items or activities, considered equally valid for everyone, everywhere. Rather, one must combine adequate information with the kind of practical wisdom (I have chosen the word intentionally) that allows one to assess the relevance of that information for the particular situation in which one finds oneself, and for the particular pleasures that one hopes to enjoy.

In just the same way, I want to argue that an approach to biblical interpretation which recognizes the potentially dangerous effects of reading certain texts in certain situations – because, for example, those texts incorporate patriarchal assumptions – need not proceed by distinguishing, in a simplistic and totalizing way, 'good' texts from 'bad' texts. What one needs is not a firm list of universalized hermeneutical rules, or a firm list of acceptable and prohibited texts, considered equally valid for everyone, everywhere. Rather, one must combine adequate information about particular biblical texts, the rhetorical situations in which they were written, and their histories of effects, with the practical wisdom that allows one to assess the relevance of that information for the particular situation in which one finds oneself, and for the particular things that one hopes to accomplish by reading the Bible in that situation.

Let us return, then, to Qohelet. It is obviously important – I would even say crucial – information, for those of us who wish to combat misogyny and the subordination of women to men, that Qohelet was written in a patriarchal society; that it takes the form of a communication between a male speaker and a male audience; that certain parts of that communication (e.g., 7.26–28) articulate misogynistic statements; and that these statements have been used to justify horrific actions taken against women by readers of the Bible (cf. Fontaine 1998b, 1998c; Christianson 1998). It will be tempting, in the light of such information, to insist that such a book should simply not be read, let alone discussed positively by biblical scholars who claim to be concerned about the development of 'safer text'. But it is important to remember the point, made earlier in this chapter, that patriarchal society has in the past often been characterized precisely by a tendency to interpret the world in dualistic categories. Both Proverbs and *Fatal Attraction*, we should recall, accomplish their representation of the world by, among other things, dividing women into the binary categories of 'good women' and 'bad women', so as to argue that the latter women must be avoided as dangerous. Clearly, we would not want to replicate such an unsatisfactory procedure by dividing biblical books simplistically into the binary categories of 'good texts' (texts in which, presumably, we would find no flaws and no potential for dangerous effects – though I am rather doubtful that any such texts actually exist) and 'bad texts' (texts which are thought to be characterized primarily by their negative messages or their potential for dangerous effects – which potential, I suspect, is actually present in all texts), so as to argue that the latter texts must always be avoided. It may very well be the case that some readers in some situations should not read Qohelet. Certainly Qohelet 7.26–28, in particular, should not be read by all readers in all situations, and I cannot myself imagine any situation whatsoever in which these verses ought to be proclaimed as an 'authoritative' statement on the nature of women or anything else. Nevertheless, to rule out the possibility that one can learn a great deal from the careful study of texts with which one, in the end, fundamentally disagrees, or which one can show to have had damaging effects in the past or to have potentially damaging effects in the present or the future, would be as foolish as a decision to restrict research into those pathogens that, by way of food or sex, cause potential harm to our bodies. It may be the case that those texts which are most troubling, or for which the most damaging effects can be imagined, are precisely the texts that most need to be taught, with all the care and critical attention that good teaching entails.

What is the attitude with which texts like Qohelet ought to be taught? Krister Stendahl, reflecting on the damaging way in which the New Testament has been read to justify the subordination of women and the persecution of Jews, observed that he increasingly understood his own role as a teacher of Bible in terms of

> what you might call the Public Health Department of biblical studies. What can be said? What can be done? What are the resources? What are the theological issues for an interpretation of the Scriptures that does not produce a harmful fallout, to use the metaphor from atomic power?... I have come to believe that the problem calls for frontal attention to what I have called the public health aspect of interpretation. How does the church live with its Bible without undesirable effects?   (Stendahl 1982: 205)

One need not adopt all of the details of Stendahl's proposals for biblical interpretation in order to be persuaded by his argument that the challenge most facing biblical interpretation today is the challenge of 'living' with the Bible – of 'opting for life' – while avoiding 'undesirable effects'. It is hardly surprising that Stendahl's 'public health' metaphor for biblical interpretation has been remembered, in print, primarily by feminist biblical scholars (e.g., Schüssler Fiorenza 1999: 31–2; Brooten 1999). After all, feminist biblical scholars, precisely as biblical scholars, continue to advocate close biblical study, but are usually explicit about avoiding the Bible's 'undesirable effects'. For a reader and teacher of the Bible such as myself, concerned as I am to 'think' food, sex and biblical interpretation together, the lure of the 'public health' imagery proves irresistible – as the title of this volume testifies. In particular, it helps us recognize that attention to potential harmful effects, and attention to possible pleasurable effects, need not be separated absolutely. As Qohelet himself argues, 'it is good for you to grasp onto this, without allowing your hand to let go of that' (7.18). The fact that a particular act of eating – let us say, the ingestion of a significant amount of honey by a person with diabetes – can have potentially dangerous effects does not lead dieticians to rule out the possibility, indeed the likelihood, that the ingestion of honey can also be, for many people in many situations, a pleasurable and nutritional experience. The fact that a particular sex act – let us say, anal intercourse without a condom between two men of discordant HIV-status – can have potentially dangerous effects does not lead safer sex educators to rule out the possibility, indeed the likelihood, that anal intercourse between men can also be, for many men in many situations, a healthy, pleasurable and rewarding experience. So, too, the fact that one can imagine quite troubling circumstances under which Qohelet might be read – let us say, when 7.26–28 is read as an accurate and divinely revealed statement about the nature of women – should not lead us to avoid opportunities for constructive theological attention to, and pleasurable use of, Qohelet. Rather, we need to create opportunities for people to have better information about biblical texts and biblical interpretation. We need to encourage readers of the Bible to take responsibility for their own roles as active agents and critical transformers of the traditions in which they stand. We need to foster the wisdom that it will always take for fallible human beings to make better decisions about the constructive use of such information, and the constructive deployment of such agency, in the vagaries of context and situation in which all of us live. Under such conditions, we may be able to encourage readers to recognize that they can follow Qohelet's own example of standing consciously in a particular tradition, while actively contesting assumptions embedded deeply in that tradition – including, no doubt, assumptions made by Qohelet itself. Under such conditions, we may once again be able to hear and proclaim safely Qohelet's message that enjoyment of the bodily pleasures of food, drink and sex is one of the best things we can do with our lives, and has been ordained by God. Under such conditions it may truly turn out to be the case that biblical interpretation will yet provide water, wine and milk for the one who thirsts, and true bread and rich food for the one who hungers (cf. Isa. 55.1–2).

BIBLIOGRAPHY

Abelove, Henry, Michèle Aina Barale, and David M. Halperin, eds. 1992. *The Lesbian and Gay Studies Reader*, New York: Routledge.

Abu-Lughod, Lila. 1986. *Veiled Sentiments: Honor and Poetry in a Bedouin Society*, Berkeley: University of California Press.

Abusch, Tzvi. 1993. 'Gilgamesh's Request and Siduri's Denial (Part I)', in Mark E. Cohen, David C. Snell and David B. Weisberg, eds., *The Tablet and the Scroll: Near Eastern Studies in Honor of W.W. Hallo*, Bethesda: CDL Press.

Ackerman, James. 1990. 'Knowing Good and Evil: A Literary Analysis of the Court History in 2 Samuel 9–20 and I Kings 1–2', *JBL* 109/1: 41–60.

Adam, A.K.M. 1995. *What Is Postmodern Biblical Criticism?* Minneapolis: Fortress Press.

Adam, A.K.M., ed. 2000. *Handbook of Postmodern Biblical Interpretation*, St. Louis: Chalice Press.

Ahlström, Gösta W. 1986. *Who Were the Israelites?* Winona Lake: Eisenbrauns.

Aho, James. 2002. *The Orifice as Sacrificial Site: Culture, Organization, and the Body*, New York: Walter de Gruyter, Inc.

Albright, William F. 1957. *From the Stone Age to Christianity: Monotheism and the Historical Process*, second edition, Baltimore: Johns Hopkins Press.

——. 1961. 'The Role of the Canaanites in the History of Civilization', in G. Ernest Wright, ed., *The Bible and the Ancient Near East: Essays in Honor of William Foxwell Albright*, Garden City: Doubleday.

——. 1968. *Yahweh and the Gods of Canaan: A Historical Analysis of Two Contrasting Faiths*, London: Athlone Press.

Alter, Robert. 1979. 'A New Theory of Kashrut', *Commentary* 68/2: 46–51.

Althaus-Reid, Marcella. 2000. *Indecent Theology: Theological Perversions in Sex, Gender and Politics*, New York: Routledge.

Altman, Dennis. 2001. *Global Sex*, Chicago: University of Chicago Press.

Altman, Lawrence K. 2001. 'Swift Rise Seen in H.I.V. Cases for Gay Blacks', *The New York Times*. http://www.nytimes.com/2001/06/01/health/01IMMU.html

Anderson, Gary A. 1992. 'Sacrifice and Sacrificial Offerings (OT)', in David Noel Freedman, *et al.*, eds., *The Anchor Bible Dictionary*, Volume 5. New York: Doubleday.

Anderson, Francis I., and David Noel Freedman. 1980. *Hosea: A New Translation with Introduction and Commentary*, Anchor Bible Commentary. Garden City: Doubleday.

Appler, Deborah A. 1999. 'From Queen to Cuisine: Food Imagery in the Jezebel Narrative', in Brenner and van Henten, eds., 1999.

Arbel, Daphna. 2000. 'My Vineyard, My Very Own, Is For Myself', in Brenner and Fontaine, eds., 2000.

Arbesmann, Rudolph. 1949–51. 'Fasting and Prophecy in Pagan and Christian Antiquity', *Traditio* 7: 1–71.

Arens, W. 1979. *The Man-Eating Myth: Anthropology and Anthropophagy*, Oxford: Oxford University Press.

Asad, Talal, ed. 1973. *Anthropology and the Colonial Encounter*, Amherst: Humanity Books.

Ateek, Naim Stifan. 1991. 'A Palestinian Perspective: The Bible and Liberation', in Sugirtharajah, ed., 1991.

Austin, J.L. 1975. *How to Do Things with Words*, second edition, edited by J.O. Urmson and Marina Sbisà. Cambridge: Harvard University Press.

Bach, Alice. 1993. 'Reading Allowed: Feminist Biblical Criticism Approaching the Millenium', *Currents in Research: Biblical Studies* 1: 191–215.

——. 1997. *Women, Seduction, and Betrayal in Biblical Narrative*, Cambridge: Cambridge University Press.

Bailey, Randall. 1995. ' "They're Nothing but Incestuous Bastards": The Polemical Use of Sex and Sexuality in Hebrew Canon Narratives', in Segovia and Tolbert, eds., 1995a.

Bal, Mieke. 1987. *Lethal Love: Feminist Literary Readings of Biblical Love Stories*, Bloomington: Indiana University Press.

——. 1988a. *Murder and Difference: Gender, Genre, and Scholarship on Sisera's Death*, trans. Matthew Gumpert. Bloomington: Indiana University Press.

——. 1988b. *Death and Dissymmetry: The Politics of Coherence in the Book of Judges*, Chicago: University of Chicago Press.

——. 1991a. *On Story-Telling: Essays in Narratology*, ed. David Jobling. Sonoma: Polebridge Press.

——. 1991b. *Reading Rembrandt: Beyond the Word-Image Opposition*, Cambridge: Cambridge University Press.

——. 1993. 'A Body of Writing: Judges 19', in Brenner, ed., 1993a.

——. 1997 [1985]. *Narratology: Introduction to the Theory of Narrative*, second edition, Toronto: University of Toronto Press.

Barr, James. 1981. 'The Bible as a Document of Believing Communities', in Hans Dieter Betz, ed., *The Bible as a Document of the University*, Chico: Scholars Press.

——. 1992. *The Garden of Eden and the Hope of Immortality*, Minneapolis: Fortress Press.

——. 1999. *The Concept of Biblical Theology: An Old Testament Perspective*, Minneapolis: Fortress Press.

Bartky, Sandra. 1988. 'Foucault, Femininity, and the Modernization of Patriarchal Power', in Irene Diamond and Lee Quinby, eds., *Feminism and Foucault: Reflections on Resistance*, Boston: Northeastern University Press.

Barton, George Aaron. 1959 [1908]. *A Critical and Exegetical Commentary on the Book of Ecclesiastes*, The International Critical Commentary, Edinburgh: T. & T. Clark.

Barton, John. 1998. 'Introduction', in John Barton, ed., *The Cambridge Companion to Biblical Interpretation*, Cambridge: Cambridge University Press.

Bassett, Frederick W. 1971. 'Noah's Nakedness and the Curse of Canaan: A Case of Incest?' *VT* 21/2: 232–7.

Batto, Bernard F. 1992. *Slaying the Dragon: Mythmaking in the Biblical Tradition*, Louisville: Westminster/John Knox Press.

Beal, Timothy K., and David M. Gunn, eds. 1997. *Reading Bibles, Writing Bodies: Identity and the Book*, New York: Routledge.

Beardsworth, Alan, and Teresa Keil. 1997. *Sociology on the Menu: An Invitation to the Study of Food and Society*, New York: Routledge.

Behar, Ruth, and Deborah Gordon, eds. 1996. *Women Writing Culture*, Berkeley: University of California Press.

Bekkenkamp, Jonneke, and Fokkelien van Dijk. 1993 [1987]. 'The Canon of the Old Testament and Women's Cultural Traditions', in Brenner, ed., 1993b.

Bell, Rudolph M. 1985. *Holy Anorexia*, Chicago: University of Chicago Press.

Berlant, Lauren, and Michael Warner. 1995. 'What Does Queer Theory Teach Us About *X*?' *Publications of the Modern Language Association of America* 3: 343–9.

——. 1998. 'Sex in Public', *Critical Inquiry* 24: 547–66.

Berquist, Jon L. 2002. *Controlling Corporality: The Body and the Household in Ancient Israel*, New Brunswick: Rutgers University Press.

Bible and Culture Collective, The. 1995. *The Postmodern Bible*, New Haven: Yale University Press.

Binger, Tilde. 1997. *Asherah: Goddesses in Ugarit, Israel and the Old Testament*, Sheffield: Sheffield Academic Press.

Bird, Phyllis A. 1997a. *Missing Persons and Mistaken Identities: Women and Gender in Ancient Israel*, Minneapolis: Fortress Press.

——. 1997b. 'The End of the Male Cult Prostitute: A Literary-Historical and Sociological Analysis of Hebrew *QADES-QEDESIM*', in J. Emerton, ed., *Congress Volume: Cambridge 1995*, Sup*VT*. Leiden: E.J. Brill.

——. 2000. 'The Bible in Christian Ethical Deliberation Concerning Homosexuality: Old Testament Contributions', in David L. Balch, ed., *Homosexuality, Science, and the 'Plain Sense' of Scripture*, Grand Rapids: Eerdmans.

Black, Fiona C. 2000. 'Unlikely Bedfellows: Allegorical and Feminist Readings of Song of Songs 7:1–8', in Brenner and Fontaine, eds., 2000.

——. 2001. 'Nocturnal Egression: Exploring Some Margins of the Song of Songs', in Adam, ed., 2000.

Bleys, Rudi C. 1995. *The Geography of Perversion: Male-to-Male Sexual Behavior Outside the West and the Ethnographic Imagination, 1750–1918*, New York: New York University Press.

Bloch-Smith, Elizabeth. 2003. 'Israelite Ethnicity in Iron I: Archaeology Preserves What Is Remembered and What Is Forgotten in Israel's History', *Journal of Biblical Literature* 122/3: 401–25.

Blok, Anton. 1981. 'Rams and Billy-Goats: A Key to the Mediterranean Code of Honour', *Man* 16: 427–40.

Boer, Roland. 1999. *Knockin' On Heaven's Door: The Bible and Popular Culture*, New York: Routledge.

——. 2000. 'The Second Coming: Repetition and Insatiable Desire in the Song of Songs', *Biblical Interpretation* 8/3: 276–301.

Boisvert, Donald L. 2000. *Out On Holy Ground: Meditations on Gay Men's Spirituality*, Cleveland: The Pilgrim Press.

Bordo, Susan. 1993. *Unbearable Weight: Feminism, Western Culture, and the Body*, Berkeley: University of California Press.

——. 1999. *The Male Body: A New Look at Men in Public and Private*, New York: Farrar, Straus and Giroux.

Borowski, Oded. 1987. *Agriculture in Iron Age Israel*, Winona Lake: Eisenbrauns.

——. 1992. 'Agriculture', in David Noel Freedman, *et al.*, eds., *The Anchor Bible Dictionary*, Volume I. New York: Doubleday.

Bourdieu, Pierre. 1979. *Algeria 1960*. Cambridge: Cambridge University Press.

——. 1984. *Distinction: A Social Critique of the Judgement of Taste*, trans. Richard Nice. Cambridge: Harvard University Press.

Boyarin, Daniel. 1993. *Carnal Israel: Reading Sex in Talmudic Culture*, Berkeley: University of California Press.

——. 1995. 'Are There Any Jews in "The History of Sexuality"?' *Journal of the History of Sexuality* 5.3: 333–55.

Brakke, David. 1995. 'The Problematization of Nocturnal Emissions in Early Christian Syria, Egypt, and Gaul', *Journal of Early Christian Studies* 3.4: 419–60.

Bratman, Steven. 2001. *Health Food Junkies: Overcoming the Obsession with Healthful Eating*, New York: Broadway Books.

Brawley, Robert L., ed. 1996. *Biblical Ethics and Homosexuality: Listening to Scripture*. Louisville: Westminster/John Knox Press.

Brenner, Athalya. 1985. *The Israelite Woman: Social Role and Literary Type*, Sheffield: Sheffield Academic Press.

——. 1989. *The Song of Songs*, Sheffield: Sheffield Academic Press.

——. 1997. *The Intercourse of Knowledge: On Gendering Desire and Sexuality in the Hebrew Bible*, Leiden: Brill.

——. 1999. 'The Food of Love: Gendered Food and Food Imagery in the Song of Songs', in Brenner and van Henten, eds., 1999.

Brenner, Athalya, ed. 1993a. *A Feminist Companion to Judges*, Sheffield: Sheffield Academic Press.

——. 1993b. *A Feminist Companion to The Song of Songs*, Sheffield: Sheffield Academic Press.

——. 1995a. *A Feminist Companion to the Latter Prophets*, Sheffield: Sheffield Academic Press.

——. 1995b. *A Feminist Companion to Wisdom Literature*, Sheffield: Sheffield Academic Press.

——. 2000. *Samuel and Kings: A Feminist Companion to the Bible* (Second Series), Sheffield: Sheffield Academic Press.

Brenner, Athalya, and Fokkelien van Dijk-Hemmes. 1993. *On Gendering Texts: Female and Male Voices in the Hebrew Bible*, Leiden: E.J. Brill.

Brenner, Athalya, and Carole R. Fontaine, eds. 1998. *Wisdom and Psalms: A Feminist Companion to the Bible* (Second Series), Sheffield: Sheffield Academic Press.

——. 2000. *The Song of Songs: A Feminist Companion to the Bible* (Second Series), Sheffield: Sheffield Academic Press.

Brenner, Athalya, and Jan Willem van Henten, eds. 1999. *Food and Drink in the Biblical Worlds*, *Semeia* 86, Atlanta: Society of Biblical Literature.

Brett, Mark G. 2000. *Genesis: Procreation and the Politics of Identity*, New York: Routledge.

Brooten, Bernadette. 1996. *Love Between Women: Early Christian Responses to Female Homoeroticism*, Chicago: University of Chicago Press.

——. 1999. 'Stendahl, Krister', *Dictionary of Biblical Interpretation*, ed. John H. Hayes. 2 volumes. Nashville: Abingdon Press.

Brown, Peter. 1985. 'The Notion of Virginity in the Early Church', in Bernard McGinn, John Meyendorff and Jean Leclercq, eds., *Christian Spirituality: Origins to the Twelfth Century*, New York: Crossroad.

——. 1988. *The Body and Society: Men, Women, and Sexual Renunciation in Early Christianity*, New York: Columbia University Press.

Brueggemann, Walter. 1997. *Theology of the Old Testament: Testimony, Dispute, Advocacy*, Minneapolis: Fortress Press.

——. 2002. *Reverberations of Faith: A Theological Handbook of Old Testament Themes*, Louisville: Westminster John Knox Press.

——. 2003. *An Introduction to the Old Testament: The Canon and Christian Imagination*, Louisville: Westminster/John Knox Press.

Brumberg, Joan Jacobs. 1988. *Fasting Girls: The History of Anorexia Nervosa*, Cambridge: Harvard University Press.

Buell, Denise Kimber. 1999. *Making Christians: Clement of Alexandria and the Rhetoric of Legitimacy*, Princeton: Princeton University Press.

Buenting, Julianne. 2003. 'Ambivalence and the Pleasures of the Flesh: Disordered Eating, Sexuality and Christian Ascesis', paper presented at the annual meeting of the American Academy of Religion, Atlanta, Georgia, November 2003.

Bulmer, Ralph. 1967. 'Why Is the Cassowary Not a Bird? A Problem of Zoological Taxonomy Among the Karam of the New Guinea Highlands', *Man* 2: 5–25.

Butler, Judith. 1990. *Gender Trouble: Feminism and the Subversion of Identity*, New York: Routledge.

——. 1993. *Bodies that Matter: On the Discursive Limits of 'Sex'*, New York: Routledge.

——. 1994. 'Against Proper Objects', *differences* 6.2–3: 1–26.

Bynum, Caroline Walker. 1987. *Holy Feast and Holy Fast: The Religious Significance of Food to Medieval Women*, Berkeley: University of California Press.

Califia, Pat. 2000. *Public Sex: The Culture of Radical Sex*, second edition. Pittsburgh: Cleis Press.

Camp, Claudia V. 1985. *Wisdom and the Feminine in the Book of Proverbs*, Sheffield: Almond Press.

—. 1991. 'What's So Strange About the Strange Woman?', in David Jobling, Peggy L. Day and Gerald T. Sheppard, eds., *The Bible and the Politics of Exegesis*, Cleveland: Pilgrim Press.

—. 1997. 'Woman Wisdom and the Strange Woman: Where is Power to be Found?', in Beal and Gunn, eds., 1997.

—. 2000. *Wise, Strange and Holy: The Strange Woman and the Making of the Bible*, Sheffield: Sheffield Academic Press.

Campbell, Edward F. 1975. *Ruth: A New Translation with Introduction, Notes, and Commentary*, The Anchor Bible, Garden City: Doubleday.

Capaldi, Elizabeth D., ed. 1996. *Why We Eat What We Eat: The Psychology of Eating*, Washington, D.C.: American Psychological Association.

Carden, Michael. 1999. 'Homophobia and Rape in Sodom and Gibeah: A Response to Ken Stone', *JSOT* 82: 83–96.

Carr, David M. 2003. *The Erotic Word: Sexuality, Spirituality, and the Bible*, Oxford: Oxford University Press.

Carroll, Michael. 1985 [1978]. 'One More Time: Leviticus Revisited', in Bernhard Lang, ed., *Anthropological Approaches to the Old Testament*, Philadelphia: Fortress Press.

Carroll, Robert P. 1995. 'Desire under the Terebinths: On Pornographic Representation in the Prophets – A Response', in Brenner, ed., 1995.

—. 1999. 'YHWH's Sour Grapes: Images of Food and Drink in the Prophetic Discourses of the Hebrew Bible', in Brenner and van Henten, eds., 1999.

Cheng, Patrick S. 2002. 'Multiplicity and Judges 19: Constructing a Queer Asian Pacific American Biblical Hermeneutic', in Liew, ed., 2002.

Christianson, Eric S. 1998. 'Qoheleth the "Old Boy" and Qoheleth the "New Man": Misogynism, the Womb and a Paradox in Ecclesiastes', in Brenner and Fontaine, eds., 1998.

Clack, Beverley. 2002. *Sex and Death: A Reappraisal of Human Mortality*, Cambridge: Polity Press.

Clark, Elizabeth A. 1986. *Ascetic Piety and Women's Faith: Essays on Late Ancient Christianity*, Lewiston: Edwin Mellen Press.

—. 1989. 'Theory and Practice in Late Ancient Asceticism', *Journal of Feminist Studies in Religion* 5.2: 25–46.

—. 1999. *Reading Renunciation: Asceticism and Scripture in Early Christianity*, Princeton: Princeton University Press.

Clark, J. Michael. 1997. *Defying the Darkness: Gay Theology in the Shadows*, Cleveland: Pilgrim Press.

Clarke, W.K.L. 1925. *The Ascetic Works of Saint Basil*, London: S.P.C.K.

Clifford, James. 1988. *The Predicament of Culture: Twentieth-Century Ethnography, Literature, and Art*, Cambridge: Harvard University Press.

Clifford, James, and George E. Marcus, eds. 1986. *Writing Culture: The Poetics and Politics of Ethnography*, Berkeley: University of California Press.

Clines, David J.A. 1995. *Interested Parties: The Ideology of Writers and Readers of the Hebrew Bible*, Sheffield: Sheffield Academic Press.

Coats, George W. 1983. *Genesis: With an Introduction to Narrative Literature*, Grand Rapids: Eerdmans.

Cohn, Robert L. 1994. 'Before Israel: The Canaanite as Other in Biblical Tradition', in Laurence L. Silberstein and Robert L. Cohn, eds., *The Other in Jewish Thought and History: Constructions of Jewish Culture and Identity*, New York: New York University Press.

Collins, John J. 2003. 'The Zeal of Phinehas: The Bible and the Legitimation of Violence', *JBL* 122/1: 3–21.

Comstock, Gary David. 1991. *Violence Against Lesbians and Gay Men*, New York: Columbia University Press.

Coogan, Michael David. 1987. 'Canaanite Origins and Lineage: Reflections on the Religion of Ancient Israel', in Patrick D. Miller, Paul D. Hanson and S. Dean McBride, eds., *Ancient Israelite Religion: Essays in Honor of Frank Moore Cross*, Philadelphia: Fortress Press.

Coote, Robert B. 1990. *Early Israel: A New Horizon*. Minneapolis: Fortress Press.

Coote, Robert B, and Keith W. Whitelam. 1987. *The Emergence of Israel in Historical Perspective*. Sheffield: Sheffield Academic Press.

Corrington, Christopher. 1999. *No Place Like Home: Relationships and Family Life among Lesbians and Gay Men*, Chicago: University of Chicago Press.

Counihan, Carole M. 1999. *The Anthropology of Food and Body: Gender, Meaning, and Power*, New York: Routledge.

Counihan, Carole, and Penny Van Esterik, eds. 1997. *Food and Culture: A Reader*, New York: Routledge.

Countryman, L. William. 1988. *Dirt, Greed and Sex: Sexual Ethics in the New Testament and Their Implications for Today*, Philadelphia: Fortress Press.

Coward, Rosalind. 1985. *Female Desires: How They Are Sought, Bought and Packaged*, New York: Grove Weidenfeld.

Crenshaw, James L. 1981. *Old Testament Wisdom: An Introduction*, Atlanta: John Knox Press.

——. 1987. *Ecclesiastes: A Commentary*, Philadelphia: Westminster Press.

Crimp, Douglas. 2002. *Melancholia and Moralism: Essays on AIDS and Queer Politics*, Cambridge: MIT Press.

Crimp, Douglas, ed. 1988. *AIDS: Cultural Analysis, Cultural Activism*, Cambridge: MIT Press.

Dalley, Stephanie. 1989. *Myths from Mesopotamia: Creation, the Flood, Gilgamesh and Others*, Oxford: Oxford University Press.

Dangerous Bedfellows, ed. 1996. *Policing Public Sex: Queer Politics and the Future of AIDS Activism*, Boston: South End Press.

Davaney, Sheila Greeve. 2000. *Pragmatic Historicism: A Theology for the Twenty-First Century*, Albany: State University of New York Press.

Davidson, Arnold I. 2001. *The Emergence of Sexuality: Historical Epistemology and the Formation of Concepts*, Cambridge: Harvard University Press.

Davis, John. 1969. 'Honour and Politics in Pisticci', *Proceedings of the Royal Anthropological Institute of Great Britain and Ireland* 1969: 69–81.

——. 1977. *People of the Mediterranean: An Essay in Comparative Social Anthropology*, London: Routledge and Kegan Paul.

Day, Peggy L., ed. 1989. *Gender and Difference in Ancient Israel*, Minneapolis: Fortress Press.

Delaney, Carol. 1987. 'Seeds of Honor, Fields of Shame', in Gilmore, ed., 1987.

——. 1991. *The Seed and the Soil: Gender and Cosmology in Turkish Village Society*, Berkeley: University of California Press.

——. 1998. *Abraham on Trial: The Social Legacy of Biblical Myth*, Princeton: Princeton University Press.

Delany, Samuel R. 1999. *Times Square Red, Times Square Blue*, New York: New York University Press.

de Lauretis, Teresa. 1984. *Alice Doesn't: Feminism, Semiotics, Cinema*, Bloomington: Indiana University Press.

——. 1987. *Technologies of Gender: Essays on Theory, Film, and Fiction*, Bloomington: Indiana University Press.

——. 1990. 'Eccentric Subjects: Feminist Theory and Historical Consciousness', *Feminist Studies* 16/1: 115–50.

D'Emilio, John. 1983. 'Capitalism and Gay Identity', in Ann Snitow, Christine Stansell and Sharon Thompson, eds., *Powers of Desire: The Politics of Sexuality*, New York: Monthly Review Press.

Derrida, Jacques. 1988. *Limited Inc.*, Evanston: Northwestern University Press.

DeVault, Marjorie L. 1991. *Feeding the Family: The Social Organization of Caring as Gendered Work*, Chicago: University of Chicago Press.

Dever, William G. 1990. *Recent Archaeological Discoveries and Biblical Research*, Seattle: University of Washington Press.

——. 1992. 'How to Tell a Canaanite from an Israelite', in Hershel Shanks, *et al.*, *The Rise of Ancient Israel*, Washington, D.C.: Biblical Archaeology Society.

——. 2001. *What Did the Biblical Writers Know and When Did They Know It?* Grand Rapids: Eerdmans.

Diaz, Rafael Miguel. 1997. 'Latino Gay Men and Psycho-Cultural Barriers to AIDS Prevention', in Martin P. Levine, Peter M. Nardi and John H. Gagnon, eds., *In Changing Times: Gay Men and Lesbians Encounter HIV/AIDS*, Chicago: University of Chicago Press.

Dijk-Hemmes, Fokkelien van. 1993a. 'Traces of Women's Texts in the Hebrew Bible', in Brenner and van Dijk-Hemmes, 1993.

——. 1993b. 'The Imagination of Power and the Power of Imagination: An Intertextual Analysis of Two Biblical Love Songs: The Song of Songs and Hosea 2', in Brenner, ed., 1993b.

Diner, Hasia R. 2001. *Hungering for America: Italian, Irish and Jewish Foodways in the Age of Migration*, Cambridge: Harvard University Press.

Dinesen, Isak [Karen Blixen]. 1958. 'Babette's Feast', *Anecdotes of Destiny*, New York: Random House.

Dollimore, Jonathan. 1998. *Death, Desire and Loss in Western Culture*, New York: Routledge.

Douglas, Mary. 1966. *Purity and Danger: An Analysis of the Concepts of Pollution and Taboo*, London: Routledge and Kegan Paul.

——. 1975. *Implicit Meanings: Essays in Anthropology*, London: Routledge and Kegan Paul.

——. 1982 [1970]. *Natural Symbols: Explorations in Cosmology*, New York: Pantheon.

——. 1993. *In the Wilderness: The Doctrine of Defilement in the Book of Numbers*, Sheffield: Sheffield Academic Press.

——. 1996a [1993]. 'The Forbidden Animals in Leviticus', in John W. Rogerson, ed., *The Pentateuch: A Sheffield Reader*, Sheffield: Sheffield Academic Press.

——. 1996b. 'Sacred Contagion', in Sawyer, ed., 1996.

——. 1999. *Leviticus as Literature*, Oxford: Oxford University Press.

Dubisch, Jill. 1986. 'Culture Enters through the Kitchen: Women, Food, and Social Boundaries in Rural Greece', in Jill Dubisch, ed., *Gender and Power in Rural Greece*, Princeton: Princeton University Press.

duBois, Page. 1988. *Sowing the Body: Psychoanalysis and Ancient Representations of Women*, Chicago: University of Chicago Press.

Duggan, Lisa, and Nan D. Hunter. 1995. *Sex Wars: Sexual Dissent and Political Culture*, New York: Routledge.

Dumont, Louis. 1980 [1970]. *Homo Hierarchicus: The Caste System and Its Implications*, revised edition, trans. Mark Sainsbury, Louis Dumont and Basia Gulati, Chicago: University of Chicago Press.

Edelman, Diana. 1996. 'Ethnicity and Early Israel', in Mark Brett, ed., *Ethnicity and the Bible*, Leiden: E.J. Brill.

Edwards, George R. 1984. *Gay/Lesbian Liberation: A Biblical Perspective*, New York: Pilgrim Press.

Eilberg-Schwartz, Howard. 1990. *The Savage in Judaism: An Anthropology of Israelite Religion and Ancient Judaism*, Bloomington: Indiana University Press.

——. 1994. *God's Phallus: and Other Problems for Men and Monotheism*, Boston: Beacon Press.

Ellison, Marvin M. 1996. *Erotic Justice: A Liberating Ethic of Sexuality*, Louisville: Westminster/John Knox Press.

Ellison, Marvin M., and Sylvia Thorson-Smith, eds. 2003. *Body and Soul: Rethinking Sexuality as Justice-Love*, Cleveland: Pilgrim Press.

Elm, Susanna. 1994. *'Virgins of God': The Making of Asceticism in Late Antiquity*, Oxford: Oxford University Press.

Exum, J. Cheryl. 1993. *Fragmented Women: Feminist (Sub)Versions of Biblical Narratives*, Valley Forge: Trinity Press International.

——. 1996. *Plotted, Shot, and Painted: Cultural Representations of Biblical Women*, Sheffield: Sheffield Academic Press.

——. 2000. 'Ten Things Every Feminist Should Know about the Song of Songs', in Brenner and Fontaine, eds., 2000.

Fabre-Vassas, Claudine. 1997. *The Singular Beast: Jews, Christians, and the Pig*, trans. Carol Volk, New York: Columbia University Press.

Falk, Marcia. 1982. *Love Lyrics from the Bible: A Translation and Literary Study of The Song of Songs*, Sheffield: Almond Press.

Faludi, Susan. 1991. *Backlash: The Undeclared War Against American Women*, New York: Crown Publishers.

Fardon, Richard. 1999. *Mary Douglas: An Intellectual Biography*, New York: Routledge.

Farquhar, Judith. 2001. *Appetites: Food and Sex in Postsocialist China*, Durham: Duke University Press.

Fausto-Sterling, Anne. 2000. *Sexing the Body: Gender Politics and the Construction of Sexuality*, New York: Basic Books.

Feeley-Harnik, Gillian. 1994. *The Lord's Table: The Meaning of Food in Early Judaism and Christianity*, second edition, Washington, D.C.: Smithsonian Institution Press.

Fernández-Armesto, Felipe. 2002. *Near A Thousand Tables: A History of Food*, New York: The Free Press.

Fewell, Danna Nolan, and David M. Gunn. 1993. *Gender, Power, and Promise: The Subject of the Bible's First Story*, Nashville: Abingdon.

Fiddes, Nick. 1991. *Meat: A Natural Symbol*, New York: Routledge.

Finkelstein, Israel. 1997. 'Pots and Peoples Revisited: Ethnic Boundaries in the Iron Age I', in Neil Asher Silberman and David Small, eds., *The Archaeology of Israel: Constructing the Past, Interpreting the Present*, Sheffield: Sheffield Academic Press.

Finkelstein, Israel, and Neil Asher Silberman. 2001. *The Bible Unearthed: Archaeology's New Vision of Ancient Israel and the Origin of Its Sacred Texts*, New York: Free Press.

Finley, M.I. 1978. *The World of Odysseus*, second revised edition, New York: Penguin Books.

Firmage, Edwin. 1990. 'The Biblical Dietary Laws and the Concept of Holiness', in J.A. Emerton, ed., *Studies in the Pentateuch*, Leiden: E.J. Brill.

Fish, Stanley. 1980. *Is There a Text in This Class? The Authority of Interpretive Communities*, Cambridge: Harvard University Press.

——. 1985. 'Consequences', *Critical Inquiry* 11: 433–58.

Flandrin, Jean-Louis, Massimo Montanari and Albert Sonnenfeld, eds. 1999. *Food: A Culinary History*, trans. Clarissa Botsford, *et al.*, New York: Columbia University Press.

Fokkelman, J.P. 1981. *Narrative Art and Poetry in the Books of Samuel:* Volume I: *King David (II Sam 9–20 & I Kings 1–2*, Assen: Van Gorcum.

Fontaine, Carole. 1995. 'A Response to "Hosea"', in Brenner, ed., 1995a.

——. 1997. 'The Abusive Bible: On the Use of Feminist Method in Pastoral Contexts', in Athalya Brenner and Carole Fontaine, eds., *A Feminist Companion to Reading the Bible: Approaches, Methods and Strategies*, Sheffield: Sheffield Academic Press.

——. 1998a [1992]. 'Proverbs', in Newsom and Ringe, eds., 1998.

——. 1998b [1992]. 'Ecclesiastes', in Newsom and Ringe, eds., 1998.

——. 1998c. '"Many Devices" (Qoheleth 7.23–8.1): Qoheleth, Misogyny and the *Malleus Maleficarum*', in Brenner and Fontaine, eds., 1998.

——. 2000. 'The Voice of the Turtle: Now It's *My* Song of Songs', in Brenner and Fontaine, eds., 2000.

Foster, Benjamin. 1987. 'Gilgamesh: Sex, Love and the Ascent of Knowledge', in John H. Marks and Robert M. Good, eds., *Love and Death in the Ancient Near East: Essays in Honor of Marvin H. Pope*, Guilford: Four Quarters Publishing.

Foucault, Michel. 1985. *The Use of Sexuality*, trans. Robert Hurley. New York: Random House.

——. 1997. *Ethics: Subjectivity and Truth. The Essential Works of Michel Foucault 1954–1984*, trans. Robert Hurley, *et al*. New York: The New Press.

Fowl, Stephen. 1998. *Engaging Scripture: A Model for Theological Interpretation*, Oxford: Blackwell.

Fox, Michael. 1985. *The Song of Songs and the Ancient Egyptian Love Songs*, Madison: University of Wisconsin Press.

——. 1999. *A Time to Tear Down and a Time to Build Up: A Rereading of Ecclesiastes*, Grand Rapids: Eerdmans.

——. 2000. *Proverbs 1–9: A New Translation with Introduction and Commentary*, The Anchor Bible, New York: Doubleday.

Frymer-Kensky, Tikva. 1989. 'Law and Philosophy: The Case of Sex in the Bible', *Semeia* 44: 89–102.

——. 1992. *In the Wake of the Goddesses: Women, Culture, and the Biblical Transformation of Pagan Myth*, New York: Free Press.

——. 2002. *Reading the Women of the Bible: A New Interpretation of Their Stories*, New York: Schocken.

Fuchs, Esther. 2000. *Sexual Politics in the Biblical Narrative: Reading the Hebrew Bible As a Woman*, Sheffield: Sheffield Academic Press.

Fulkerson, Mary McClintock. 1998. '"Is There a (Non-Sexist) Bible in This Church?" A Feminist Case for the Priority of Interpretive Communities', in L. Gregory Jones and James J. Buckley, eds., *Theology and Scriptural Imagination*, Oxford: Blackwell.

Fuss, Diana. 1991. 'Inside/Out', in Diana Fuss, ed., *Inside/Out: Lesbian Theories, Gay Theories*, New York: Routledge.

Gabaccia, Donna. 1998. *We Are What We Eat: Ethnic Food and the Making of Americans*, Cambridge: Harvard University Press.

Gagnon, Robert A.J. 2001. *The Bible and Homosexual Practice: Texts and Hermeneutics*, Nashville: Abingdon.

García-Treto, Francisco O. 1996. 'The Lesson of the Gibeonites: A Proposal for Dialogic Attention as a Strategy for Reading the Bible', in Ada María Isasi-Díaz and Fernando F. Segovia, eds., *Hispanic/Latino Theology: Challenge and Promise*, Minneapolis: Fortress Press.

Garnsey, Peter. 1999. *Food and Society in Classical Antiquity*, Cambridge: Cambridge University Press.

Geertz, Clifford. 1973. *The Interpretation of Cultures*, New York: Basic Books.

——. 1988. *Works and Lives: The Anthropologist as Author*, Stanford: Stanford University Press.

Gibson, J.C.L. 1977. *Canaanite Myths and Legends*, Edinburgh: T. & T. Clark.

Gilmore, David. 1987. 'Introduction: The Shame of Dishonor', in Gilmore, ed., 1987.

——. 1990. *Manhood in the Making: Cultural Concepts of Masculinity*, New Haven: Yale University Press.

Gilmore, David, ed. 1987. *Honor and Shame and the Unity of the Mediterranean*, Washington, D.C.: American Anthropological Association.

Ginsburg, Christian D. 1970. *The Song of Songs and Coheleth (Commonly Called the Book of Ecclesiastes)*, New York: Ktav.

Giovannini, Maureen. 1981. 'Woman: A Dominant Symbol With the Cultural System of a Sicilian Town', *Man* 16: 408–26.

——. 1987. 'Female Chastity Codes in the Circum-Mediterranean: Comparative Perspectives', in Gilmore, ed., 1987.

Gnuse, Robert. 1997. *No Other Gods: Emergent Monotheism in Israel*, Sheffield: Sheffield Academic Press.

Goiten, S.D. 1993 [1957]. 'The Song of Songs: A Female Composition', in Brenner, ed., 1993b.

Goode, Erica. 2001. 'With Fears Fading, More Gays Spurn Old Preventive Message', *The New York Times*. http://www.nytimes.com/2001/08/19/health/19RISK.html

Goody, Jack. 1982. *Cooking, Cuisine and Class: A Study in Comparative Sociology*, Cambridge: Cambridge University Press.

Gordis, Robert. 1955. *Koheleth – The Man and His World*, New York: Bloch Publishing.

Goss, Robert E. 2002. *Queering Christ: Beyond Jesus Acted Up*, Cleveland: Pilgrim Press.

——. 2003. 'Gay Erotic Spirituality and the Recovery of Sexual Pleasure', in Ellison and Thorson-Smith, eds., 2003.

Goss, Robert, and Mona West, eds. 2000. *Take Back the Word: A Queer Reading of the Bible*, Cleveland: Pilgrim Press.

Gottwald, Norman K. 1979. *The Tribes of Yahweh: A Sociology of the Religion of Liberated Israel, 1250–1050 B.C.E.* Maryknoll: Orbis Books.

Goulder, Michael. 1986. *The Song of Fourteen Songs*, Sheffield: Sheffield Academic Press.

Gregor, Thomas. 1985. *Anxious Pleasures: The Sexual Lives of Amazonian People*, Chicago: University of Chicago Press.

Grimm, Veronika E. 1996. *From Feasting to Fasting, the Evolution of a Sin: Attitudes to Food in Late Antiquity*, New York: Routledge.

Gudorf, Christine E. 1994. *Body, Sex, and Pleasure: Reconstructing Christian Sexual Ethics*, Cleveland: Pilgrim Press.

Hackett, Jo Ann. 1989. 'Can A Sexist Model Liberate Us? Ancient Near Eastern "Fertility" Goddesses', *Journal of Feminist Studies in Religion* 5/1: 65–76.

Hadot, Pierre. 1995. *Philosophy as a Way of Life*, edited and with an Introduction by Arnold Davidson, trans. Michael Chase. Oxford: Blackwell.

Halperin, David M. 1990. *One Hundred Years of Homosexuality and Other Essays on Greek Love*, New York: Routledge.

——. 1995. *Saint Foucault: Towards a Gay Hagiography*, Oxford: Oxford University Press.

Halpern, Baruch. 1987. ' "Brisker Pipes Than Poetry": The Development of Israelite

Monotheism', in Jacob Neusner, Baruch A. Levine and Ernest S. Frerichs, eds., *Judaic Perspectives on Ancient Israel*, Philadelphia: Fortress Press.

Harper, Phillip Brian. 1999. *Private Affairs: Critical Ventures in the Culture of Social Relations*, New York: New York University Press.

Harrington, Hannah K. 2001. *Holiness: Rabbinic Judaism and the Graeco-Roman World*, New York: Routledge.

Harris, Rivkah. 2000. *Gender and Aging in Mesopotamia: The Gilgamesh Epic and Other Ancient Literature*, Norman: University of Oklahoma Press.

Hastrup, Kirsten. 1995. *A Passage to Anthropology: Between Experience and Theory*, New York: Routledge.

Haynes, Stephen R. 2002. *Noah's Curse: The Biblical Justification of American Slavery*, Oxford: Oxford University Press.

Heldke, Lisa. 2003. *Exotic Appetites: Ruminations of a Food Adventurer*, New York: Routledge.

Henshaw, Richard A. 1994. *Female and Male: The Cultic Personnel: The Bible and the Rest of the Ancient Near East*, Allison Park, PA: Pickwick Publications.

Hertzberg, Hans Wilhelm. 1964. *I & II Samuel: A Commentary*, Old Testament Library, trans. J. S. Bowden. Philadelphia: Westminster Press.

Herzfeld, Michael. 1980. 'Honor and Shame: Some Problems in the Comparative Analysis of Moral Systems', *Man* 15: 339–51.

——. 1985. *The Poetics of Manhood: Contest and Identity in a Cretan Mountain Village*, Princeton: Princeton University Press.

——. 1987. ' "As in Your Own House": Hospitality, Ethnography, and the Stereotype of Mediterranean Society', in Gilmore, ed., 1987.

Hesse, Brian. 1990. 'Pig Lovers and Pig Haters: Patterns of Palestinian Pork Production', *Journal of Ethnobiology* 10/2: 195–225.

Hesse, Brian, and Paula Wapnish. 1997. 'Can Pig Remains Be Used for Ethnic Diagnosis in the Ancient Near East?', in Neil Asher Silberman and David Small, eds., *The Archaeology of Israel: Constructing the Past, Interpreting the Present*, Sheffield: Sheffield Academic Press.

——. 1998. 'Pig Use and Abuse in the Ancient Levant: Ethnoreligious Boundary Building with Swine', in Sarah M. Nelson, ed., *Ancestors for the Pigs: Pigs in Prehistory*, Philadelphia: University of Pennsylvania Museum of Archaeology and Anthropology.

Hiebert, Theodore. 1996. *The Yahwist's Landscape: Nature and Religion in Early Israel*, Oxford: Oxford University Press.

Hillers, Delbert. 1985. 'Analyzing the Abominable: Our Understanding of Canaanite Religion', *Jewish Quarterly Review* 75/3: 253–69.

Hollibaugh, Amber L. 2000. *My Dangerous Desires: A Queer Girl Dreaming Her Way Home*, Durham: Duke University Press.

Hooks, Stephen M. 1985. 'Sacred Prostitution in Israel and the Ancient Near East', PhD dissertation: Hebrew Union College.

Hooper, Antony. 1976. ' "Eating Blood": Tahitian Concepts of Incest', *Journal of the Polynesian Society* 85: 227–41.

Hopkins, David C. 1985. *The Highlands of Canaan: Agricultural Life in the Early Iron Age*, Sheffield: Almond Press.

Houston, Walter. 1993. *Purity and Monotheism: Clean and Unclean Animals in Biblical Law*, Sheffield: Sheffield Academic Press.

Humphreys, Laud. 1999 [1970]. 'Tearoom Trade: Impersonal Sex in Public Places', in Leap, ed., 1999.

Humphreys, W. Lee. 2001. *The Character of God in the Book of Genesis: A Narrative Appraisal*, Louisville: Westminster/John Knox Press.

Hunt, Mary. 1991. *Fierce Tenderness: A Feminist Theology of Friendship*, New York: Crossroad.

Iggers, Jeremy. 1996. *The Garden of Eating: Food, Sex, and the Hunger for Meaning*, New York: Basic Books.

Inhorn, Marcia C. 1994. *Quest for Conception: Gender, Infertility, and Egyptian Medical Traditions*, Philadelphia: University of Pennsylvania Press.

Inness, Sherrie A. 2001. *Dinner Roles: American Women and Culinary Culture*, Iowa City: University of Iowa Press.

Inness, Sherrie A., ed. 2001a. *Cooking Lessons: The Politics of Gender and Food*, Lanham: Rowman and Littlefield.

——. 2001b. *Pilaf, Pozole, and Pad Thai: American Women and Ethnic Food*, Amherst: University of Massachusetts Press.

Jakobson, Janet R., and Ann Pellegrini. 2003. *Love the Sin: Sexual Regulation and the Limits of Religious Tolerance*, New York: New York University Press.

Jagose, Annamarie. 1996. *Queer Theory: An Introduction*, New York: New York University Press.

Japhet, Sara. 1979. 'Conquest and Settlement in Chronicles', *JBL* 98: 205–18.

Jennings, Theodore W., Jr. 2003. *The Man Jesus Loved: Homoerotic Narratives from the New Testament*, Cleveland: Pilgrim Press.

Johnson, Luke T. 1996. *Scripture and Discernment*, Nashville: Abingdon.

Jones-Warsaw, Koala. 1993. 'Toward a Womanist Hermeneutic: A Reading of Judges 19-21', in Brenner, ed., 1993a.

Jordan, Mark D. 1997. *The Invention of Sodomy in Christian Theology*, Chicago: University of Chicago Press.

——. 2002. *The Ethics of Sex*, Oxford: Blackwell.

Joüon, Paul. 1991. *A Grammar of Biblical Hebrew*, translated and revised by T. Muraoka, Rome: Pontifical Biblical Institute.

Kahn, Miriam. 1994 [1986]. *Always Hungry, Never Greedy: Food and the Expression of Gender in a Melanesian Society*, Prospect Heights: Waveland Press.

Katz, Jonathan Ned. 1995. *The Invention of Heterosexuality*, New York: Dutton.

Keefe, Alice. 1993. 'Rapes of Women/Wars of Men', in Claudia Camp and Carole R. Fontaine, eds., *Women, War, and Metaphor: Language and Society in the Study of the Hebrew Bible*, Semeia 61. Atlanta: Scholars Press.

——. 1995. 'The Female Body, the Body Politic and the Land: A Sociopolitical Reading of Hosea 1–2', in Brenner, ed., 1995a.

——. 2001. *Woman's Body and the Social Body in Hosea*, London: Sheffield Academic Press.

Keuls, Eva C. 1985. *The Reign of the Phallus: Sexual Politics in Ancient Athens*, Berkeley: University of California Press.

King, Christopher. 2000. 'A Love as Fierce as Death: Reclaiming the Song of Songs for Queer Lovers', in Goss and West, eds., 2000.

King, Edward. 1993. *Safety in Numbers: Safer Sex and Gay Men*, New York: Routledge.

King, Philip J., and Lawrence E. Stager. 2001. *Life in Biblical Israel*, Louisville: Westminster/John Knox Press.

Kipnis, Laura. 1999 [1996]. *Bound and Gagged: Pornography and the Politics of Fantasy in America*, Durham: Duke University Press.

——. 2003. *Against Love: A Polemic*, New York: Pantheon Books.

Knapp, Caroline. 2003. *Appetites: Why Women Want*, New York: Counterpoint.

Kramer, Larry. 1997. 'Sex and Sensibility', *The Advocate* 27.

Kristeva, Julia. 1982. *Powers of Horror: An Essay on Abjection*, trans. Leon S. Roudiez. New York: Columbia University Press.

Kwok Pui-Lan. 1995. *Discovering the Bible in the Non-Biblical World*, Maryknoll, NY: Orbis Books.

Laclau, Ernesto, and Chantal Mouffe. 1985. *Hegemony and Socialist Strategy: Towards a Radical Democratic Politics*, London: Verso.

LaCocque, André. 1990. *The Feminine Unconventional: Four Subversive Figures in Israel's Tradition*, Minneapolis: Fortress Press.

——. 1998. *Romance She Wrote: A Hermeneutical Essay on Song of Songs*, Harrisburg: Trinity Press International.

Landy, Francis. 1983. *Paradoxes of Paradise: Identity and Difference in the Song of Songs*, Sheffield: Almond Press.

Lawrence, Marilyn, ed. 1987. *Fed Up and Hungry: Women, Oppression and Food*, New York: Peter Bedrick Books.

Leach, Edmund. 1964. 'Anthropological Aspects of Language: Animal Categories and Verbal Abuse', in Eric H. Lennenberg, ed., *New Directions in the Study of Language*, Cambridge: MIT Press.

Leap, William L., ed. 1999. *Public Sex/Gay Space*, New York: Columbia University Press.

Lee, John Alan. 1990. 'Impersonal Sex and Casual Sex', in Wayne Dynes, ed., *Encyclopedia of Homosexuality*, Volume I. New York: Garland Publishing.

Leick, Gwendolyn. 1994. *Sex and Eroticism in Mesopotamian Literature*, New York: Routledge.

Leith, Mary Joan Winn. 1989. 'Verse and Reverse: The Transformation of the Woman, Israel, in Hosea 1–3', in Peggy L. Day, ed., *Gender and Difference in Ancient Israel*, Minneapolis: Fortress Press.

Lelwica, Michelle Mary. 1999. *Starving for Salvation: The Spiritual Dimensions of Eating Problems among American Girls and Women*, Oxford: Oxford University Press.

Lemche, Niels Peter. 1991. *The Canaanites and Their Land: The Tradition of the Canaanites*, Sheffield: Sheffield Academic Press.

——. 1998. *The Israelites in History and Tradition*, Louisville: Westminster/John Knox Press.

Levenson, Jon D. 1978. 'I Samuel 25 as Literature and History', *CBQ* 40: 11–28.

——. 1993. *The Hebrew Bible, The Old Testament, and Historical Criticism: Jews and Christians in Biblical Studies*, Louisville: Westminster/John Knox Press.

Levenson, Jon D., and Baruch Halpern. 1980. 'The Political Import of David's Marriages', *JBL* 99/4: 507–18.

Lévi-Strauss, Claude. 1963. *Totemism*, trans. Rodney Needham. Boston: Beacon Press.

——. 1969. *The Elementary Structures of Kinship*, revised edition, trans. James Harle Bell, John Richard von Sturmer, and Rodney Needham. Boston: Beacon Press.

Leyerle, Blake. 1995. 'Clement of Alexandria on the Importance of Table Etiquette', *Journal of Early Christian Studies* 3.2: 123–41.

Lichtheim, Miriam. 1973. *Ancient Egyptian Literature:* Volume I: *The Old and Middle Kingdoms*, Berkeley: University of California Press.

——. 1976. *Ancient Egyptian Literature: A Book of Readings:* Volume II: *The New Kingdom*, Berkeley: University of California Press.

Liew, Tat-siong Benny, ed. 2002. *The Bible in Asian America*. Semeia 90–91, Atlanta: Society of Biblical Literature.

Linafelt, Tod. 1992. 'Taking Women in Samuel: Readers/Responses/Responsibilities', in Danna Nolan Fewell, ed., *Reading Between Texts: Intertextuality and the Hebrew Bible*, Philadelphia: Westminster Press.

——. 1999. 'Ruth', in Tod Linafelt and Timothy K. Beal, *Ruth and Esther*, Collegeville: Liturgical Press.

Lindisfarne, Nancy. 1994. 'Variant Masculinities, Variant Virginities: Rethinking "Honour and Shame"', in A. Cornwall and N. Lindisfarne, eds., *Dislocating Masculinity: Comparative Ethnographies*, New York: Routledge.

Long, Ron. 2002. 'A Place for Porn in a Gay Spiritual Economy', *Theology and Sexuality* 16: 21–31.

Longman, Tremper. 1998. *The Book of Ecclesiastes*, Grand Rapids: Eerdmans.

Long, Burke O. 1997. *Planting and Reaping Albright: Politics, Ideology, and Interpreting the Bible*. University Park: Pennsylvania State University Press.

Longo, Oddone. 1999. 'The Food of Others', in Flandrin, Montanari and Sonnenfeld, eds., 1999.

McCarter, P. Kyle, Jr. 1984. *II Samuel*, Anchor Bible Commentary, Garden City: Doubleday.

McClintock, Anne. 1995. *Imperial Leather: Race, Gender and Sexuality in the Colonial Contest*, New York: Routledge.

McKane, William. 1970. *Proverbs: A New Approach*, Philadelphia: Westminster Press.

MacKinnon, Catharine. 1992. 'Does Sexuality Have a History?', in Domna C. Stanton, ed., *Discourses of Sexuality: From Aristotle to AIDS*, Ann Arbor: University of Michigan Press.

McKinlay, Judith E. 1996. *Gendering Wisdom the Host: Biblical Invitations to Eat and Drink*. Sheffield: Sheffield Academic Press.

McKnight, David. 1973. 'Sexual Symbolism of Food Among the Wik-Mungkan', *Man* 8/2: 194–209.

McLaren, Margaret A. 2002. *Feminism, Foucault, and Embodied Subjectivity*, Albany: State University of New York Press.

McNutt, Paula. 1999. *Reconstructing the Society of Ancient Israel*, Louisville: Westminster/John Knox Press.

McWhorter, Ladelle. 1999. *Bodies and Pleasures: Foucault and the Politics of Sexual Normalization*, Bloomington: Indiana University Press.

Malson, Helen. 1998. *The Thin Woman: Feminism, Post-Structuralism and the Social Psychology of Anorexia Nervosa*, New York: Routledge.

Marcus, George E., and Michael M.J. Fischer. 1986. *Anthropology as Cultural Critique: An Experimental Moment in the Human Sciences*, Chicago: University of Chicago Press.

Martin, Dale B. 1993. 'Social-Scientific Criticism', in Steven L. McKenzie and Stephen R. Haynes, eds., *To Each Its Own Meaning: An Introduction to Biblical Criticisms and Their Application*, Louisville: Westminster/John Knox Press.

——. 1995a. 'Heterosexism and the Interpretation of Romans 1:18–32', *Biblical Interpretation* 3.3: 332–55.

——. 1995b. *The Corinthian Body*, New Haven: Yale University Press.

——. 1996. '*Arsenokoitēs* and *Malakos*: Meanings and Consequences', in Brawley, ed., 1996.

Matthews, Victor H. 1992. 'Hospitality and Hostility in Genesis 19 and Judges 19', *Biblical Theology Bulletin* 22/1: 3–11.

Matthews, Victor H., and Don C. Benjamin. 1993. *Social World of Ancient Israel 1250–587 BCE*, Peabody: Hendrickson.

——. 1997. *Laws and Stories from the Ancient Near East*, second edition, New York: Paulist Press.

Mays, James Luther. 1969. *Hosea: A Commentary*, Old Testament Library, Philadelphia: Westminster Press.

Mead, Paul S., *et al.* 1999. 'Food-Related Illness and Death in the United States', *Emerging Infectious Diseases* 5/5: 607–25.

Meigs, Anna S. 1984. *Food, Sex, and Pollution: A New Guinea Religion*, New Brunswick: Rutgers University Press.

Mennell, Stephen. 1996 [1985]. *All Manners of Food: Eating and Taste in England and France from the Middle Ages to the Present*, Urbana: University of Illinois Press.

Merkin, Daphne. 1987. 'Ecclesiastes', in David Rosenberg, ed., *Congregation: Contemporary Jewish Writers Read the Jewish Bible*, San Diego: Harcourt Brace Jovanovich.

Mettinger, Tryggve N.D. 1990. 'The Elusive Presence: YHWH, El and Baal and the Distinctiveness of Israelite Faith', in Erhard Blum, Christian Macholz, and Ekkehard Stegemann, eds., *Die Hebräische Bibel und ihre zweifache Nachgeschichte: Festschrift für Rolf Rendtorff*, Neukirchen-Vluyn: Neukirchener Verlag.

Metz, Johann Baptist. 1986. *The Emergent Church: The Future of Christianity in a Postbourgeois World*, trans. Peter Mann. New York: Crossroad.

Meyers, Carol. 1988. *Discovering Eve: Ancient Israelite Women in Context*, Oxford: Oxford University Press.

——. 1991. '"To Her Mother's House": Considering a Counterpart to the Israelite *Bêt 'āb'*, in David Jobling, Peggy L. Day and Gerald T. Sheppard, eds., *The Bible and the Politics of Exegesis*, Cleveland: Pilgrim Press.

——. 1993 [1986]. 'Gender Imagery in the Song of Songs', in Brenner, ed., 1993b.

Milgrom, Jacob. 1991. *Leviticus 1–16: A New Translation with Introduction and Commentary*, Anchor Bible Commentary, New York: Doubleday.

——. 2000. *Leviticus 17–22: A New Translation and Commentary*, Anchor Bible Commentary, New York: Doubleday.

Moberly, R.W.L. 1988. 'Did the Serpent Get It Right?' *Journal of Theological Studies* 39.1: 1–27.

Modleski, Tania. 1991. *Feminism Without Women: Culture and Criticism in a 'Postfeminist' Age*, New York: Routledge.

Moore, Stephen D. 1989, *Literary Criticism and the Gospels: The Theoretical Challenge*, New Haven: Yale University Press.

——. 1998. 'Que(e)rying Paul: Preliminary Questions', in David J.A. Clines and Stephen D. Moore, eds., *Auguries: The Jubilee Volume of the Sheffield Department of Biblical Studies*, Sheffield: Sheffield Academic Press.

——. 2001. *God's Beauty Parlor: And Other Queer Spaces In and Around the Bible*, Stanford: Stanford University Press.

Mullen, E. Theodore, Jr. 1993. *Narrative History and Ethnic Boundaries: The Deuteronomistic Historian and the Creation of Israelite National Identity*, Atlanta: Scholars Press.

——. 1997. *Ethnic Myths and Pentateuchal Foundations: A New Approach to the Formation of the Pentateuch*, Atlanta: Scholars Press.

Murphy, Roland. 1990. *The Tree of Life: An Exploration of Biblical Wisdom Literature*, New York: Doubleday.

Musurillo, Herbert. 1956. 'The Problem of Ascetical Fasting in the Greek Patristic Writers', *Traditio* 12: 1–64.

Nestle, Marion. 2002. *Food Politics: How the Food Industry Influences Nutrition and Health*, Berkeley: University of California Press.

——. 2003. *Safe Food: Bacteria, Biotechnology, and Bioterrorism*, Berkeley: University of California Press.

Newsom, Carol. 1989. 'Woman and the Discourse of Patriarchal Wisdom: A Study of Proverbs 1–9', in Day, ed., 1989.

Newsom, Carol, and Sharon H. Ringe, eds. 1998 [1992]. *Women's Bible Commentary*, expanded edition. Louisville: Westminster/John Knox Press.

Niditch, Susan. 1998 [1992]. 'Genesis', in Newsom and Ringe, eds., 1998.

Nissinen, Martti. 1998. *Homoeroticism in the Biblical World: A Historical Perspective*, trans. Kirsi Stjerna. Minneapolis· Fortress Press.

Nussbaum, Martha. 1990. 'Therapeutic Arguments and Structures of Desire', *differences* 2/1: 46–66.

Oden, Robert A., Jr. 1987. 'Religious Identity and the Sacred Prostitution Accusation', in *The Bible Without Theology: The Theological Tradition and Alternatives to It*, San Francisco: Harper & Row.

Odets, Walt. 1995. *In the Shadow of the Epidemic: Being HIV-Negative in the Age of AIDS*, Durham: Duke University Press.

Ohnuki-Tierney, Emiko. 1993. *Rice as Self: Japanese Identities Through Time*, Princeton: Princeton University Press.

Okie, Susan. 2001. 'Sharp Drop in AIDS Toll May Be Over', *The Washington Post Online*, http://www.washingtonpost.com/wp-dyn/articles/A6758–2001Aug13. html

O'Leary, Timothy. 2002. *Foucault and the Art of Ethics*, London and New York: Continuum.

Olyan, Saul. 1994. '"And with a Male You Shall Not Lie the Lying Down of a Woman": On the Meaning and Significance of Leviticus 18:22 and 20:13', *Journal of the History of Sexuality* 5.2: 179–206.

——. 2000. *Rites and Rank: Hierarchy in Biblical Representations of Cult*, Princeton: Princeton University Press.

Ortner, Sherry B. 1996. *Making Gender: The Politics and Erotics of Culture*, Boston: Beacon Press.

Ostriker, Alicia. 2000. 'A Holy of Holies: The Song of Songs as Countertext', in Brenner and Fontaine, eds., 2000.

Overholt, Thomas W. 1996. *Cultural Anthropology and the Old Testament*, Minneapolis: Fortress Press.

Pagels, Elaine. 1988. *Adam, Eve, and the Serpent*, London: Weidenfeld and Nicolson.

Pardes, Ilana. 1992. *Countertraditions in the Bible: A Feminist Approach*, Cambridge: Harvard University Press.

Parker, Richard. 1994. 'Sexual Cultures, HIV Transmission, and AIDS Prevention', *AIDS* 8, Supplement 1.

Patton, Cindy. 1996. *Fatal Advice: How Safe-Sex Education Went Wrong*, Durham: Duke University Press.

Penley, Contance, ed. 1988. *Feminism and Film Theory*, New York: Routledge.

Peterson, John L. 1997. 'AIDS-Related Risks and Same-Sex Behaviors among African American Men', in Martin P. Levine, Peter M. Nardi and John H. Gagnon, eds., *In Changing Times: Gay Men and Lesbians Encounter HIV/ AIDS*, Chicago: University of Chicago Press.

Phillips, Anthony. 1980. 'Uncovering the Father's Skirt', *VT* 30/1: 38–43.

Pilcher, Jeffrey M. 1998. *Que vivan los tamales! Food and the Making of Mexican Identity*, Albuquerque: University of New Mexico Press.

Pillsbury, Richard. 1998. *No Foreign Food: The American Diet in Time and Place*, Boulder: Westview Press.

Pitt-Rivers, Julian. 1977. *The Fate of Shechem or the Politics of Sex*, Cambridge: Cambridge University Press.

Polaski, Donald. 1997. '"What Will Ye See in the Shulamite": Women, Power and Panopticism in the Song of Songs', *Biblical Interpretation* 5: 64–81.

Pollock, Donald. 1985. 'Food and Sexual Identity Among the Culina', *Food and Foodways* 1: 25–42.

Polzin, Robert. 1993. *David and the Deuteronomist: A Literary Study of the Deuteronomic History*. Part Three: *2 Samuel*, Bloomington: Indiana University Press.

Pope, Harrison G., Katharine A. Phillips, and Roberto Olivardia. 2000. *The Adonis Complex: The Secret Crisis of Male Body Obsession*, New York: Free Press.

Pope, Marvin H. 1977. *Song of Songs: A New Translation with Introduction and Commentary*, Anchor Bible Commentary, Garden City: Doubleday.

Rad, Gerhard von. 1962. *Old Testament Theology: Volume I: The Theology of Israel's Historical Traditions*, New York: Harper & Row.

——. 1972. *Genesis: A Commentary*, revised edition. Philadelphia: Westminster Press.

Rappoport, Leon. 2003. *How We Eat: Appetite, Culture, and the Psychology of Food*, Toronto: ECW Press.

Rashkow, Ilona. 1993. *The Phallacy of Genesis: A Feminist-Psychoanalytic Approach*, Louisville: Westminster/John Knox Press.

——. 2000. *Taboo or Not Taboo: Sexuality and Family in the Hebrew Bible*, Minneapolis: Fortress Press.

Ringgren, Helmer. 1947. *Word and Wisdom: Studies in the Hypostatization of Divine Qualities and Functions in the Ancient Near East*, Lund: Hakan Ohlssons Boktryckeri.

Rogerson, John. 1984 [1978]. *Anthropology and the Old Testament*, Sheffield: Sheffield Academic Press.

Rosaldo, Renato. 1989. *Culture and Truth: The Remaking of Social Analysis*, Boston: Beacon Press.

Rotello, Gabriel. 1997. *Sexual Ecology: AIDS and the Destiny of Gay Men*, New York: Dutton.

Rousselle, Aline. 1988. *Porneia: On Desire and the Body in Antiquity*, trans. Felicia Pheasant. Oxford: Blackwell.

Rubin, Gayle. 1976. 'The Traffic in Women: Notes on the "Political Economy" of Sex', in Rayna Reiter, ed., *Toward An Anthropology of Women*, New York: Monthly Review Press.

——. 1984. 'Thinking Sex: Notes for a Radical Theory of the Politics of Sexuality', in Vance, ed., 1984.

Rubin, Gayle, with Judith Butler. 1994. 'Interview: Sexual Traffic', *differences* 6/2&3: 62–99.

Rudy, Kathy. 1997. *Sex and the Church: Gender, Homosexuality, and the Transformation of Christian Ethics*, Boston: Beacon Press.

Russell, Sabin. 2001. 'Young Gays Contracting HIV at "Explosive" Rate, CDC Says', *San Francisco Chronicle*, http://www.sfgate.com/cgi-bin/article.cgi?f=/c/a/2001/06/01/MN28551.DTL

Sack, Daniel. 2000. *Whitebread Protestants: Food and Religion in American Culture*, New York: St. Martin's Press.

Said, Edward. 1978. *Orientalism*, New York: Random House.

——. 1988. 'Michael Walzer's *Exodus and Revolution*: A Canaanite Reading', in Edward Said and Christopher Hitchens, eds., *Blaming the Victims: Spurious Scholarship and the Palestinian Question*, London: Verso.

Sawyer, John F.A., ed. 1996. *Reading Leviticus: A Conversation with Mary Douglas*, Sheffield: Sheffield Academic Press.

Schifter, Jacobo. 2000. *Public Sex in a Latin Society*, New York: Haworth Press.

Schlosser, Eric. 2001. *Fast Food Nation: The Dark Side of the All-American Meal*, Boston: Houghton Mifflin.

Schneider, Jane. 1971. 'Of Vigilance and Virgins: Honor, Shame and Access to Resources in Mediterranean Societies', *Ethnology* 10/1: 1–24.

Schneider, Laurel. 2000. 'Queer Theory', in Adam, ed., 2000.

——. 2001. 'What if It is a Choice? Some Implications of the Homosexuality Debates for Theology', *Chicago Theological Seminary Register* 91/3: 23–32.

Schroer, Silvia, and Thomas Staubli. 2000. 'Saul, David and Jonathan – The Story of a Triangle? A Contribution to the Issue of Homosexuality in the First Testament', in Brenner, ed., 2000.

Schumann Antelme, Ruth, and Stéphane Rossini. 2001. *Sacred Sexuality in Ancient Egypt*, trans. Jon Graham. Rochester, VT: Inner Traditions International.

Schüngel-Straumann, Helen. 1995. 'God as Mother in Hosea 11', in Brenner, ed., 1995a.

Schüssler Fiorenza, Elisabeth. 1984. *Bread Not Stone: The Challenge of Feminist Biblical Interpretation*, Boston: Beacon Press.

——. 1992. *But She Said: Feminist Practices of Biblical Interpretation*, Boston: Beacon Press.

——. 1998. *Sharing Her Word: Feminist Biblical Interpretation in Context*, Boston: Beacon Press.

——. 1999. *Rhetoric and Ethic: The Politics of Biblical Studies*, Minneapolis: Fortress Press.

Schwartz, Regina M. 1997. *The Curse of Cain: The Violent Legacy of Biblical Monotheism*, Chicago: University of Chicago Press.

Scott, R.B.Y. 1965. *Proverbs, Ecclesiastes: Introduction, Translation, and Notes*, Garden City: Doubleday.

Sedgwick, Eve Kosofsky. 1990. *Epistemology of the Closet*, Berkeley: University of California Press.

Segal, Lynne. 1994. *Straight Sex: The Politics of Pleasure*, London: Virago.

Segal, Lynne, and Mary McIntosh, eds. 1992. *Sex Exposed: Sexuality and the Pornography Debate*, London: Virago.

Segovia, Fernando F. 2000. *Decolonizing Biblical Studies: A View from the Margins*, Maryknoll: Orbis Books.

Segovia, Fernando F., and Mary Ann Tolbert, eds. 1995a. *Reading From This Place:* Volume I: *Social Location and Biblical Interpretation in the United States*, Minneapolis: Fortress Press.

——. 1995b. *Reading From This Place:* Volume II: *Social Location and Biblical Interpretation in Global Perspective*, Minneapolis: Fortress Press.

Seidman, Steven. 1991. *Romantic Longings: Love In America, 1830–1980*, New York: Routledge.

——. 1992. *Embattled Eros: Sexual Politics and Ethics in Contemporary America*, New York: Routledge.

Seitz, Christopher R. 1998. *Word Without End: The Old Testament as Abiding Witness*, Grand Rapids: Eerdmans.

Seow, Choon Leon. 1997. *Ecclesiastes: A New Translation with Introduction*, The Anchor Bible, New York: Doubleday.

Setel, T. Drorah. 1985. 'Prophets and Pornography: Female Sexual Imagery in Hosea', in Letty M. Russell, ed., *Feminist Interpretation of the Bible*, Philadelphia: Westminster Press.

Sharon, Diane M. 2002. *Patterns of Destiny: Narrative Structures of Foundation and Doom in the Hebrew Bible*, Winona Lake: Eisenbrauns.

Shaw, Teresa M. 1998. *The Burden of the Flesh: Fasting and Sexuality in Early Christianity*, Minneapolis: Fortress Press.

Sherwood, Yvonne. 1996. *The Prostitute and the Prophet: Hosea's Marriage in Literary-Theoretical Perspective*, Sheffield: Sheffield Academic Press.

——. 2000. *A Biblical Text and its Afterlives: The Survival of Jonah in Western Culture*, Cambridge: Cambridge University Press.

Shore, Sally Rieger, trans. 1983. *John Chrysostom: On Virginity; Against Remarriage*, New York: Edwin Mellen Press.

Shutt, R.J.H. 1985. 'Letter of Aristeas: A New Translation and Introduction', in James H. Charlesworth, ed., *The Old Testament Pseudepigrapha:* Volume 2: *Expansions of the "Old Testament" and Legends, Wisdom and Philosophical Literature, Prayers, Psalms, and Odes, Fragments of Lost Judeo-Hellenistic Works*, Garden City: Doubleday.

Siker, Jeffrey. 1996. 'Gentile Wheat and Homosexual Christians: New Testament Directions for the Heterosexual Church', in Brawley, ed., 1996.

Simkins, Ronald A. 1994. *Creator and Creation: Nature in the Worldview of Ancient Israel,* Peabody: Hendrickson.

Simoons, Frederick J. 1994. *Eat Not This Flesh: Food Avoidances from Prehistory to the Present*, second edition, Madison: University of Wisconsin Press.

Skinner, John. 1910. *A Critical and Exegetical Commentary on Genesis*, New York: Charles Scribner's Sons.

Smith, Mark. 1990. *The Early History of God: Yahweh and the Other Deities in Ancient Israel*, San Francisco: Harper & Row.

Snitow, Ann, Christine Stansell, and Sharon Thompson, eds., 1983. *Powers of Desire: The Politics of Sexuality*, New York: Monthly Review Press.

Soler, Jean. 1997 [1973]. 'The Semiotics of Food in the Bible', in Carole Counihan and Penny Van Esterik, eds., 1997.

Somerville, Siobhan B. 2000. *Queering the Color Line: Race and the Invention of Homosexuality in American Culture*, Durham: Duke University Press.

Speiser, E.A. 1964. *Genesis*, The Anchor Bible, Garden City: Doubleday.

Spurlin, William J. 1998. 'Sissies and Sisters: Gender, Sexuality and the Possibilities of Coalition', in Mandy Merck, Naomi Segal and Elizabeth Wright, eds., *Coming Out of Feminism?* Oxford: Blackwell.

Stager, Lawrence E. 1985. 'The Archaeology of the Family in Ancient Israel', *Bulletin of the American Schools of Oriental Research* 260: 1–35.

Steinhauer, Jennifer. 2001. 'Secrecy and Stigma Keep AIDS Risk High for Gay Black Men', *The New York Times*, http://www.nytimes.com/2001/02/11/health/11AIDS.html.

Stendahl, Krister. 1982. 'Ancient Scripture in the Modern World', in Frederick E. Greenspahn, ed., *Scripture in the Jewish and Christian Traditions: Authority, Interpretation, Relevance*, Nashville: Abingdon.

Stoler, Ann Laura. 1997. 'Carnal Knowledge and Imperial Power: Gender, Race, and Morality in Colonial Asia', in Roger Lancaster and Micaela di Leonardo, eds., *The Gender/Sexuality Reader: Culture, History, Political Economy*, New York: Routledge.

Stone, Ken. 1995. 'Gender and Homosexuality in Judges 19: Subject-Honor, Object-Shame?', *JSOT* 67: 87–107.

——. 1996. *Sex, Honor and Power in the Deuteronomistic History*, Sheffield: Sheffield Academic Press.

——. 1997a. 'Biblical Interpretation as a Technology of the Self: Gay Men and the Ethics of Reading', in Danna Nolan Fewell and Gary A. Phillips, eds., *Bible and Ethics of Reading*, Semeia 77: 139–55.

——. 1997b. 'The Hermeneutics of Abomination: On Gay Men, Canaanites, and Biblical Interpretation', *Biblical Theology Bulletin* 27/2: 36–41.

——. 1999. 'Safer Text: Reading Biblical Laments in the Age of AIDS', *Theology and Sexuality* 10: 16–27.

——. 2000. 'The Garden of Eden and the Heterosexual Contract', in Goss and West, eds., 2000.

——. 2001a. 'Homosexuality and the Bible or Queer Reading? A Response to Martti Nissinen', *Theology and Sexuality* 14: 107–18.

——. 2001b. 'Queer Commentary and Biblical Interpretation: An Introduction', in Stone, ed., 2001.

——. 2002. 'What Happens When "Gays Read the Bible"?', in Sean Freyne and Ellen van Wolde, eds., *The Many Voices of the Bible*, Concilium, London: SCM.

——. In press. 'Queering the Canaanite', in Marcella Althaus-Reid and Lisa Isherwood, eds., *The Sexual Theologian: Essays on Sex, God and Politics*, London: Continuum.

Stone, Ken, ed. 2001. *Queer Commentary and the Hebrew Bible*, Sheffield/Cleveland: Sheffield Academic Press/Pilgrim Press.

Streete, Gail Corrington. 1997. *The Strange Woman: Power and Sex in the Bible*, Louisville: Westminster/John Knox Press.

Strossen, Nadine. 1995. *Defending Pornography: Free Speech, Sex, and the Fight for Women's Rights*, New York: Scribners.

Stuart, Elizabeth. 1995. *Just Good Friends: Towards a Theology of Lesbian and Gay Relationships*, London: Mowbray.

Sugirtharajah, R.S., ed. 1991. *Voices from the Margin: Interpreting the Bible in the Third World*, Maryknoll: Orbis Books.

Tambiah, S.J. 1969. 'Animals Are Good to Think And Good to Prohibit', *Ethnology* 8: 423–59.

Tamez, Elsa. 2000. *When the Horizons Close: Rereading Ecclesiastes*, trans. Margaret Wilde, Maryknoll: Orbis Books.

Tanner, Kathryn. 1997. *Theories of Culture: A New Agenda for Theology*, Minneapolis: Fortress Press.

Tarlin, Jan. 1997. 'Utopia and Pornography in Ezekiel: Violence, Hope, and the Shattered Male Subject', in Beal and Gunn, eds., 1997.

Terry, Jennifer. 1999. *An American Obsession: Science, Medicine, and Homosexuality in Modern Society*, Chicago: University of Chicago Press.

Thistlethwaite, Susan Brooks. 1985. 'Every Two Minutes: Battered Women and Feminist Interpretation', in Letty M. Russell, ed., *Feminist Interpretation of the Bible*, Philadelphia: Westminster Press.

Thorson Smith, Sylvia. 1988. *Pornography: Far from the Song of Songs*, Louisville: Office of the General Assembly, Presbyterian Church U.S.A.

Thurston, Thomas M. 1990. 'Leviticus 18:22 and the Prohibition of Homosexual Acts', in Michael L. Stemmeler and J. Michael Clark, eds., *Homophobia and the Judaeo-Christian Tradition*, Dallas: Monument Press.

Tolbert, Mary Ann. 1983. 'Defining the Problem: The Bible and Feminist Hermeneutics', in Mary Ann Tolbert, ed., *The Bible and Feminist Hermeneutics, Semeia* 28. Chico, CA: Scholars Press.

——. 1990. 'Protestant Feminists and the Bible: On the Horns of a Dilemma', pp. 5–23 in Alice Bach, ed., *The Pleasure of Her Text: Feminist Readings of Biblical and Historical Texts*, Philadelphia: Trinity Press International.

——. 1991. 'A Response from a Literary Perspective', in R. Alan Culpepper and Fernando F. Segovia, eds., *The Fourth Gospel from a Literary Perspective, Semeia* 53: 203–12.

——. 1993. 'Social, Sociological, and Anthropological Methods', in Elisabeth Schüssler Fiorenza, ed., *Searching the Scriptures:* Volume 1: *A Feminist Introduction*, New York: Crossroad.

——. 1995a. 'Reading for Liberation' in Segovia and Tolbert, eds.

——. 1995b. 'When Resistance Becomes Repression: Mark 13:9-27 and the Poetics of Location', in Segovia and Tolbert, eds., 1995b.

——. 1998. 'A New Teaching with Authority: A Re-evaluation of the Authority of the Bible', in Fernando F. Segovia and Mary Ann Tolbert, eds., *Teaching the Bible: The Discourses and Politics of Biblical Pedagogy*, Maryknoll: Orbis Books.

Treichler, Paula A. 1999. *How to Have Theory in an Epidemic: Cultural Chronicles of AIDS*, Durham: Duke University Press.

Trible, Phyllis. 1978. *God and the Rhetoric of Sexuality*, Philadelphia: Fortress Press.

——. 1984. *Texts of Terror: Literary-Feminist Readings of Biblical Narratives*, Philadelphia: Fortress Press.

Trubek, Amy B. 2000. *Haute Cuisine: How the French Invented the Culinary Profession*, Philadelphia: University of Pennsylvania Press.

Tubb, Jonathan N. 1998. *Canaanites*, Norman: University of Oklahoma Press.

Turner, Dwayne C. 1997. *Risky Sex: Gay Men and HIV Prevention*, New York: Columbia University Press.

Turner, William B. 2000. *A Genealogy of Queer Theory*, Philadelphia: Temple University Press.

Vance, Carole S. 1984. 'Pleasure and Danger: Toward a Politics of Sexuality', in Vance, ed., 1984.

Vance, Carole S., ed. 1984. *Pleasure and Danger: Exploring Female Sexuality*, London: Routledge and Kegan Paul.

Van Eijk, Ton H.J. 1972. 'Marriage and Virginity, Death and Immortality', in J. Fontaine and C. Kannengiesser, eds., *Epektasis: Mélanges patristiques offerts au cardinal J. Daniélou*, Paris: Beauchesne.

Vasey, Michael. 1995. *Strangers and Friends: A New Exploration of Homosexuality and the Bible*, London: Hodder & Stoughton.

Visser, Margaret. 1986. *Much Depends on Dinner: The Extraordinary History and Mythology, Allure and Obsessions, Perils and Taboos, of an Ordinary Meal*, New York: Grove Press.

——. 1991. *The Rituals of Dinner: The Origins, Evolution, Eccentricities, and Meaning of Table Manners*, New York: Penguin Books.

Wagner, M. Monica. 1950. *Saint Basil: Ascetical Works*, The Father of the Church: A New Translation, New York: Fathers of the Church, Inc.

Walls, Neal. 2001. *Desire, Discord and Death: Approaches to Ancient Near Eastern Myth*, Boston: American Schools of Oriental Research.

Walsh, Carey Ellen. 2000a. *The Fruit of the Vine: Viticulture in Ancient Israel*, Harvard Semitic Monographs. Winona Lake: Eisenbrauns.

——. 2000b. *Exquisite Desire: Religion, the Erotic, and the Song of Songs*, Minneapolis: Fortress Press.

Warner, Michael. 1999. *The Trouble With Normal: Sex, Politics, and the Ethics of Queer Life*, New York: Free Press.

——. 2002. *Publics and Counterpublics*, New York: Zone Books.

Warrior, Robert Allen. 1991. 'A Native American Perspective: Canaanites, Cowboys, and Indians', in Sugirtharajah, ed., 1991.

Washington, Harold C. 1995. 'The Strange Woman (אשה זרה / נכריה) of Proverbs 1–9 and Post-Exilic Judaean Society', in Brenner, ed., 1995b.

Watney, Simon. 1989. *Policing Desire: Pornography, AIDS and the Media*, second edition. Minneapolis: University of Minnesota Press.

——. 1994. *Practices of Freedom: Selected Writings on HIV/AIDS*, Durham: Duke University Press.

Webb, Stephen H. 2001. *Good Eating*, Grand Rapids: Brazos Press.

Weems, Renita. 1989. 'Gomer: Victim of Violence or Victim of Metaphor', *Semeia* 47: 87–104.

——. 1991. 'Reading *Her Way* through the Struggle: African American Women and the Bible', in Cain Hope Felder, ed., *Stony the Road We Trod: African American Biblical Interpretation*, Minneapolis: Fortress Press.

——. 1995. *Battered Love: Marriage, Sex, and Violence in the Hebrew Prophets*, Minneapolis: Fortress Press.

——. 1998 [1992]. 'Song of Songs', in Newsom and Ringe, eds., 1998.

West, Gerald. 1999. *The Academy of the Poor: Towards a Dialogical Reading of the Bible*, Sheffield: Sheffield Academic Press.

Westenholz, Joan Goodnick. 1989. 'Tamar, *Qedesa, Qadistu*, and Sacred Prostitution in Mesopotamia', *Harvard Theological Review* 82/3: 245–65.

Westenholz, Joan Goodnick, ed. 1998. *Sacred Bounty, Sacred Land: The Seven Species of the Land of Israel*, Jerusalem: Bible Lands Museum Jerusalem.

Westermann, Claus. 1984 [1974]. *Genesis 1–11: A Commentary*, trans. John J. Scullion. Minneapolis: Augsburg.

——. 1985 [1981]. *Genesis 12–36: A Commentary*, trans. John J. Scullion. Minneapolis: Augsburg.

Whitelam, Keith W. 1996. *The Invention of Ancient Israel: The Silencing of Palestinian History*, New York: Routledge.

——. 2002. 'Palestine During the Iron Age', in John Barton, ed., *The Biblical World*, 2 volumes. New York: Routledge.

Whybray, R.N. 1982. 'Qoheleth, Preacher of Joy', in David Clines, David Gunn and Alan Hauser, eds., *Art and Meaning: Rhetoric in Biblical Literature*, Sheffield: Sheffield Academic Press.

Wiessner, Polly, and Wulf Schiefenhövel, eds. 1996. *Food and the Status Quest: An Interdisciplinary Perspective*, Providence: Berghahn Books.

Wikan, Unni. 1987. 'Shame and Honour: A Contestable Pair', *Man* 19: 635–52.

Williams, Linda. 1999 [1989]. *Hard Core: Power, Pleasure, and the 'Frenzy of the Visible'*, expanded edition. Berkeley: University of California Press.

Wilson, Robert R. 1984. *Sociological Approaches to the Old Testament*, Philadelphia: Fortress Press.

Winkler, John J. 1990. *The Constraints of Desire: The Anthropology of Sex and Gender in Ancient Greece*, New York: Routledge.

Winston, David. 1979. *The Wisdom of Solomon: A New Translation with Introduction and Commentary*, The Anchor Bible, Garden City: Doubleday.

Witt, Doris. 1999. *Black Hunger: Food and the Politics of U.S. Identity*, Oxford: Oxford University Press.

Wittig, Monique. 1992. *The Straight Mind and Other Essays*, Boston: Beacon Press.

Wold, Donald J. 1998. *Out of Order: Homosexuality in the Bible and the Ancient Near East*, Grand Rapids: Baker.

Wolff, Hans Walter. 1974. *Hosea: A Commentary on the Book of the Prophet Hosea*, trans. Gary Stansell, ed. Paul D. Hanson, Philadelphia: Fortress Press.

Wood, Simon P. 1954. *Clement of Alexandria: Christ the Educator*, New York: Fathers of the Church, Inc.

Wright, G. Ernest. 1952. *God Who Acts: Biblical Theology as Recital*, Chicago: Henry Regnery Company.

Yee, Gale. 1995. 'Ideological Criticism: Judges 17–21 and the Dismembered Body', in Gale Yee, ed., *Judges and Method: New Approaches in Biblical Studies*, Minneapolis: Fortress Press.

——. 1998 [1992]. 'Hosea', in Newsom and Ringe, eds., 1998.

——. 2003. *Poor Banished Children of Eve: Woman as Evil in the Hebrew Bible*, Minneapolis: Fortress Press.

Young, Iris Marion. 1990. *Justice and the Politics of Difference*, Princeton: Princeton University Press.

Zaretsky, Eli. 1986 [1976]. *Capitalism, the Family, and Personal Life*, revised and expanded edition, San Francisco: Harper & Row.

INDEX

INDEX OF REFERENCES

OLD TESTAMENT PASSAGES

INDEX OF MODERN AUTHORS

Parker, R. 10
Patton, C. 8
Pellegrini, A. 16
Penley, C. 95
Peterson, J. 10
Phillips, A. 56, 57
Phillips, K. 92
Pilcher, J. 50
Pillsbury, R. 50
Pitt-Rivers, J. 78, 104, 119
Polaski, D. 98
Pollock, D. 3, 5, 8, 18, 22
Polzin, R. 75, 94
Pope, H. 92
Pope, M. 99, 100, 101, 107

Rappoport, L. 51
Rashkow, I. 56, 123
Ringgren, H. 133
Rogerson, J. 17
Rosaldo, R. 18
Rossini, S. 123
Rotello, G. 9, 68
Rousselle, A. 28
Rubin, G. 6, 16, 82–3, 90, 91–3, 98, 105, 108, 112
Rudy, K. 69, 87–8
Russell, S. 9

Sack, D. 4
Said, E. 64
Sawyer, J. 46
Schiefenhövel, W. 51
Schifter, J. 69, 72, 77
Schlosser, E. 10–11
Schneider, J. 104, 123
Schneider, L. 15, 88
Schroer, S. 14
Schumann Antelme, R. 123
Schüngel-Straumann, H. 126
Schüssler Fiorenza, E. 12–13, 14,

25, 86, 148
Schwartz, R. 12, 64, 75, 83
Scott, R. 131
Sedgwick, E. 64, 112
Segal, L. 90, 106
Segovia, F. 18, 25
Seidman, S. 69, 85, 90
Seitz, C. 23–6, 29, 31, 32, 33, 40, 43, 44
Seow, C. 137, 138, 139–40, 142, 143
Setel, T.D. 106, 111
Sharon, D. 7
Shaw, T. 27, 28, 29, 30, 31
Sherwood, Y. 25, 111, 112, 116, 126–7
Shutt, R. 46
Siker, J. 65
Silberman, N. 58, 61
Simkins, R. 37
Simoons, F. 5
Skinner, J. 79
Smith, M. 116, 123
Snitow, A. 90
Soler, J. 7
Somerville, S. 51
Speiser, E. 66
Spurlin, W. 112
Stager, L. 33
Stansell, C. 90
Staubli, T. 15
Steinhauer, J. 9
Stendahl, K. 148
Stoler, A. 64
Stone, K. 7, 14, 15, 17, 42, 48, 54, 64, 71, 80, 104, 111, 119, 142
Streete, G. 7
Strossen, N. 106
Stuart, E. 140
Sugirtharajah, R. 25, 48